A Cruel Paradise

JOURNALS OF AN INTERNATIONAL RELIEF WORKER

A Cruel Paradise

JOURNALS OF AN INTERNATIONAL RELIEF WORKER

Leanne Olson

INSOMNIAC PRESS

Edited by Mike O'Connor.
Copy edited by Lisa Marshall and Kate Harding.
Designed by Mike O'Connor.

Canadian Cataloguing in Publication Data

Olson, Leanne, 1963-
    A cruel paradise: journals of an international relief worker

ISBN 1-895837-82-0

1. Olson, Leanne, 1963-   - Diaries. 2. War relief. 3. Nurses-Canada-Diaries. I. Title.

HV639.O47 1999   363.3'988'092   C99-931678-8

The publisher gratefully acknowledges the support of the Canada Council and the Ontario Arts Council.

Printed and bound in Canada

THE CANADA COUNCIL | LE CONSEIL DES ARTS
FOR THE ARTS | DU CANADA
SINCE 1957 | DEPUIS 1957

ONTARIO ARTS
COUNCIL
CONSEIL DES ARTS
DE L'ONTARIO

Insomniac Press, 393 Shaw Street,
Toronto, Ontario, Canada, M6J 2X4
www.insomniacpress.com

This book is for Rink, of course, who was with me through it all.
And for my family and my friends from the field.
You know who you are,
and you know I could never have done it without you.
Thank you.

It's also for Darcy and Mac
who gave me the idea to write this book in the first place.

Table of Contents

INTRODUCTION

It is the names I remember, even after this time. They roll off my tongue like pearls off a string; Gbalatuah, Gbarnga, Fenutoli, Sanniquellie, Ripac, Toposku, Doboj, Banja Luka, Bujumbura, Ngozi, Musema, Mweso, Birambizo, Mokoto. They are names I once knew well. The roads I travelled, the homes I lived in. Like cards from a deck, each one is different and each has its story to tell. The massacre in Mokoto, the incident in Birambizo where we were nearly killed, the checkpoint where we were stopped in Topusko, the afternoon in jail in Gbarnga.

The first time I came back from a war zone I had so many stories to tell, so much to express. The experience was all so new. Later, after a few more wars and a couple more years, I stopped talking so much. I could still tell a great story, but I stopped trying to explain what it was really like. There were things I had such strong opinions about, issues I could discuss for hours, but only to someone who'd been there, and so few people had been there. So few people could truly relate to the work I'd done.

I found out that my family and friends, for all their good intentions, shared little interest in what I had to say. They were unaware of the effects of early UN intervention in conflict areas, knew nothing about the unequal distribution of resources as a cause of famine, drew blank stares when I spoke of businesses and governments fuelling the war effort in Liberia, of ethnic cleansing in Bosnia, or of massacres in Zaire. They liked a good story, but only the CNN headlines — not the truth behind the headlines.

To say that I was a bit naive when I first started working as an international relief worker would be an understatement of monumental proportions! I knew nothing. But I learned more in a few years than I could ever have imagined. I pushed myself to the limit in ways I had never expected. Life as an international relief worker changed me profoundly. For that kind of life one makes a sacrifice: friends disappear, family ties loosen, and the sense of home, of the place you belong, becomes the place where you lay down a backpack — be it for days or weeks or months.

My work created a distance, distance of experiences, of time, of tragedy and of too many things I could never mention in all the letters I sent home over the years. It was a distance made of the *real* stories, sitting there between the lines of those letters, never acknowledged.

I would like to try to go back between those lines now and tell you the story of what it's *really* like to be a nurse working in a war zone and what it's *really* like to be an international aid worker. It's a job I held for nearly four years and a hell of a way to make a living. It was all the things one would imagine: a great adventure, an exotic life, an amazing challenge, a rewarding experience. It was also the hardest job I've ever done, the most frustrating and, at times, the most dangerous. This is my personal story, and every aid worker in the world has his or her own. I would not ask you to see this as 'typical' of all relief workers' experiences. Nothing about this kind of work is typical.

This is not just a story of tragedy and sorrow. In every war, no matter how ugly or how cruel, there remains a part of the human spirit that will not be broken. A part that survives, grows strong, adapts and simply will not surrender. In my projects there was always laughter — even joy — friendship, love and hope. Strangers became friends, staff members became colleagues, students became teachers, and we all grew and changed in some way. Nobody ever comes away from a war unchanged, not those who perpetrate it, nor their victims, not those of us there to help. It was sometimes a dangerous job, but people worked with a passion and a belief in their work that one rarely sees in the 'real' world. I met friends who became family and enemies who became friends. I worked with civilians and military, with rebels and combatants, with heros and fools. I worked in the cities, in the jungle and the bush, in hospitals, shacks, health centres, homes and schools. I remember times of utter boredom and times when the adrenaline rushed and everything seemed possible. It was terrifying, it was exciting, it was insane. We were living on the edge — and you should have seen the view!

THE BEGINNING

When people see my nursing photos from years ago, they always ask why I decided to give up my 'nice, safe job' in the city hospital. My reply is that my job in 1993 may have been comfortable, but it was certainly not safe.

At that time, the Canadian government had begun a complete restructuring of the health system, and even though I had ten years' worth of nursing experience, I had no seniority in my job. I had worked in numerous places — Texas, Zaire, Nicaragua, Zimbabwe and a few different hospitals in Winnipeg, Manitoba — and had had a lot of fun with my work but never stayed long in one place. In 1993, I had been working in the adult emergency department of Health Sciences' Centre in Winnipeg for about a year, and my job was one of the first to go. I transferred to the Children's Hospital emergency room, but only on a part-time basis. Soon, that position, too, was in jeopardy, and I needed to find a new job quickly.

So why relief work? I have no idea. That is such an unanswerable question, although people ask all the time. I did it for the challenge, for the adventure, for fun, because I felt a moral and ethical responsibility to do it. I did it as an expression of my personal faith. I did it for the change. Who knows anymore? I did it because somebody had to and I could.

A friend in the hospital suggested I call Medecins Sans Frontieres (MSF). Medecins Sans Frontieres or in English, Doctors Without Borders, is an emergency medical relief agency with over twenty years' experience. It began in France, but when I joined there were six operational departments — in France, Holland, Belgium, Luxembourg, Switzerland and Spain. The English speakers ended up with MSF-Holland. The Canadian chapter was only about three years old and focussed on recruitment and fundraising for the MSF-Holland desk. At that time, I had never even heard of it. .

I applied to MFS-Holland through the Canadian agency, and in October I flew to Toronto for an interview. Unfortunately, nobody had told me about the 'casual' dress code. I spent a small fortune and went to a dozen friends for advice on how to achieve the 'dressed-for-success' look: new haircut, new power skirt and blazer, new high heels, the works. Ben, from the human resources department, showed up in jeans and a T-shirt. I was mortified! I didn't quite achieve the impression I wanted to, and it took some persuasion to get them to see past the conservative look, which turned out to be a dismal mistake.

The interview was long and fairly intensive. Two hours worth of questions covered everything from my nursing and travel experiences to my ability to work in strenuous situations to my experiences working with different cultures. I recall being asked how I would respond in a security situation; I replied, honestly, that I wouldn't have a clue, never having really experienced one. Little did I know that I'd become something of an expert in a few years.

By the end of the interview, no clear decision had been made. I wasn't sure if I had 'passed' or not. I returned to Winnipeg, and to work, and basically forgot about the organization. In November, I phoned the office, only to be informed that all new 'volunteers' were obliged to attend a two-week training course in Amsterdam prior to accepting a mission with MSF. I was also told there were no vacancies for the course until the following spring. I still wasn't certain if they considered me an appropriate applicant.

To my amazement, on December 20, 1993, my thirtieth birthday, I received a call from the Toronto office asking me to attend the course in Amsterdam in January. I was also told to be prepared to leave for a mission immediately afterwards if I did well in the course. I had two weeks to move out of my apartment, arrange my life for the possibility of a six-month absence to God knows where, and quit my job.

Chaos is the only word that describes the blur of activity during those two weeks. My head nurse couldn't believe that I really didn't know if or when I'd be back. I left a written letter of resignation with a friend in case I wouldn't be returning to Canada. (As it turned out, I didn't return, my friend handed my letter in, and the head nurse hasn't forgiven me yet.) I moved in with my sister and her boyfriend, packed my bags for whatever country in the world I might go to and said my goodbyes. Panicking, I changed my mind at least a dozen times. If I'd had another week to think about it, I might never have left.

On January 15, 1994, I arrived in Amsterdam to attend the two-week Health Emergency Preparedness/Logistics Training Course, offered by MSF to all new recruits. The HEP/LTC is a very intensive course designed to give trainees a quick, essential overview of life in the world of international aid. The course covers a variety of topics: :emergency health care in refugee camps, primary health care clinics, the role of MSF expatriates as teachers and supervisors, the ordering of supplies and materials, how to train trainers, cultural sensitivity, operating communication equipment — handsets, satellite phones, computers, high frequency and very high frequency radios — handling security situations, dealing with stress, et cetera. Every aspect of the program included a great deal of role-playing and teamwork. There were about forty people from around the world attending the course, and we were told repeatedly that the key word for MSF was 'flexibility, flexibility and flexibility.' They weren't kidding.

One evening, I set off to a nearby forest as part of a team of five people with a map, a compass and a handset. Our goal: to find two items hidden somewhere in the forest, in the dark, in a place we'd never been to before, in the freezing rain. We succeeded in about three hours, finding first a tent, which we had to drag back to the base, and next a bottle of red wine. One of the guys on the team managed to open it with his pen, and I knew then he'd turn out to be the perfect logistician. That wine was consumed long before we arrived back at the base.

After-hours were spent in the local pub, drinking, talking and getting to know the instructors. It was also an important part of our evaluation; the instructors noted how well individuals interacted, socialized, and became a part of the group. It was fascinating to get to know people from such varied backgrounds and, in spite of the very long and tiring days, we managed to have a lot of fun together.

One item we often discussed was how to deal with the stress of living and working in dangerous situations. We were told to be aware of how individuals dealt with stress and to recognize some common symptoms: excessive drinking or drug use, sleeplessness, mood swings, changes in relationships, obsessive behaviour regarding the project, failure to maintain a professional standard, high risk-taking behaviour and many other signs. We were also warned about the dangers of beginning relationships between the national and expat teams, primarily because in case of an evacuation, only the expat staff leaves, and bringing the national staff along is out of the question. An entire module was handed to us; there would come a time when I would see myself in every page of it. But then I believed — as we all did, being so new and enthusiastic — that I could handle anything. In fact, I believed I was invincible, and if anything bad were to happen, it wouldn't be to me. That was then.

The first week we covered general information, but during the second, the group split into the medical and the logistical teams. The medical teams were fairly straightforward: doctors and nurses studying tropical diseases, vaccination campaigns, how to set up and run medical centres, deal with nutrition issues and run feeding programs.

The logisticians had a different program altogether. For starters, I had never heard the term *logistician*, and had no idea what one was, looked like, or did. I did learn that although MSF is an emergency medical organization, it ends up hiring more logisticians than medical personnel. Logisticians have a variety of backgrounds and a variety of talents. Some have mechanical, engineering, or water and sanitation backgrounds. Others come without any degree but with a wide range of experiences, from mechanics to carpentry, computers to office management. A logistician's job is, simply put, to do whatever is necessary to support the medical program. The medical personnel cannot manage without good logistical support. It's essential that the two parts work together as a whole, but sometimes that's easier said than done.

The logisticians assume a huge amount of responsibility. They are in charge of everything that makes a program work — ordering supplies, arranging living arrangements, dealing with local staff, and making sure there are enough cars, drugs, personnel, food and materials. A good logistician can really make or break a project, and I have had the pleasure of working with some excellent ones. In fact, I married my favourite logistician.

I was pleased to complete the course as a volunteer. Throughout the course, we'd heard various stories from the other expats, and when the course was finished, all of us had some idea about where we'd like to go. I wasn't certain, but there were two places that really didn't appeal to me. One was Liberia and the other was Bosnia. Of course my first mission would be to Liberia, and my second, Bosnia.

BACKGROUND

Before I can get started on my first mission with MSF, I should provide some background information. For starters, MSF is one of numerous non-governmental organizations, or NGOs, doing international relief work. Unlike the International Red Cross (ICRC), MSF is not always obliged to work with the permission of the government. In times of war, the government is usually in such a chaotic state that it can hardly be relied upon to care for the population. Of course, all NGOs do their best to work within whatever national systems are in place, but often that's not possible. MSF will work without a system, and will set up its own if necessary. The organization will also do cross-border operations if there is a need. MSF specializes in *emergencies*, and less so on long-term or developmental programs. Basically, when the fighting gets bad, and everyone else is fleeing the country, MSF is going in. Which leads me to believe that you've got to be just a little bit mad to want to do this kind of work!

Though MSF aims to provide medical care, the organization has expanded in a variety of directions and is able to respond within forty-eight hours to natural or man-made disasters anywhere in the world. Services have grown to include refugee health care, water and sanitation programs, preventative health care, hospital rehabilitation, drug distribution, AIDS programs, feeding and nutrition programs, emergency health programs and dozens more. The variety and complexity of the projects the organization undertakes is based on its excellent reputation and years of experience. MSF probably has the best logistical capacity of any medical relief NGO in the world. Over the years, the agency has developed numerous kits that can be packed and ready to ship within hours, containing everything necessary to set up clinics, run a measles vaccination campaign for 10,000 kids, or start up a cholera camp in hours, plus a whole lot more. A single kit can weigh several tons and contain dozens of boxes of materials.

There are hundreds of NGOs world-wide. Some are world renowned, like MSF, Oxfam, CARE, Action Contre la Faime (ACF), Save the Children Fund (SCF), et cetera. Others are small, perhaps a single group from one small town. Some are religiously oriented, but most of the major players are strictly neutral. Some specialize in particular areas — food, water and sanitation, health or education. Some work only in emergencies, others only in development. Most are staffed by volunteers.

My favourite word, volunteer. It conjures up images of good-hearted, well-meaning, clean-cut youngsters braving all sorts of dangers to save the world. Well, it wasn't exactly like that. For starters, most medical volunteers with MSF are well-trained professionals: doctors, nurses and nutritionists with years of experience. Most are in their twenties and thirties. And, for most volunteers, one mission is all they do. Only about thirty percent ever continue in the aid business. Well-meaning idealists become realists very quickly in this field.

Secondly, with MSF, a volunteer does receive a salary of sorts, albeit a small one. When I started I received slightly more than $800 Canadian a month. After my first year, my wage increased. Depending on how quickly one moves up to coordination positions and how many extra training courses one takes, the salary increases. But absolutely *nobody* is in it for the money.

Some of the World Health Organization or UN agencies pay far better wages than NGOs, as most NGOs depend on public support and fundraising. Granted, there are numerous governmental departments that fund relief work, such as the European Commission, USAID, and hundreds more, yet fundraising remains a major issue, and getting people to believe in your work requires good public relations and a lot of hard work.

When one becomes an expatriate for MSF — a person who accepts a position in a project somewhere overseas — much has to be done prior to the actual departure. Each operational desk has a constant overview of what's happening with projects throughout the world. As new personnel are required in each field, requests are sent to Amsterdam. Those requests can be for medical personnel, logisticians, nutritionists, financial controllers, surgeons, or whatever else is necessary. MFS-Amsterdam then contacts its sister offices in Toronto, London and elsewhere, and the hunt for staff begins.

When the office verifies that an applicant is acceptable for a position, a quick briefing is done to inform the applicant of exactly what position he or she will be filling. This is always a bit tricky, since job descriptions change frequently, and the person an applicant is supposed to replace might decide at the last minute to extend his or her work term for another three months. Often, the communication is so poor that you never really know what you might be doing except that it's in 'nutrition,' or some other broad area. About a hundred things change between accepting a job and arriving in the field, which used to drive the perfectionist in me crazy. But that's the nature of working in an emergency.

Once you're accepted, the real fun begins. Vaccinations have to be upgraded and anti-malarial medication started if necessary. Visas, passports and any other paperwork must be in order prior to leaving the country. For me, the journey was inevitably long. From Winnipeg, my first stop was always Toronto, for a briefing about my new job, the country politics, the current security situation, my position in the team and the specifics of the medical program. Then I was off to Amsterdam for a more in-depth briefing. In Amsterdam I was required to meet with the medical, logistical, financial and public relations departments as well as the country coordinator or desk manager. A photo ID card would be issued there, and I was regularly given a couple of MSF T-shirts, the standard field uniform, to take along. Then there was the mail for the rest of the team, extra supplies, money for the project, and about a thousand other things I had to remember to bring to the airport. I've travelled with everything from computers to radio handsets, textbooks to care packages, food to vaccines. And nearly always with money.

One of the major problems with working in conflict areas is that the basic infrastructure of the area breaks down quickly. Roads, borders, schools, banks and hospitals close, supply routes are interrupted or impassable and normal systems grind to a halt. Therefore, for most projects, money has to be brought in by person. The currency of international aid is American dollars, which can most easily be converted to local currencies if necessary, although some countries refuse to accept U.S. dollars. The plain truth is, salaries, supplies and materials must be paid for somehow, and that means there must be regular access to funds. No funds, no project. This issue alone could fill an encyclopedia, but the fact remains that promised funding and actual cash-in-hand money can be months apart. Entire projects can fail or succeed based on a scribble in a donor's chequebook.

My airfare as a volunteer was paid for by MFS, and all insurance costs were covered for several weeks after a project was finished. MSF offers coverage for health, life, disability, et cetera. I had no idea that on my very first mission I would require nearly all of those.

LIBERIA
Chapter 1

When MSF asked me to accept a position in Liberia, I agreed instantly. Though the country wasn't exactly what I had in mind, it was such an honour to be chosen to work with the agency that I didn't dare refuse. Besides, at that point I knew nothing about working with MSF, and didn't really have a clue what I was getting into. Most first-missioners don't know what to ask or how to ask it, they just hope they end up with a good team and pray someone will be there to show them the ropes.

I hung around Amsterdam for a couple of weeks waiting for the final arrangements. I stayed with Gerda, a friend from the course, who would also be joining me in Liberia. I was excited, scared and impatient, and I kept asking myself over and over if I really knew what I was doing. I didn't, of course.

To be honest, the beginning of my first mission was a disaster. I flew to Abidjan in the Ivory Coast, and from there I was supposed to fly to Man, a border town where MSF had a base of operations. From Man I would then drive across the border to Gbarnga in Liberia. That was the plan. Well, you know what they say about the best laid plans?

In reality, when I arrived at Abidjan airport the first week in February, there was not a soul from MSF there to greet me. Unable to speak a word of French, I tried to fend off persistent taxi drivers and prayed to see *any* NGO car arrive. Finally, a driver with an MSF T-shirt did show up. Chatting away in a language I couldn't understand, he whisked me off to a comfortable house somewhere in the suburbs. I was met by a guard at the gate and two national staff members about to go off duty. Mercifully, one of them spoke English and was able to direct me to my room, assuring me that Louise, the project coordinator, would be back shortly. Obviously, we had different ideas of 'shortly'. My first important lesson: time has very different interpretations in Africa than it does in Canada.

Hungry and exhausted, I managed to find the shower but no food, not even a piece of bread. I later discovered that this oversight wasn't meant to torture new arrivals, it was just that food never lasts long in the heat and, as a result, is bought fresh daily. Unfortunately, this was the end of the day, and Louise wasn't the sort who snacked between meals.

Eventually, Michiel, the Dutch logistical coordinator from Monrovia, showed up and took me out to dinner at a gorgeous Vietnamese restaurant. My hunger satisfied, my initial excitement crept back. I plied Michiel with about a hundred questions — poor guy — until I realized he was in the Ivory Coast for a break, and I wasn't really giving him one.

Back at the house, I finally met Louise, a fellow Canadian who was the logistical coordinator for Abidjan. Liberia looked to be a fairly complicated project. To begin, it was a cross-border operation. Though there was a team living and working in Gbarnga in Liberia, most of the supplies and materials that had to come from Europe arrived via the Ivory Coast. There were few flights into Monrovia in those days, and getting there was a dangerous undertaking. If supplies could be brought across the frontline between Monrovia and Gbarnga (a very iffy thing), that was the first choice. If not, then requests went on to Man or Abidjan, and Louise took care of getting orders sorted from her end. Usually, either by road or plane, supplies were brought to the MFS base in the border town of Man, then driven across the border into Liberia. That way nobody had to try crossing the frontline.

I also received an updated report on the situation from Louise. I learned that prior to the war Liberia had a population of some 2.6 million people. Since the war had begun in 1989, some 700,000 people had fled the country. The bloody fighting, started largely by Charles Taylor and his supporters, brought massacres and atrocities to every region of the country. Charles Taylor, who had helped lead the uprising that started the war in 1989, was based in Gbarnga and already calling himself the president of 'Greater Liberia'. In 1997 he did become the elected president of Liberia, more likely due to the public's fear of continued violence and further bloodshed than anything else. Much of the fighting was ethnically based.

The intervention of the UN-supported Economic Communiy of West Africa Ceasefire Monitoring Group (ECOMOG) troops, almost all Nigerian, was initially seen as a positive action. However,

ECOMOG soon got dragged into the conflict and became yet another faction warring against Taylor. An economic embargo was started in 1993 against the territory held by Taylor, which was all of 'Greater Liberia' — about eighty percent of the country. The aid agencies advocated against the inclusion of humanitarian aid in the embargo. Finally, due to a horrific famine in the area, some of the agencies began to work in Taylor's territory regardless of the restrictions. By the time their programs began, some 5,000 children had died of starvation.

After a couple of days in Abidjan, it was time to head for Man. Two days and two attempts to catch a flight there ended in failure. One time we were told that the pilot was too drunk because of a party the night before and he simply never showed up. Finally, to my horror, Louise put me on the night bus. Every seat was full, and the hold was loaded with baggage, but that didn't stop the driver from piling more bags and boxes on the roof of the bus. When that was fully loaded, people continued to fill the aisles with more baggage, children, chickens, and goats. Packages and bundles of goods were even hanging out the windows.

Lesson number two: there is no such thing as a full bus in Africa. Mine left three hours after expected departure time. A tire had to be changed, and it took hours, several discussions and a town-wide hunt for the right size tire before we were ready to depart. Even worse, as I got into my seat, I noticed I was being followed by a very large and threatening-looking woman. Muttering a few words in French, she dropped a baby in my lap and disappeared! A gift? A terrible mistake? The girl, about nine months old, took one look at what was probably her first white face and started wailing. At that point, I was about ready to join her. Afraid to leave my bags and supplies alone, I was reluctant to get off the bus to search for her mother, so I tried leaning out the bus window and shouting for mom. My fellow travellers just laughed and smiled. My sorry attempts at high-school French got me nowhere. I was getting desperate!

Finally, the others started to board, and Mom showed up with a few chickens, an enormous bundle of goods, two more children and a goat. The woman positively beamed at me while retrieving the kid. My own relief knew no bounds.

We headed off on a bus that had missed at least half a century's worth of safety checks. Mostly windowless, with one headlight and a decided tilt to the left, the bus (with a driver who looked about eighteen years old) took off at an alarming speed. He turned his transistor radio up as loud as possible, and at first several fierce arguments started, but eventually singing broke out and all was well.

Halfway to Man, sometime around 1 a.m., the bus stopped for a 'restroom' break. The restroom was a ditch on the side of the road, which everyone but me was quite comfortable using. I crossed my legs desperately, decided dehydration was not a bad way to die, and prayed for the driver to hurry.

Near the ditch, there were dozens of people at roadside stands selling everything from bags of water to cooked meats and vegetables to radios. It was like market day at one in the morning! I couldn't believe it. My fellow travellers were enjoying the transactions, but I was getting desperate for a real toilet. Eventually, we got back on the road again. The goat slept well, but none of the children did — weeping and wailing for the next several hours, accompanied by a radio that would not stop.

An eternity later, when it was nearly dawn, we arrived in the station at Man. Bleary-eyed with exhaustion, I had never in my life been so grateful to see anyone as I was to see two staff members in a pick-up truck bearing MSF stickers. They collected my bags, drove me to the base, showed me my room and, more importantly, the toilet, then left me to my own devices. I was asleep in about ten seconds.

When I awoke, I met two expats, Nikky and Wilma, who were in Man on their first break in weeks. Because the project was considered a 'hardship' project, expats were sent out of the country to Man every six weeks for a little R&R. The work was exhausting and difficult in an area of constant fighting, and there was no way to take a break inside the country. These four to five day weekends were essential for the physical and mental well-being of the expats.

Nikky, the nutritionist, was responsible for the overall working of the twelve feeding centres MSF was managing. Wilma was working at one such feeding centre, and I was to be her replacement, also becoming Nikky's assistant. They were both quite patient with me considering the thousands of questions I asked them that morning, but they eventually told me I'd pretty much have to see it myself to get the hang of things. How right they were!

I spent the evening in Man, and we had a lovely dinner in town. The next morning, loaded with supplies, medicines, materials, tires, coldboxes of food and countless forms and requisitions, we headed across the border to Liberia.

The border crossing wasn't as bad as I feared. The Ivorian soldiers conducted their standard search and recorded our names and numbers in their ledgers but let us go without too much trouble. The Liberian side was a different matter. Although MSF had been crossing at that point for months, it was a bureaucratic hassle each time. It took ages to be allowed to pass, after copious paperwork had been filled in and the vehicles thoroughly searched. The contents of our shipments were matched with the manifest, and at least two or three people had to sign or stamp some form or other. The Liberians loved paperwork; the more official and abundant it was, the better!

This was my first experience with a country at war, and I would later learn that it was typical. When a country is at war, the infrastructure deteriorates. The wealthy are often the first to go; if you're able to evacuate, you take what you can and run. Then farms and factories close down, plantations stop running, schools and shops close. Those left behind end up jobless, broke and desperate to feed their families. If the war comes to your village, you never get the chance to harvest your crops or gather your money and belongings. People have been displaced with nothing but the clothes on their backs. They can lose everything in an instant: homes, family, money, jobs, security.

Corruption becomes commonplace and, though not excusable, perhaps somewhat understandable. People who own nothing see NGO workers as rich, mostly white, expats driving expensive cars with expensive equipment. Workers live in the nicest houses and can afford to have electric generators, good food, medicines, materials and nicer clothes than the local people will ever have. It's easy to see why NGOs can become a target. Some of the most ridiculous regulations are implemented by whatever person or group is in charge, and NGOs find themselves paying ridiculous amounts for licences or permits or import taxes. It's all mostly illegal, and just a way to line some officials' pockets.

In principle, none of the NGOs pay bribes. The prevailing view is that as a humanitarian organization, the agency should be given free access to all areas to offer help and support to a population in need. Period. In reality, there have been times where working without a specific permit or travelling without an invented visa is impossible. As for the method of bribery, it depends entirely on the situation. Sheets of writing paper and cigarettes have worked in Liberia. Condoms used to be given out to the combatants in Zaire. I have given medicine to people stricken with fever or malaria at the checkpoints, or transported them to the nearest clinic for medical attention. In Bosnia, I once gave a strong antihistamine to a man by the name of Curly, and it must have worked well. Later, I was able to avoid a sticky situation because Curly remembered I'd once helped him out. Determining how much one must legitimately do to continue the project and how much is some official's nonesense, to be avoided at all costs, is a matter of experience and intuition. This, for me, was not an easy lesson to learn.

On that first trip past the border to Liberia, I found the soldiers intimidating and was glad I was not alone. I was shocked to see how young some of the boys at the checkpoints were. Some were eight or nine years old, and I learned later that many had been taken by force and conscripted into the army. They could barely hold their AK-47s. Many were using drugs, and their behaviour was quite irrational. Dealing with these boys was a risky business, and there were at least a dozen checkpoints along the road.

In the late afternoon, we arrived in Gbarnga. MSF had set up a base on the Cuttington University compound (CUC), also known as Charlie base. The base had a large office, one warehouse for food and another for medical supplies, and four houses for some fifteen expats. I was devastated when the coordinator's first words were "Where are we going to put you?" So much for great expectations! Eventually, one of the expats reluctantly agreed to set me up in her house. It was not a very auspicious beginning.

In fact, the first three weeks were a bit of a nightmare. Everybody kept saying what an emergency the situation was, but nobody seemed to have a clear idea of what my position should be. I also wasn't that impressed with the coordinator. For starters, she refused to take her anti-malarial pills, so she was suffering from her third bout of malaria. She wore short, tight dresses and didn't strike me as very professional or as an exemplary role model for a first-missioner. I also didn't receive proper security guidelines for a couple of weeks. It wasn't until a month later, when the new coordinators arrived, that things sorted themselves out and I actually assumed a real position on the team.

I have so many scattered impressions of those first weeks — trying to learn all the Dutch names of my colleagues; getting used to living without running water or electricity; cold sponge baths from a fifty-gallon barrel; rain that poured down in a solid sheet; having to sleep under my mosquito net nightly; the eerie feeling of travelling in Africa and seeing no cattle, or chickens, or animals of any kind on the roads. The famine had reduced the livestock rather quickly, and was only beginning to get under control. What food there was was dreadful: mostly rice, beans and canned goods. Later, when the emergency situation was under control, some time was finally spent on improving the diet and living conditions of the expat team.

Adapting to my new position was overwhelming. In all, there were some 200 national staff I needed to know — drivers, medical staff, feeding centre staff, doctors, nurses, house staff, cooks and cleaners, logistical support staff, warehouse managers, well-diggers, and dozens of others. It took me ages to figure out who was who.

Fortunately, Wilma took me under her wing, and it was with her that I began my job as supervisor of the Grand Bassa feeding centre at Joshua Harmon Farm. It was the centre furthest away from the base, about a three-hour drive each way. We left the base at 7:30 a.m. to go to work and usually had to take several staff members with us. There was only one functioning hospital near Gbarnga, Phebe Hospital, and because of the distance, we also used to transport patients from our area to the hospital if necessary. Then, each morning there would be a lineup of people with written notes from one of the expats asking to please return a patient from the hospital to his village. I don't recall a single morning that the landcruiser ever left for the field empty.

As I mentioned earlier, MSF was running, along with medical clinics, about twelve therapeutic feeding centres and numerous other supplementary feeding programs. Once released from a therapeutic centre, a child must continue to receive weekly supplementary food — usually a high-calorie, high-protein cereal mix. The program ensured that every child's progress was monitored and gave us a good overview of the nutritional status of the population. Other agencies provided a general food distribution service, ensuring that every family received a sufficient supply of food each month. The malnutrition rate at that time was way above the accepted level; about forty to fifty percent of the population was malnourished. By the time MSF left the area, that percentage had decreased greatly, and the rice harvest was almost ready.

Sadly, the sole cause of the famine was the war. Forced to flee their homes because of fighting, thousands of people were left without gardens or fields, and many died before feeding centres could be opened and food brought in. Local resources were completely used up. All livestock and farm animals had long since been eaten, and many people were reduced to eating what they could find in the forest.

The continued fighting meant that many Liberians could not return to their homes or villages and were forced to settle in camps or in the homes of friends and relatives elsewhere. Those villages not affected by the fighting became very crowded, with up to thirty people living in a single home, and hundreds setting up makeshift camps in schools and churches.

The Save the Children Fund (SCF) was in the area doing a general food distribution in Grand Bassa County and running some medical clinics. The International Red Cross (ICRC) was also providing food distribution in other counties, such as Bong and Margibi. ICRC also ran family tracing programs and assisted in supplying the displaced with plastic sheeting for homes, tools for farming, casseroles for cooking and other emergency supplies. Few other NGOs were working in National Patriotic Front of Liberia (NPFL)-held territory. I got to know almost all of the other expats, and because there were no more than about thirty of us, we became good friends. It turned out to be a much easier task to coordinate just three or four agencies than the dozens or even, in some cases, hundreds working in other areas.

The disadvantage here, though, was that we were all stretched to our limits, and the workload was very difficult to manage. General food distribution remained inadequate, and the clinics could serve only a small part of the population. The constant insecurity meant entire regions could be cut off for days, weeks, or months at a time, severely limiting any possibility of consistent care. The morbidity and mortality rates of the population in Greater Liberia remained high throughout the war, as just getting to the target population oftentimes proved impossible.

On my first trip to Grand Bassa County, I passed about twenty-four checkpoints and was introduced to three generals and a colonel with the NPFL. The big boss was General Nixon Gaye. He was only about twenty-four years old but quite a cold-blooded killer, from what I heard. The population was terrified of him, and he had no qualms about holding them hostage to get what he wanted, or kidnapping their children and young men to force them into his war. He was under the command of Charles Taylor.

The frontline of battle ran between the capital of Monrovia and Gbarnga, at a town called Kakata. It was often very difficult to get permission from both factions to cross that line to get supplies into Gbarnga, so most of the agencies worked out of the Ivory Coast. Our security in NPFL territory depended solely on the Liberian soldiers. The UN people had not arrived when MSF started work, and though some arrived later, they did little to provide security to NGOs. Like it or not, we needed the support of Nixon Gaye and his men in order to do our job.

Gaye could be a very charming fellow, but he was also very demanding. MSF was obliged at times to allow him to ride with us to Gbarnga for one of his numerous meetings with his bosses. He also constantly asked for rides for his friends and his soldiers, but we all did our best to keep him out of the program as much as possible. It wasn't easy. There were a few times I had to go to him and ask for his help with a security issue or report that one of his men had been causing problems at the centre. Mostly, I tried hard to stay well away from him.

Despite the situation, I remember how incredibly beautiful that first trip to my feeding centre was. Lush and green, heavily forested, the area we drove through was magnificent. We travelled through part of the Firestone rubber plantation, with acres of rubber trees planted in rows. It was like stepping into a story — I fully expected to see Gandalf and the hobbits at any moment.

The roads were terrible, though, and more than once in the rainy season we got stuck. I quickly learned just how tough driving in Liberia could be. As several villages and at least six other MSF feeding centres or clinics were en route, we'd travel together in convoys when possible, which helped increase our sense of security.

When we arrived at the end of the road, I discovered that we had to cross the Farmington River to get to the feeding centre. It was a wide, deep, fast-moving river, and I had no desire whatsoever to cross it on the little Save the Children Fund raft at my disposal. A wooden canoe that was available seemed a better idea, but my driver begged me not to take it. We had just passed through Margibi County and driven alongside Mount Gibi, which was a source of powerful witchcraft to the people. I was told that the canoe was cursed, and that several people had died in it. Who was I to argue? I took the raft.

Set up on a rocky promontory on the other side was the medical centre. Behind it was the makeshift therapeutic feeding centre, and near it was a large, fenced enclosure which opened once a week for some 7,000 people to receive their supplementary rations. Wilma casually introduced me to several workers, whose names I promptly forgot as I was pretty overwhelmed with the whole situation.

In those first weeks, I had so much to learn! Just getting a grasp on how the feeding centre worked was enough to fill my days. Malnutrition, I soon found out, is a complex and complicated disease. The therapeutic centre admitted children who were less than 75 percent of the normal weight for their height. They were kept in the therapeutic centre to receive twenty-four-hour care, which included special feedings every four hours until their conditions stabilized. Severely malnourished kids faced death unless they were carefully rehydrated and fed, very slowly. Some of the children spent weeks, even months, in the centre until their general health improved. They also received medications to prevent infections and treat parasites, special doses of vitamins and vaccinations. Their recovery was a long, difficult process.

To complicate matters further, there was a supervisor at the centre named Roland, whom I didn't trust at all. As it turned out, he was giving quite a few bags of food to the military to ensure the 'security' of the centre. I could understand his dilemma, but the drain on our supplies soon became a real burden on the centre, which was already in a bad state of neglect. I constantly had to check out the supply room for food, and to make matters worse, the heat was spoiling the food far too quickly. As well, the whole area needed to be cleaned out and sprayed for bugs. The well was almost dry, so a new one would have to be built; the latrines were filthy; the garbage pit was full and not being burned properly.

The place was also in a state of disarray, managerially. The doctor at the centre was intending to leave, and we needed at least one good nurse capable of diagnosing patients to replace him. Two of the cooks never showed up to work on my first day, and there was no firewood for the kitchen. The raft, which was the sole means of transport to the centre, was breaking apart, and the new one was only half finished. There had been a lot of fighting two days before I arrived, and several of the staff and patients had fled. I could go on, but suffice to say that I realized 'supervision' covered a lot of ground I hadn't thought about.

Wilma was reassuring, but I was feeling pretty insecure about the whole thing. It didn't help that that very night the team had a big security meeting. On March 7, the interim government in Monrovia was supposed to take power during this, the latest cease-fire. Nobody expected the cease-fire to last, and most people were expecting further trouble. In the face of a possible emergency, it was essential to review the security and evacuation guidelines. It was necessary, but not conducive to feeling very safe. Great, just great.

However, within a couple of weeks and after numerous trips to Grand Bassa, I was beginning to feel a bit better about the situation. I began to know the staff at the centre better and to see ways we could improve our lot. I came to recognize people at the checkpoints, and they began to know my face. I learned a lot more about the war and the present situation as the staff confided in me. I studied the maps, did a lot of background reading, and slowly began to fill in the gaps.

Still, things within the team needed to be improved. The stress of handling the emergency had taken its toll on people. Security was not great. None of the vehicles had radios because the NPFL hadn't allowed the team to have them yet, meaning there was no way of contacting the base if something went wrong. The coordinator was tired — ill with malaria again — and was having a hard time handing over her program to Anne, the incoming coordinator; it can be a very difficult thing to relinquish responsibility for a program you have learned to love, and it's hard sometimes to stay objective. The whole team was tired, worn out, run down, and in need of fresh blood. I was helping Nikky part of the time and supervising the one feeding centre for the rest, but still, nobody seemed to know what my real job was or where I should be placed. I was beginning to wonder if Liberia was the right place for me.

Chapter 2

From my journal, February 26, 1994:

Well, it started off as a great day and ended up a disaster. First conflict — got to the Gbarnga police gate, and they wanted to see Harris's (the driver's) 'police clearance'. It's being processed along with all the others, but none of the drivers have the official form yet. Forty minutes of hassling to get us through.

Then Anne and Gert, one of the nurses, never showed up for the 6 p.m. curfew. Turns out Nixon Gaye hijacked one of our trucks and threatened the driver. He wanted to transport his *football team* to Gbarnga. The driver went as far as Peter Town and stopped, refusing to go any further, at which point Anne and Gert showed up. They were able to finally negotiate for the release of both the driver and the truck, but I guess it pissed off Nixon Gaye to no end.

Then there was supposed to be a big farewell party for Wilma and Egbert, who are both leaving. I had to be the one to tell them it was cancelled. Until the issue with General Nixon was resolved, nobody would be allowed to travel to the field. The staff from Grand Bassa has been planning a special farewell for months, but now no one is going anywhere. It's such a shame.

Eventually, the coordinator spoke with Nixon, sorted things out, and we went back to work. I moved up to Wilma's old room in the guesthouse. It was far more peaceful than the previous one. Denis, a French Canadian, arrived to be the new logistician. I went with him for a stroll about the university campus and started to become familiar with my new home.

The 'guesthouse', where we lived, was a large four-bedroom house where guests had once been entertained. It backed up against a swamp, and the noise of insects and frogs kept me awake for several nights until I finally became accustomed to their clatter. We had a large yard, where the volleyball court was to be, and a garden in the back. Unlike the other houses, ours required a ten-minute walk down the hill to the main base, so we lived in more of a 'neighbourhood' than the others.

One bizarre evening, the house filled up with thousands of flying termites. They were big, ugly, worm-like creatures with wings. We were apparently in the way of their annual mating season, and being the only house with electricity, we had light to attract them into our place. The next day, the staff had to sweep up those that didn't survive.

We also had snakes around the place. Once, the guards very excitedly called us to see them capture a large but harmless cassava snake. They shared it with the neighbours for dinner. Another time, we ended up with a deadly green mamba on the stoop, which was a bit more of a challenge to exterminate. Luckily, nobody was hurt.

I was now on my own in the feeding centre and feeling more secure. Debbie, my roommate and one of the nurses managing the clinics, became a very close friend. She was always in amazingly good spirits, and I enjoyed her lively personality. I was finally settling into a routine, getting to know my teammates, the house staff, and my feeding centre staff. The cultural differences between the various expats soon became quite obvious, though, particularly between the rather serious Dutch and the more relaxed, louder Americans, Canadians and Australians.

March 5, 1994:

Survived the first week on my own. Ran out of corn-soya blend cereal at the feeding centre on Wednesday, but am starting to get the hang of things. Denis came for a visit to the feeding centre, and helped make a plan for improvements of the well, new kitchen, warehouse, garbage ditch, et cetera.

Poor Anne is having a rotten time of things, with the outgoing coordinator wanting to extend her work term and refusing to hand over responsibilities. Debbie is leaving Saturday for a week's holiday, and another expat is finishing her mission. There's a big farewell party tomorrow. I was so hoping to sleep in, but some of the workers here for the EPI (Expanded Program of Immunization) workshop have to get home, and after the trouble last week, the coordinator wants an expat in every car. We have to be ready to leave at 6 a.m.!

Dineke, the project coordinator, the big boss from Monrovia, is coming here for a week, until after the interim government takes its seats two days from now. Hopefully, it will be a peaceful transition, but I doubt it.

By this point, I had been asked to assist with the EPI team. EPI is the World Health Organization (WHO) standard of vaccination for developing countries. It's a rapid vaccination routine designed so that children from birth to five years can be fully vaccinated within a year. The statistics of children dying from preventable diseases are alarming in developing nations. In Liberia at that time, less than thirty-two percent of people were fully vaccinated. One of the expats who was about to leave had just gotten started on an EPI team, and I was asked to take it over.

I began with only six or seven people, although before I left, we would have a twelve-person team, and they would be running the show themselves. At first, I didn't know the schedule or the routine, or an awful lot about EPI, and I had to teach myself as much as I could as quickly as possible. Fortunately, every project includes an MSF library, which contains books covering just about every aid-related topic you can imagine. My standard copies of *Clinical Guidelines* and *Essential Drugs* became my bibles, and I would have been lost without them.

Our EPI team's first assignment together was on March 7, a screening for a supplementary feeding program in Fenutoli. There was already a therapeutic centre there to receive any severely malnourished children identified in the screening.

Scores of mothers and fathers arrived, together with some 700 children. It was a logistical nightmare to try to maintain order but, somehow, it worked remarkably well. The children were first lined up outside the centre. One by one they were then brought in to have a mid-upperarm circumference (MUAC) measurement done. The MUAC is used to do a quick initial assessment of how thin a child is. The band goes aroundthe child's arm, and a measurement is read in millimetres to see if the child is thin enough to qualify. It's usually done in surveys when there's not enough time to weigh and measure everyone.

After that, the kids would walk under a stick placed at a certain height. Age is hard to know in Africa, so the standard by which children are admitted is weight and height. The stick would determine if they fell under a certain height, which would be the norm for a child of five years or less. If they were too tall, they were excluded, unless they looked extremely thin; then, of course, an exception was made. Those too small to be walking were measured on a height board specially designed to hold a child straight for an accurate measurement.

Children who could walk under the stick were then weighed, either by a scale hanging from a post in the medical centre or on a standing scale, depending on size. If they were under eighty or eighty-five percent of their normal weight, they were admitted to the supplementary feeding program. If they were under seventy or seventy-five percent of their normal weight, they went into the therapeutic centre for more intensive care.

Whether admitted to the program or not, each child still received the vaccinations. If they didn't have a vaccination card, one was issued to them so they could be brought in again for the next dose the following month. After that, any sick child was sent to the medical centre to be seen by the medical personnel.

It took dozens of staff to measure and weigh each child, fill in the medical charts and enter the children's names into the ledgers. All of the staff had to be trained in the techniques for this, and one day's work required weeks of preparation. Not only did the staff have to know their work, but the community had to be contacted so that parents knew when and where they could bring their children in for treatment. No point in doing a screening if nobody shows.

Afterwards, each child would have his or her ear or nail painted with gentian violet, a stain that is hard to wash out, so that nobody could sneak back in for a second try.

It was a long, hot, dusty, crowded, loud and chaotic day. But it was a success. A lot of hungry children were accepted into the feeding program, and the most vulnerable kids were treated in the therapeutic centre.

The bad news was that although there had been singing in the streets on the day the interim government took their seats in Monrovia, the peace process wasn't going to last, as many had suspected. The ECOMOG, the West Africa peacekeeping troops, crossed Kakata at the frontline to start setting up their disarmament procedures in NPFL territory. Procedures lasted about a day before fighting broke out in Kakata. A local NGO in Gbarnga was robbed of money and food which was to be distributed in town. A hijacking occurred near Kakata. A Lutheran World Services truck from Gbarnga was looted of its extra fuel in town. The nutritional surveys for the Grand Bassa and Bong areas were cancelled. In Yarnwellie, a town on the road to Grand Bassa that I passed every day, a SCF truck was stoned and the drivers' documents were confiscated by General Gaye's men. Driving past Totota, along the main road just outside Cuttington University compound, we saw four men stripped naked and tied to a pole in the town centre, being beaten for some infraction or other. We didn't dare stay to see what happened, as the crowd was pretty agitated.

The UN Observer Mission in Liberia (UNOMIL), the UN peacekeeping troops, had arrived in Monrovia but were refusing to cross the frontline and enter NPFL territory without some security guarantees, which of course Charles Taylor couldn't provide. One of the factions in Lofa County elected a new leader and claimed Lofa as their territory. A lot of the generals from Margibi County ended up in Gbarnga, but it sure wasn't for peace talks.

Chapter 3

March 15, 1994:

It's been general food distribution time in Grand Bassa for these last few days. Absolute chaos! The road has been quiet, but there's been fighting in Compound Two, not far from the feeding centre, between the NPFL and the Liberian Peace Council (LPC). Four people from LPC were killed yesterday. Then there's United Liberation Movement for Democracy (ULIMO), the Lofa Defence Force (LDF), and the Armed Forces of Liberia (AFL) thrown into the mix. Yet when I actually asked one of the kids at the checkpoint what he was fighting for, he told me 'freedom'. When I asked him to be a little more specific, he couldn't respond. I doubt any of these kids care what the fight is about. They've been forced to fight and have been given a gun and some power. It's a scary thing to happen to a child.

My new baby at the therapeutic feeding centre (TFC) is doing well. Her name is Handful, since that's about all she is! She's six months old and weighed 2.8 kilograms when she arrived. She's up to 3.2 kilograms now and is looking beautiful.

Some of the drivers are still very edgy driving here. The whole area around Mount Gibi is haunted, full of witchcraft and mysteries. I've been told that if I tried to climb to the top of Mount Gibi without the permission of the elders, I'd simply disappear. I actually had to take the canoe today because the raft was occupied by SCF workers and their food. We almost tipped over midway, so I waited for the raft to cross back. No sense in aggravating the spirits if I don't have to.

The convoy got in from Monrovia today, and I finally got my first mail from home. Finally! And we now have enough corn-soya blend cereal for the feeding centres tomorrow.

March 19, 1994:

What a hell of a week! Roland's been stealing from the centre for ages, but I just can't prove it yet. What he doesn't steal, the soldiers do. I heard that just after people had received their month's food distribution from Save the Children Fund, the soldiers stopped them right in the road and confiscated it all.

The well is almost dry at the feeding centre, and the new one still isn't finished, so Denis came and chlorinated what water was left in the old one. It is so hot these days, about 35° C. I'm really getting tired of this six-hour commute everyday. The good thing is that Emanuel, one of the drivers, has taught me to drive a landcruiser. I was expecting it to be much harder than it is.

Fighting in Monrovia continues, and two MSF-France national nurses have been killed just across the frontline. Peace talks are at a standstill, and the prospect of disarmament is a joke.

To top it all off, yesterday Nixon Gaye's response to accusations of his men stealing food was to ask for a ride to town! I can tell you where I'd like to drive the son of a bitch to!

Poor Denis, this wasn't his week either. The twenty-ton truck he was driving from Monrovia to Gbarnga overturned on the tarmac road. We managed to salvage most of the supplies, but it took all our vehicles, and we had to leave the field early to help. I even had to bring the general to the road to try to maintain some order.

By the end of March, a lot of changes had taken place within the team. Anne took over as the new medical coordinator, and a man named Ton as the new logistical and field coordinator. With the nutritional emergency now well in hand, some care was finally taken to improve the living status of the expat team.

Some staff were reassigned, a new cook was hired, and better food was ordered from Amsterdam, Monrovia and Man. We started a vegetable garden in the backyard, and the quality and quantity of the food improved dramatically. New house staff were hired and arrangements made so that we no longer ran out of essentials in the house, like water for cooking, cleaning and drinking. The staff ensured that the kerosene in the lamps was filled regularly and that enough candles were available. Ton even ordered a reasonable supply of beer and, for the first time since I had arrived, the mood of the team improved.

Ton also started building a volleyball court in the yard of the guesthouse, where I was now living with Debbie, Nikky and Denis. That volleyball court was to become the centre of many social events in Cuttington University compound and was a real morale booster. With a 6 p.m. curfew, volleyball became our after-hours entertainment of choice.

I soon became the official supervisor of the EPI team. I still managed the TFC and SFP in Grand Bassa, but more time was spent in getting EPI up and running. In my new role, I slowly began to get to know the EPI staff and found them to be a hard-working, professional and dedicated group. I also started talking with Henrietta, the supervisor, to try to start making an actual schedule for the work. As MSF was working in at least three counties, we were hoping to carry out a full vaccination campaign in every place where we had either a feeding centre or a health centre. This meant that we would have to go to each centre at least once a month for three consecutive months to fully vaccinate as many kids as possible.

Arranging this was not easy. For starters, we had to implement a proper cold chain to make sure our food and drug supplies were properly refrigerated, which is no easy task in a place without electricity. As for obtaining supplies, we had a good relationship with the UNICEF representative in Gbarnga, and as long as we handed her our monthly reports she gave us as many vaccination cards, needles, syringes and vaccines as we needed. Of course, things always went wrong. Sometimes the shipment for UNICEF never made it in, or we ran out of kerosene for our three lousy refrigerators and couldn't keep the temperature stable, ruining some of the vaccines. Or there wasn't a car available for us to drive into town to pick up our supplies when we needed them. Or there weren't enough ice packs for the day, because the generator was on the blink and the big freezer thawed out overnight. Or about a thousand other things.

Then there was the problem of trying to choose a good day for each town in order to get as many people to come for the vaccination as possible. That meant finding out what the population was in each town so we could estimate how many children under the age of five we could expect. With no population census available and huge numbers of displaced people, this was next to impossible. Sometimes we really miscalculated, but we were generally clever enough to know who to speak to and which questions to ask, and after a while we were accurate to a surprising degree. When possible, we tried to go to towns on market day to ensure that most of the women and children would be present.

Once the day was set, I then had to ensure that we had enough vaccines, needles, syringes, vaccination cards, ledger books, pens, cold boxes, cookies and other supplies ready to go at 7:30 in the morning. The cookies were a donation from SCF, a wonderful treat to give to the kids after they had received their vaccinations. I often took over cookie distribution when other staff members were doing the real work. The cookies came packed in big metal tins, circa 1963, but were still surprisingly tasty. A lot of the kids were very afraid of our white faces, but nobody ever refused a cookie.

By now we had radios installed in all of the vehicles. I was responsible for two landcruisers, since I needed both for the vaccines and the staff. One of the trucks was a donation from UNICEF, and the other was 'Charlie 5'. I became very attached to Charlie 5, until one day it was stolen by the soldiers.

A new feeding centre had opened up in a university complex in Gbalatuah, north of Gbarnga, near the Lofa county frontline. Uriah Morgan was the nurse-supervisor, an excellent nurse who cared deeply for his patients. The centre was clean, new and well-run. I went to the opening party with Gert and it was great fun, with speeches, dancing, singing and even a soccer game. In time, the centre grew to accomodate a couple of hundred patients from its initial few dozen.

The one thing that didn't change, however, was the very poor security situation. At two of our feeding centres, Bopolu and Blumo, MSF staff were beaten up and food looted from the centre. The NPFL started a forced recruitment of young boys and men that went on for weeks in that area. Staff in Grand Bassa were terrified. Two people were 'arrested' and forcibly recruited into Nixon's army. One escaped and went into hiding, and the other was eventually released. I saw General Jack-the-Ripper (as he called himself) with a pick-up truck full of weapons in Yarnwellie on my way to Bassa. There was no sign of him when I returned.

We started hearing rumours; Nixon Gaye was in Abidjan, some 100, 300, 500 men and boys were taken from their homes at night. The big generals were either out of the country or in Gbarnga, so they had the excuse of supposedly not being there at the time. People were scared, and tensions were rising.

April 2, 1994:

Margibi is a ghost town! There are estimates that up to 1,000 young boys and men have now been abducted. The stories abound — they are working in the diamond mines, working on Nixon's sugar cane and rice farms, they have been recruited into the army and are training in the Firestone plantation. Randolf, my outreach worker, was badly harassed on his way home. Sumo Leo and Bindo Bondo, two other outreach workers, have disappeared. I hope they've gone bush, but maybe they've been forcibly taken. Nobody knows. The people are terrified. On Friday, we didn't have a single patient in the feeding centre. The roads are filling up with those on the run.

I'm getting scared. Those of us working in the area have been quietly trying to sneak some of the boys out, and I'm afraid it's a huge risk and we might get caught. But what can we do?

I was frightened. For the first time, I realized how precarious our situation was. Along with a few other expats, I tried sneaking some young men out of Bassa and Margibi before they became the next victims of the general. I took one man along as a fake patient, even starting a drip to make it look good, because that impressed the soldiers. I took another along as a caregiver, as we always took a caregiver along to feed and care for the patient in Phebe Hospital. This poor kid was terrified. As the patient was legitimate, I made the young man promise to actually stay and look after the old lady until she was released, which he did.

Another time, I took a national staff member, Arthur, out. We told the soldiers at the checkpoint that he was coming for an inservice in CUC. But he left with a small bag of his belongings and half a bag of rice, which of course made the soldiers suspicious. During a long conversation with the checkpoint guards, my heart was pounding, and I was so nervous I could hardly breathe. Arthur was equally distressed, and there was a moment when we thought they wouldn't let us pass. But finally they dropped the gate and let us through. We all breathed a sigh of relief when we got out to the main road and left Margibi behind.

Chapter 4

The radios in the vehicles turned out to be a lifesaver. Barely a week after they were installed, Debbie called the base with a frantic message that she'd had an accident on the road to Shankpalai, where our new clinic was located. She had gotten stuck on a bridge, which partially collapsed, leaving the landcruiser hanging off the side. Unable to leave the car because of a poisonous snake on the bridge, Debbie called for help. Vehicles from the base went to her aid, using their winches to pull the disabled vehicle to safety, sliding the car off the bridge until it ended up beneath the uncollapsed portion. It took them hours to free her, but she eventually made it back to base, safe but late.

In the beginning of April, the rains began visibly building up. Denis and I used to sit on the porch for hours in the evening and watch the thunderclouds roll in. With the lightning and thunder, and the mists hanging low on the ground, it was spectacular. One night, over dinner, we could hear the people from the village singing just after a big soccer game, while half of the sky was filled with stars and the other half was flashing lightning. The music accompanying the fantastic display seemed dreamlike. Moments like those were so lovely and peaceful, you could almost believe there wasn't a war going on. Except, of course, for the missing people, the threatened and frightened staff and the constant undercurrent of tension.

For Easter, the entire staff gathered for dinner, an unusual occurrence as we were spread out over four houses and rarely ate together. Usually, we only assembled as a group for morning arguments over the day's destination and the evening's return or for the regular security meetings. But after that, it soon became a habit to spend Sunday afternoons together as a team, for brunch or volleyball gamesor to watch movies. The guesthouse had a TV, and it was quite a social event when we could get a film and use the generator to power the VCR for a couple of hours.

That Easter, we decorated the table with flowers, everybody dressed up, and I still remember now how special our dinner together was. After our feast, the UNOMIL people from town invited us to the one and only local disco, Club Mahogany. I wasn't overly impressed with the club, nor with the UNOMIL people. Ton used to say UNOMIL actually stood for 'Unbelievable Number of Mustaches in Liberia'. To be honest, most of the new UN crew did have mustaches, but I don't think they would have appreciated the joke.

The next morning, Deb and I went to Wohrn for the Easter service. It was three hours of dancing, singing, spiritual revival and praying. One song still stands out in my memory to this day:

I don't worry no more
No, I don't worry no more.
I pray to Jesus, He answers my prayer,
So I don't worry no more.

How these people, who had just had their husbands, brothers and sons taken from them, could possibly sing after what they had been through was incomprehensible to me. I could not imagine what it must have been like to lose a son and to be completely helpless. I knew that there was no justice in Liberia, no authority to turn to, and not a soul who would help you. I was awed by the people's courage in bearing that and by the way they stayed faithful to a God they could not see, who at that point did not even seem to be listening.

I once asked one of my Liberian colleagues how he could stand such a life, to have to run at a moment's notice, leaving or losing everything. He told me that you just put your life in the care of your feet and run. He laughed when he told me this. It was my first glimpse of what it was like to be a displaced person. It put a face on the thousands of immigrants applying for refugee status in countries around the world, and it humbled me to realize that, despite their situation, there are those who will not allow themselves to be broken. They will pick up the pieces and go on, sing again, laugh and pray for better days. Some will even learn to forgive. I do not know if I could be that strong or that brave. I hope I never have to find out.

April 10, 1994:

Did EPI this entire week. They're a good team, and Henrietta manages well. Later this week I'm going to Man for my first break. Has it been seven weeks already? I can't believe it! I've never worked this hard in my life. I'm up at 6:30 for breakfast, which is fruit and bread, then down to base at 7 to pack my two cars, gather staff and supplies, then find out who else is going in my direction so we can travel together. And there are always a dozen people who need a ride, or need help, or need a job: or there's trouble with the number of vaccines; or I have to bring drug supplies along to the clinics for Deb or Stephanie, et cetera. Then off we go for a two to three hour drive. Then it's the set-up of the whole program — which building can we use, where to put the guys who have to do all the writing and charting, where the preparers can go to start preparing the vaccines — then we need chairs for the vaccinators to sit on, then the cold boxes have to be ready and information given to the women and children arriving in the line-up.

I usually try to get the team to take a break at noon for some food. Mistakes are not permitted in this kind of work, and it has to be a very well organized operation in order to run properly. It's exhausting work, and most days I'm ready to leave before my team is.

The work was pretty straightforward but, from a logistical point of view, not that easy. I had three or four registrars who set up tables and chairs and started the day by registering every woman and child who arrived for their vaccinations. Each child was listed in at least two different ledgers — some for the daily record, some according to age, others according to the type of vaccine they received. Each person took a few minutes to list and then had to be given a vaccination card if they didn't already have one.

Next came the vaccination preparers. Again, three or four people were in charge of preparing at least a dozen doses of each vaccine. Each dose had to be correctly drawn up and placed on an ice pack to keep the vaccine stable. The ice packs melted quickly and had to be changed regularly, and the doses had to be easily available to the vaccinators. Label cards were placed near each ice pack to avoid any mix-up.

Then came the vaccinators; at least two for the children and one for the women. The vaccinators had to check each child's card to ensure that they would receive the correct dose in the correct spot. Some children received all vaccines, including polio, measles, tuberculosis, and the trio of diphtheria, pertussis and tetanus (DPT). I've seen a good vaccinator hold a child down in a headlock and fully vaccinate the kid in under a minute!

After the kids were finished, the mothers went to their own line for tetanus shots. The plan was to have every woman of childbearing age receive a minimum of five doses of tetanus. They were to receive three during or before their first pregnancy and two after. Again, the EPI is set up so that a woman should be fully vaccinated within three years at the most.

The details that needed attending were mind-boggling. I had to keep an eye on the supply of chairs, benches, pens, needles, syringes, icepacks, cotton, pails, water for washing the skin prior to injections, and about a dozen other things. I had to make sure there was rope to arrange the line-up outside the school/clinic/feeding centre/hut/tree we were using that day. Every used syringe had to be placed in its pail, and every child had to be checked again before leaving the facility to verrify that they had received their injections and their mothers knew that we'd be back in one month to continue the regime. After all that, the successfully vaccinated children could get their cookies. The mothers then received certificates naming them good moms because they had their children vaccinated. Mothers took such pride in receiving this paper. It always amazed me that they would flee their homes, under fire sometimes, but still remember to take their vaccination and health cards.

The staff never brought food with them, but the work was very tiring and we needed to eat somewhere in the middle of all the chaos. I got into the habit of bringing along a bag of rice from our warehouse and paying a local woman a small fee to cook us lunch, usually rice with cassava leaves, cooked up in a spicy pili pili sauce. It is a very hot dish, but delicious. The staff really appreciated a midday meal, and we soon had our own spoons and plates to add to our daily materials. That's one thing we never forgot.

Near the end of the day, the number of vaccines, needles, syringes and doses used had to be counted and properly disposed of. The used needles and syringes were thrown in the latrines or buried in a pit to prevent the people from reusing them. It usually took nearly an hour to do the clean-up and count. Then everything and everyone was reloaded. By this time I would have to visit either the feeding centre or the health centre to pick up requisitions for supplies, reports, sick patients that had to go to Phebe and sometimes staff members who were going into Gbarnga for a weekend to take their own breaks. I also had to deal with any security information, and problems with staff or the military. Some days, this took up more of my time than supervision of the EPI itself.

When the team went home, I went to the office. Any issues that had to be discussed with either Anne or Ton were brought up then. We had a constant shortage of computers, and with the lack of generator hours, getting them charged was always a problem. Whenever I got my hands on one, I started on my reports.

I usually made it back to the house for dinner around 6:30 and occasionally had time for a volleyball game. The evening was spent by candlelight or kerosene lamp, more often than not doing reports, working on surveys, trying to find out population figures and planning the numerous workshops and inservices that needed to be arranged as the program expanded. Bedtime was about 9:30 p.m. , after the cold daily splash bath, and the alarm was set for 6:30 a.m. to start it all over again.

Mercifully, though, Anne and Ton refused to allow the team to work on Sundays. We all did a half day of office work on Saturday, but they tried hard to keep us out of the field on weekends, although there were times when we were required to work.

I cannot express the importance of having a team that not only works well together but also realizes the importance of maintaining the health and high spirits of the entire team. There is nothing worse than returning to your house at the end of an exhausting day and having lousy food to eat, no water to drink and no clean clothes for the morning. The day-to-day work is hard enough that if your living arrangements aren't decent, it makes life harder than it already is. It doesn't cost much to make a volleyball court, or to ensure that a supply of beer is available and decent food is purchased.

By western standards, our living quarters with MSF were pretty poor. By local standards, however, they were pretty good, and there was a reason for that. MSF knows that if they want their people to put in twelve-hour days, six or seven days in a row, for months on end, those people will need compensation. Since the pay is lousy, a few small extras go a long way towards making a team feel comfortable: food that includes chicken or meat once in awhile. A case of beer that you can enjoy together after work. Having a full barrel of water in your bathroom for washing everyday. Having the water containers full, so that your drinking water has been filtered. The occasional bag of crisps or cookies around the house. Clean sheets and clean clothes. When possible, a group trip to a restaurant in town. These little things can do so much for the morale of the team. I have learned that a good cook is more precious than a good nurse. I can train a nurse to be good. I can't train a cook!

April 12, 1994:

There was a big storm a couple of nights ago. It tore the roof off the ICRC (International Red Cross) house. One poor guy lost his clothes, his room, everything. Now he's a true refugee.

We had dinner and a movie the other night. Very nice. The guys even made Irish coffee for us all. Weird — watching movies in an abandoned university compound with no electricity except our one generator, a few houses full of refugees as neighbours and an odd assortment of teammates that come from Holland, Canada, USA, Australia, Ireland, Britain and France.

Boy, does it rain when it rains here! The house got struck by lightning last night. The lightning ripped through a cement wall after rebounding off a pole outside. Good thing no one was hurt. You can hear the rain coming from miles away, and it washes over the house in a sheet.

We couldn't get into Margibi yesterday. They cut us off at the bridge. Fighting in Compound Two. NPFL? LPC? Who knows? Rumour is that Nixon Gaye hijacked General Varney's car and four people were killed, four others injured. Varney's an even bigger fish than Nixon, so God only knows what retaliation he's got planned.

Ended up with the EPI team in Upper Bong instead. Beautiful area: narrow trails, lots of jungle, very green and lush. Quiet day, though, since it wasn't planned. Some fighting at the Belefuania checkpoint. Heard gunshots. Apparently someone looted some oil from a woman who was the NPFL commander's girlfriend. Oops! Thank God tomorrow I'm off to Man. I am so tired. I am so tired.

Chapter 5

April 18, 1994:

Well, Man was wonderful! I went shopping at an actual market with everything in it — cows, chickens, goats, everything! I ate real food — fresh bread with ham and cheese and tomatoes, croissants and baguettes and fresh mangoes — while swinging in the hammock. Went out for dinner every night. Hot showers and cold beer. Yes, there is a God!

We went to the cascades, the waterfall in Man. There's a rope bridge across the river, which they say is built and rebuilt by six witches from the villages. They build it in one week and then turn into monkeys, spiders and birds so they can climb up the trees to attach it. The new bridge goes up in one night and nobody ever knows when or how often it is replaced.

A couple of MSF-Belgium people came and hung out with us in Man. The last night we went out with Steve, a Canadian fellow, and Philippe, a *gorgeous* Frenchman from ACF (Action Contre la Faime). They were working in Harper but got their cars stolen and wanted to go to Gbarnga to try to sort things out. Since they came with food, we let them in. Any expat from any organization is welcomed if they come with food, drinks, reading material — or a need.

We drove with our new friends in convoy back to Gbarnga. Of

course, since they were travelling in an ACF vehicle, we were stopped at every bloody gate along the way. Good thing the soldiers know MSF and we could vouch for these guys.

We made it home in time for a great dinner and set Steve and Philippe up at Steph's house, since it's got the only free room.

I hear they're letting us back into Margibi and Bassa tomorrow, maybe only temporarily. People say they want food to come in so that the soldiers can loot it. It's 'General Ba-bating' (General bad, bad thing) and 'General Jack the Ripper' responsible for these doings.

I'm glad that Gerda has taken over the feeding centre. I'm really enjoying EPI, and I can't imagine doing both anymore.

And now we've been turned back from Upper Bong. Apparently ULIMO is fighting in Lofa and Upper Bong. Who knows? We see the ECOMOG troops, the Tanzanians, everywhere for all the good they're doing. Sure as hell no one is disarming. It seems the country is falling into ruin and everything is escalating. I could just cry, it is so discouraging. God, these poor people. I really could just close my eyes and cry.

The situation reports, better known as sitreps, going from Gbarnga to Monrovia and on to Amsterdam, continued to indicate a worsening security situation. Areas were closed to us more often, and the fighting moved from place to place, with less periods of calm in between.

When we returned to Bassa, the staff had plenty of stories. The biggest one was that the NPFL had stolen a *tank* from ECOMOG and tried to transport it one night. House-to-house searches continued in Gbarnga, with market women being killed because they were married to Mandingos. They say hundreds have been buried at the checkpoint by Wainsu. Roland from my EPI team called it the 'Holy Ground', saying that if you ever got taken there, you'd better pray to God for help because without divine intervention, your life was over. The NPFL weren't big on mercy. ULIMO, The United Liberation Movement for Democracy, was fighting amongst themselves, and there were rumours of a new faction in the fray. More checkpoints along the road. Concerns that the convoys from Monrovia would no longer get through. Troops from Ganta fighting in Sanniquellie.

We were being asked for identification cards at the gates and had to issue them to all our staff. ICRC tried to get to Bong through Sonoya and ended up having to spend the night at a checkpoint in Totota. We went where we could, when we were allowed, and life went on.

A letter to a friend, April 26, 1999:
Dear Darcy,

Am sitting here in the semi-dark waiting for night. We have no electricity and no running water anymore. Our three generators all died at once. The one in our backyard blew up. It was kind of entertaining, and fortunately didn't interfere with our volleyball game.

We had a big tournament this last weekend. My EPI team lost out in the first round, but I dare say we were formidable opponents. We all had a lot of fun. This volleyball court in our yard has become the social gathering point of the project now.

Things are going OK. The security situation remains dicey. The soldiers are moving troops, and there is fighting at the Guinea border. Two counties have been closed to us for a week but have since reopened. Lots of movement of people, though.

Anyhow, we're managing. My head's still above water. We're being very careful, and everyone keeps a bag packed for emergency evacuation if we need it.

At least things have improved in the market. They have bubblegum now! Still, I'm not too optimistic. The UN says they're pulling out if all the soldiers don't disarm by May 21. At which point the country might just go to hell.

Anyhow, no news is good news. At least not around here.

Chapter 6

By May, I felt like a real expat. I was an actual relief worker, and I was loving it. The work was extremely challenging, and I was always busy with something or other, but I also found out that life could be a lot of fun.

We had an excellent relationship with the other NGOs, especially the Save the Children crew — Ros, Rob, and Kathy — because there were only three of them. They lived almost across the street in the Phebe Hospital compound, and we used to go there frequently to visit. For starters, they had a better generator and a fridge, which meant cold beer. They also had a lovely hut built in their backyard with a couple of hammocks that we enjoyed swinging in while listening to music. Once, Deb went a bit overboard with the swinging and ended up on the ground. She needed three stitches to sew her head up.

There were regular parties amongst the three organizations — MSF, SCF and ICRC — and we used to get together for movies and to share books, which were like gold in Liberia. MSF just sort of adopted the three SCF workers, and almost every day one of them showed up at our compound or someone from MSF was at theirs. One time, the SCF dog, Convoy, showed up at our compound. Ton sent a driver to bring Convoy back in a landcruiser with a note attached to his collar which read: "Keep your dog on a leash".

It was funny to see how quickly the usual process of making friends was discarded. These people were in the war with you, and they became like family, usually very quickly. There wasn't a lot of time for the getting-to-know-you niceties. If a fellow NGO worker needed help, they got it. We went to SCF for food supplies if our convoy couldn't make it in from Monrovia. We shared the results of the nutritional surveys with the ICRC for their food distribution surveys, and they helped us arrange our EPI days to coincide with their general food distribution.

Any information concerning the security situation was quickly shared. When ICRC and SCF had their vehicles stolen, we all went on standby until the matter was resolved. When MSF had a security situation in a particular area, the others often steered clear until reassurances from the NPFL made it safe to return.

And there was always space for another international aid worker at the table. Alongside the regular interagency meetings, we had some great dinner parties with ICRC, and one time all thirty of them came over to watch movies at the guesthouse. SCF had some great dinners, too. One farewell dinner consisted of a roasted pig *and* a roasted goat. How they got their hands on that meat remains a mystery. They never did reveal their secret.

There was a camaraderie amongst the expats, a way of caring for each other that is not so easy to find in the 'real' world. We looked out for each other, and we helped each other when we could. People could usually overlook the cultural differences and the personality quirks that normally would drive you mad. Though there were times I really didn't 'click' with some individuals, I can honestly say there were few people that I didn't respect or couldn't work with.

I also became very attached to my national staff. For starters, they worked well together, which was very important, and there was no rivalry between them. They were dedicated to the work, willing to participate and teach in workshops, and the end result was a significant increase in the number of vaccinated children. Anne once sent them a very encouraging letter saying how pleased she was to see a thirty-percent increase in Margibi county in the number of fully vaccinated children and women. The letter stayed on the wall of the EPI office for months.

The national staff also got involved in making posters for the feeding centres and clinics to advertise upcoming vaccination campaigns, and sent letters to the areas to encourage all women and children to attend. Sometimes the younger, teenaged women would be very reluctant to receive their first tetanus shot. If Marietta couldn't persuade them and Henrietta couldn't threaten them, we'd get the womanizing 'TT' Toe to charm them into agreeing. His real name was Wampole, but as he was responsible for giving all the tetanus toxoid shots to the women, we nicknamed him TT. He definitely had a way with the ladies.

If we were overloaded with patients, the national staff would rather have me call the base and get extra supplies than have to quit and return another day. They worked on weekends to catch up on the program if we had been refused permission in a certain area. I never realized then how lucky I was to have such a good relationship with my staff, or what a nightmare it could be if you didn't.

True, I used to get hassled for loans of money quite regularly, but the borrowers almost always tried their best to repay me. I also received some amusing love letters from national staff members, and more than one fellow was interested in pursuing a serious relationship with me. Though other expats working with me did establish relationships with the national staff, I think I was wise to avoid that particular pitfall.

In the beginning of the program, the national staff actually received only food each month in exchange for their work. As the emergency situation stabilized, they received part of their salary in food and part in wages, and by the end of the program, the market was functioning sufficiently well for them to be able to receive money. But still, I could hardly complain about my wages when I saw how dedicated the national staff was.

Every morning MSF sent two vehicles out to collect the local staff; one to Gbarnga town and another to Sergeant Kollie town, each of which was about four or five kilometres away. If they missed the car, they had to walk to base. The vehicles would arrive at the base, loaded down with staff, and the morning ritual of the 'handshake' began.

In Liberia, the normal handshake ends with two people snapping their middle fingers together as they part. It was a source of great amusement to the national staff as new expats arrived and went through the trials of learning this technique. And heaven forbid you should forget shaking somebody's hand in this event! The day could not begin without at least twenty-five proper handshakes each morning. Everybody milled around shaking hands in their MSF T-shirts, which they took extreme pride in wearing. Anne and Ton made sure that all the national staff received new ones as they became available, and that even Denis's day boys received one.

The day boys were a group of workers hired by the logistician on a daily basis to assist with whatever needed to be done around the compound. They didn't have a job description or a contract like most of the other staff, but they kept the warehouse free of rats, swept the grounds, made culverts during the rainy season, cut grass, unloaded the trucks when the convoy arrived, and did countless other essential but often dirty tasks around the base. Usually they'd be sitting under the tree by the EPI room first thing in the morning. They always assured me that my tree was well looked after by them, and they were very good security guards!

I had an agreement with the team that I was allowed to play my own tapes on the way into the field, and they could play theirs on our cassette player on the way back. Fierce arguments used to occur over whose tape would get played, and even the expats used to fight over which vehicle had the best tape player. Nothing like six hours in the car and no music to aggravate a bad day! Music became a very important aspect of the work, and when I left Liberia it was with dozens of tapes that I'd never heard before arriving. To this day, certain music brings me immediately back to Liberia and the friends I've left behind.

However, there were some disadvantages to working and living in such close proximity to my co-workers. The most irritating and annoying aspect to me was the total lack of privacy. With guards surrounding the house twenty-four hours a day, house staff around constantly, dozens of local staff and plenty of nosy neighbours, I could hardly go to the bathroom without ten people knowing. It was impossible to take a walk off MSF grounds without being followed by two dozen kids who just wanted to hold my hand and walk with me. I couldn't go to the marketplace to shop without being followed or solicited about something, or asked about work, or trailed to my vehicle. Even at night, the sound of the guards walking the perimeter just outside my window was a constant reminder that I was never alone. There was no such thing as a private personal relationship. The moment any relationship started, the whole expat and national staff knew all about it.

As well, it was difficult to find any time for myself. Even on a Sunday, our one day off, people came to visit or to play volleyball, or the local staff would come and invite you to church with them, or somebody showed up wanting money to pay their hospital bill or asking for someone to look at their sick child. It wasn't often possible to refuse. For me, my only escape was to read. I went through about fifty novels while I was in Liberia. It didn't matter *what* I read — trashy romances or serious biographies — books were my only private escape.

Once I got my hands on a big, fat spy novel and the rest of the team, including the SCF people, had to draw lots to see who would get to read it next. Ros from SCF won and he took the book with him on vacation. Unfortunately, upon his return the pilot made a slight miscalculation when landing in Monrovia, and the plane went right off the end of the runway into a soccer field. Ros waited patiently while everybody else injured themselves rushing off the plane, but when he saw smoke and flame filling the cabin behind him, he figured he'd waited long enough. His carry-on bag, with the coveted book in it, was in an overhead compartment, and there was no longer time for him to find it. He had to leave the bag behind.

The rest of us heard he'd been on the plane that crashed, but nobody heard from him. We spent an anxious day waiting for news while the entire office staff went to the airport, fearing the worst. Ros failed to find them after he got safely out of the plane, however, so he hitched a ride to the office in Monrovia. When they all finally caught up with each other, he'd had a drink or two and wasn't too bothered by his neck injury. He sent a message to Gbarnga which said, in part, "Sorry about the book."

Chapter 7

Probably one of my scariest moments in Liberia came when I was thrown in jail. Travel tip: a Liberian jail cell is not a good place to spend an afternoon!

We had gone out with the team to Shankpalai. On the way home, we drove in a little convoy of three vehicles with Stephanie and her crew, who had been doing prenatal care at the clinic.

We arrived at the main police gate outside Gbarnga. The 'gate' in this case was a rope stretched across the road and manned by armed soldiers. After another irritating conversation about where we'd been and where we were going (as if they hadn't heard this story every day for how many months?), one of the soldiers, who looked about fourteen, dropped the rope. The first vehicle, which I was in, drove through. He suddenly tried to lift up the rope as the second car was halfway through.

Immediately there was a great deal of shouting and several soldiers grabbed their weapons and surrounded the second car. One soldier was asking why the driver had tried to 'run the gate' and wondered what we were trying to hide. Thinking the whole situation was a bit ridiculous, I explained to the soldiers that they had already dropped the gate for the first car, so it was natural for the next one to follow.

This simple explanation did nothing to allay their anger. And there's nothing like a large group of drunk and angry soldiers with big guns to thwart your attempts at reason. They promptly arrested the drivers of both vehicles, in spite of my protests.

I was instructed to wait in the car, but having heard about the things that go on in a Liberian jail, I figured my drivers didn't have much of a chance alone. I went with them up the hill to the station while Stephanie stayed behind in her car and tried to contact the base.

By this time, my drivers were nervous, and I wasn't very calm myself. My heart was pounding, and I was vividly imagining a gruesome ending to all this. I finally managed to get the soldiers to agree to go get their commander, because clearly nobody there was in charge. I also discovered that Liberian soldiers believe that the louder and faster you talk, the better your argument. Liberian English is a pidgin dialect that's way beyond my capacity to follow. Needless to say, the noise of a dozen shouting, drunk and annoyed soldiers was pretty intimidating. While we waited, a discussion started as to whether or not the drivers should be consigned to a cell. In the end, that's exactly what happened. I explained that I was responsible for my drivers, that I couldn't leave them, I couldn't drive to the base alone and that it was nearly curfew and we *really* had to leave. I also tried to explain to them that if anything happened to MSF people, *somebody* would be in a lot of trouble, hoping they knew I meant them and not me. Instead, I ended up in the cell with my drivers!

Seeing several dark and ominous stains on the walls and some poor but accurate drawings of torture, I had no doubt that the stories I'd heard were true. The message saying 'Abandon all hope' written over the door also did nothing to quell my fear. The only positive thing about the situation was that the lock to the cell was broken, so all the guards could do was shut the door. But the armed, red-eyed guard outside it brokered no chance for escape. One of my drivers was almost in tears, begging me not to leave them, as he was certain they'd be killed if I left.

Finally, someone arrived who claimed to be in charge. He let me out of the cell to speak to him. I once again explained the situation and told him that we were in no way intending to overstep a gate, but the soldier had been either too quick or too slow with the rope. Because a number of the men were rather intoxicated, this explanation took a long time, and a lot of patience.

In the meantime, Stephanie, bless her, had instructed her pregnant passenger to start moaning. If there's one thing that most Liberian men fear, it's anything to do with childbirth; the men don't like dealing with 'female' troubles. One of the soldiers came in saying that the woman was about to deliver her baby, and we'd better hurry up. I casually told him that I was sure we could resolve this little problem shortly, so Steph could go ahead and leave without me. The commander told his guy to instruct Stephanie that she could leave. Of course, he soon returned, saying she refused to leave without me and the drivers. Since I had known all the time she wouldn't leave without me, offering to let her go had been a safe bet to hurry the process up.

In the end, after a while, my drivers were released from their cell, and I agreed that the coordinators would come see the general tomorrow to 'pay the fine' for overstepping a checkpoint.

It was with great relief that we got out of there. Stephanie's patient, however, was brought to the hospital for a C-Section; I think she rather enjoyed her convincing performance. We got to base just past curfew.

The next day, Anne and Ton returned to the police gate to sort it out. The end result was that the persons who detained us were taken out behind the station and severely beaten by the general's men. Justice, Liberian style. I had no idea that the persons responsible for stopping us would receive that punishment, and for a long time therafter it bothered me. I'd have to be very careful what I said and who I threatened if I didn't know what the outcome would be for those involved. I know of one expat (not in Liberia) who complained to a military commander about harassment from one of his soldiers, and the commander shot and killed the soldier right in front of the expat.

My first incarceration. My name is down in the Gbarnga police station book, and I have a criminal record. That was one of the trickiest security incidents I had been involved in, and I feel lucky to have gotten through it unharmed. Between the rampant alcohol and drug problems among the soldiers and the brutal punishments given to those who anger the wrong people, the Liberian justice system is a dangerous thing to be caught up in.

May 15, 1994:

It's a farewell party for one of the loggies (logisticians) tonight. He got the dancers from the cultural centre to come and dance at his party. They were really good, all wearing beautiful costumes. Liberia has a lot of secret societies — the leopard society, the snake society, the lightning society, et cetera. Many of our national staff members have gone to the bush schools to be initiated. I hear that some of the schools are quite brutal. Lots of witchcraft, black magic and sorcery. The graduates come out with ritual scars on their faces, necks and chests, which indicates their passage.

Apparently, there was a professor from Cuttington University who wrote a book about the whole thing, and they retaliated by killing his daughter. In Gibi, they say that some enemies of the society have been drowned in the Farmington River, and I'm still never happy crossing it on that stupid raft!

Anyhow, the dancers all wore masks, and the most imposing figure was the devil himself. So the devil danced for us, and the staff were all afraid. Just the sight of him sent the house staff scurrying inside. Now there's a terrific storm so maybe the lightning society had something to do with it.

Apparently, there is a lot of pressure on young people to join these societies, and most of the good Christian churches are filled with society members. I'd love to find out more about it, but it's not exactly safe to go poking about in other people's beliefs. There's a lot here that nobody shares, and I guess it isn't any of our business. The tribes guard their secrets well.

I won't be that sorry to see this particular loggie go. I'll never forget the time he had to take me to the hospital late one evening and made such a stink about it. A little girl had died of malnutrition complications in one of our feeding centres here on the campus. I couldn't just leave her body there with the other children overnight. He was so angry with me for insisting he drive me to the hospital. Well, there was nobody else available, and I hadn't learned to drive the landcruiser yet, so what was I supposed to do? I was so upset. It was the first time in my life I'd seen a child die from starvation. Such a stupid, stupid waste. I held her in my arms the whole way, and the hospital was angry that I'd brought her. I had to *pay* them to get them to keep her for one night until we could contact her family and bury her the next day. He just shrugged and said 'That's life.' So it is, but I didn't appreciate the attitude.

By mid-May I had suffered through the usual tropical diseases common to expats in Africa. I had come to Liberia terrified of catching diseases that I later learned to view as minor inconveniences. I'd already had giardia, parasites, scabies and the usual 'traveller's diarrhea'. All of them are easily treatable, and none of them are too life-threatening, as opposed to malaria, which I also had the misfortune to catch. Even though I was taking my prophylactics regularly, the risk of catching malaria in Liberia is very high, and several expats had caught it. I was no exception.

May something?

It's Friday, anyway, and that's all I know. I've got malaria. Finished treatment with chloroquine this morning, but still have a positive smear. I don't *ever* want to be this sick again. Twenty-four hours of non-stop nausea. If only I could just throw up and get it over with! First the itching, the heat rash, the fevers, the chills, the sweats and now the nausea. I'm lying here too sick to even get up. Henrietta has to manage EPI without me. And poor Little Henrietta from my EPI team, she was six months pregnant and lost the baby. I can't even go to see her. I'm exhausted, but can't sleep, can't eat, and feel like shit. This is miserable.

It was worse than miserable actually. For a week I lay in bed, hardly getting up. My malaria smear finally came back negative, but even then I didn't seem to be improving. Everyone was so good to me. My staff stayed late after work to update me on their activities, and Roland, a vaccinator from my EPI team, brought me pineapples, my favourite, to try to tempt me to eat. Marietta came by and told me to 'stop reducing', alarmed by how much weight I was losing. Even Ton, usually rather reserved, showed up with a can of ice cold Pepsi that he had scrounged from the SCF fridge. It tasted wonderful.

I recall one moment, while lying in my bed, when I watched a lizard on the wall stalk a spider up on the ceiling. I spent about an hour watching them, hoping the gecko would win because a) I hated spiders, and b) I was too tired to get up and do something about it myself. Eventually, I moved out of our guesthouse and down to Steph's house, closer to the base, so people could check up on me more often. Many of the staff came to visit me, and I had some good talks with people despite my feverish state.

Within a week or so, I realized I was sicker than I had at first suspected. I really hadn't eaten for a week and my weight had dropped to forty-six kilograms. Anne ordered me to the Ivory Coast for tests. Easier said than done.

First, I had to get to Man, and the drive was a horror! I could barely walk across the bridge bordering Liberia, and the minute I arrived there, I threw up in the bushes. The soldiers barely took the time to stamp my visa. They took one look at my yellow eyes and skin and sent me on my way. I spent the night in Man and caught the first flight to Abidjan. By this time I was pretty sure what I had was hepatitis. I was right.

How appalling it was to be in charge of the vaccination program and to catch hepatitis! It was my own fault for not taking my gammaglobulin when it was due a month earlier. The vaccines had arrived incountry just a bit too late. Besides, I recall eating at a village once where they served river crabs. It was a very special treat, but the crabs came from a not-too-clean river and hadn't been properly washed or cooked. Even though I knew that, it's impossible to refuse a meal sometimes, particularly when people are trying to do something special for you. Whether or not it was the shellfish I'll never know, but the end result was clear.

Louise made arrangements to bring me and two other colleagues to the hospital in Abidjan. Thomas and Koert both had very bad malaria, and I was indeed diagnosed with hepatitis.

Koert and I spent a week in the Polyclinique Internationale Sainte Anne Marie, where he received IV quinine, and I a multitude of vitamins and a special diet. We were very well cared for in the hospital, and I must add that some of my male nurses were rather good looking. Koert and I used to take our IV poles out for a walk in the hallway every day, and within a week we were well enough to be released. MSF wisely decided I should be medevacked home to Canada. I was terribly disappointed, and when Louise told me the news I spent the day in tears. But it was the correct decision, as I was not in any shape to do my job.

When we got out of the hospital, I had a couple days to wait before I had to leave for Canada and Koert had to go back to Monrovia. We decided to spend a day at the beach. Unfortunately, my yellow skin turned rather orange in the sun, and I think I frightened a lot of people on the flight home. No one wants to sit next to a skinny orange woman who has obviously been out in the bush too long!

The flight was miserable, with my feeling awful and the plane fully packed so that the only space I got was in the smoking section. I was delayed again in Paris, and by the time I got to customs in Toronto, I must have looked as bad as I felt. The team from Gbarnga had forwarded some clothes, and things and I had left with just one small bag and a lot of beautiful letters from everyone wishing me a safe journey, better health and a quick return. The woman at the customs desk asked me why I only had a small bag after being away for four months. The words 'home for sick leave' got me out of there in a hurry. Thirty-six hours, which felt like two centuries, later I finally arrived in Winnipeg.

There, I spent a month eating everything in sight and catching up with friends. I missed Liberia every day, and it was all I could talk about. I was addicted to the work by now, and I drove everybody nuts talking about it. It was odd to see how some people reacted to my work. They couldn't understand why I'd risk my health and safety for people I didn't know and would probably never see again. Some thought I was a fool, some saw me as some kind of hero and others didn't want me to speak about my work at all.

My parents worried about my future career and security. I had no money and likely wouldn't for as long as I did this, and I had no prospects for employment afterwards. It was impossible to tell them that those things that had once been so important to me no longer mattered. I felt more alive than I had in my entire life, and I *loved* my job. I was doing something good, and decent, and *right*. The insecurity, the illnesses, the exhaustion, were all part of the job. It was a war, and in a war, things happen. I could accept it. I took the danger for granted by then, and never really thought of what effect it must have had on people when I spoke of my afternoon in jail as a joke. They thought I was mad! Everyone kept telling me how brave I was — *that* was the joke. Courage is a relative thing. When the shit really hits the fan, the expats leave. The national staff can't. Who has courage then?

At the end of my month, as lovely as it had been, I was dying to return. I achieved my target weight of fifty kilograms and took the next flight out.

A letter to a friend, July 9, 1994:
Dear Darcy,

Greetings! Disease, war, pestilence, rain, cold showers, warm beer, giant cockroaches sharing my bedroom — it's nice to be home. It was a long flight, and once again I had to catch the bus from Abidjan to Man, as the plane had crashed the week before, killing everyone on board, including a relief worker — a nurse from a French agency. Then I spent seven hours in the landcruiser. The road was a nightmare! At one point the river overflowed and we drove through about two feet of water. Another time we were stuck in a hole so deep that the edge of it was level with the windshield! Saw two big, twenty-ton trucks from a convoy stuck in mud up to their axles. I really thought we'd be stuck for good a couple of times, but we finally made it.

Everyone welcomed me with a beautiful homecoming party; a wonderful barbecue, flowers, banners. The next day my EPI team also held a party for me. I don't think they really expected me to return.

I was out in the field again yesterday. Along the main tarmac road there are now about ten displaced camps for over 30,000 people. The fighting is getting worse. They've cut down huge tracts of forest to build shelters and burned out a lot of bush to plant rice. It sure doesn't look promising.

The fighting is getting bad in Grand Bassa. The ICRC and SCF have had their cars stolen. And one of ours was wrecked in a bad accident. The driver just got out of the hospital the other day. They've tried twice to loot our vehicles lately, but so far we've been lucky.

The World Food Program had thirty-five tons of rice and beans looted from their warehouse. The agencies have stopped general food distribution for now. A somewhat drastic but effective protest.

And now the rains have started full force. The roads are such a mess. At least they've fixed the major bridges, like the one I got stuck on before.

Anyhow, I'm glad to be back. Work is keeping me busy. I have yet another job in addition to EPI — supervision of the eight supplementary feeding programs they have in Upper Bong. Never a dull moment with MSF. I'm working my ass off, but I love it.

Chapter 8

There had been a few changes while I was away. Gerda was taking over the health centres, and Iris, a new arrival, was to replace her in the feeding centres. I had been given the position of supervisor of the supplementary feeding program in Upper Bong. The EPI team had done well without me for a month and no longer required close supervision. They started doing more and more work on their own, in keeping with the plan of becoming entirely self-sufficient within the MSF structure.

The supplementary program was another challenge. My colleague, Saah Jackta, was experienced with the area and the program, but the security situation was poor. My role was mostly to supervise and to provide some added security, as the presence of expat staff allows teams in and out of tense areas.

Food is a dangerous weapon in a conflict area. It can be used to control a population, to remove a population, to feed an army and for a lot of reasons besides its intended purpose of keeping people from starving to death in an emergency. Because of the danger of food being misused or diverted by others, we ran our program in Upper Bong differently. We prepared as many individual bags of corn-soya blend cereal (CSB) as we needed for each town, filled the landcruiser with bags, and drove directly to the area ourselves. Our target group was, as usual, children under five who still needed additional food until they reached a normal weight.

When we arrived, each child was weighed and measured, their measurements charted and their names noted in the ledger. When they achieved their targeted weight, they were given an additional week's supply and discharged from the program. The others received a bag of CSB was sufficient for the following week. We tried to return every week to the same area to make sure that the kids weren't receiving too much food at a time. By using the ration method, we hoped to avoid having so much food in one town that it would become a target for the soldiers. However, we still had a lot of problems with looting.

I had several meetings with various battalion leaders because we often heard from families that the soldiers were stealing the children's food. Stealing food from five-year-olds! Disgusting as it was, it didn't really surprise me. Once, I was in an hour long meeting where the commander dared me to try to prove my allegations. In the end he promised he'd find the *real* culprit and beat him until he confessed. However, meetings such as this one were futile, and there were times when my frustration with these people was hard to control.

On July 13, the road to Monrovia closed. An ECOMOG truck full of Tanzanians was attacked at the frontline. Ten escaped, and one was captured, but apparently all were badly beaten and the truck was destroyed. Three SCF workers stuck in Margibi had their vehicle stolen. It was later seen in Salala, not too far from CUC, with bullet holes in it, being driven by none other than Nixon Gaye. The next day, except for Debbie, Ton, and Gert, the team evacuated for the first of what would become repeated evacuations, to Man. It was the beginning of the end.

It was a horrible time to have to go. When things get really bad and we are needed the most, that's the time when we have to leave. It wasn't possible to take any of the national staff with us. It was a very serious and difficult decision, but we were at a far greater risk than the national staff simply because of our position as foreigners in the situation. And we could not take national staff members across international borders, as we would be making them refugees. That's not a choice too many people would ever want to make. But the staff knew how grave the situation was. They laid no blame on us but spoke no words of reassurance either. They stood silently watching us in preparation for our departure. Both teams cried when the cars pulled out of base.

In some ways, though, I think the evacuation of the expat team was far less traumatic for the national staff than it was for us. Expats come and go, and the staff had seen these evacuations before. For me, it was my first evacuation, but it certainly wouldn't be the last.

As it was, we spent a week in Man. Iris and I went to town a few times, and we planned a nice barbecue for everyone. We talked with Anne or Ton on the radio daily, and we waited for news. All the NGOs had suspended their work in the area until SCF got their car and workers back.

While we waited, we prepared for the next big workshop, a water and sanitation inservice, that we'd all be participating in. We also passed the time playing tennis at the very colonialist country club, swimming and having dinner with friends. But mostly we just waited.

Around that time, I heard some bad news from home. My sister-in-law's father was diagnosed with leukemia, and my uncle from British Columbia was very ill and in hospital. The news worried me, but my family's concerns seemed so very far from my own. I felt as if everybody's life was going on without me in it, and my place in the hearts of my family and friends was becoming smaller and smaller. I began to miss the experiences of families — weddings, funerals, illnesses, new jobs, new homes, new loves and other life changes that I would have no part of. It was the start of the distance between my family and me that I never really found a way around.

Chapter 9

July 25, 1994:

So much has happened since we've returned from Man and resumed our program. Spent a few days last week in Gbalatuah. Nice to have the team together again. Gert's farewell party was in Gbalatuah, and it was great! I took loads of photos. Gert received some lovely gifts from his workers. Even I got a couple. There was food and singing, the place was decorated with palm leaves, we even had a soccer match. Brought a woman to Phebe hospital. She delivered her baby on the Commissioner's doorstep! Poor Moses got a bit nervous. Unfortunately, I found out the lady later died in hospital.

Trouble in Fenutoli. General Prince of the 'Death Squad' (these guys watch far too many American films) has been threatening Mary, the supervisor of the feeding centre. Deb and Iris tried to go speak with him and sort it out, but with no success.

Today was a heinous day! I went with Jackta to the supplementary feeding program. Tomorrow is Independence Day, and we're all staying put, expecting trouble so we had to do all five places in one shot: Wainsu, Belefuania, Naama, Gbansue and Jowah. Had another argument with these idiotic soldiers about stealing food from the kids. I get so sick of it sometimes! And then we had this poor pregnant woman who practically delivered her baby in the car. I was actually sitting up back there and we just made it to the hospital before we had to deliver her. Thank goodness a few of the nurses came to help. I've never had to do that before, and it scared the shit out of me.

Got back to base, late, to find that the whole place has gone to hell. Five or six cars were looted today near Salala. ICRC, SCF — again— CRS (Catholic Relief Services). Some expats were left stranded and had to walk to the UNOMIL compound in Konola and were helicoptered out. Eleven ICRC trucks had their fuel looted in Salala, so two expats, Barbara and Enzo, are sleeping in Salala tonight. Happy birthday, Enzo! Simon, an SCF guy from Monrovia, also got stuck and is spending the night in the UNOMIL compound. They're sending Nixon (in his looted SCF car) to retrieve the other five vehicles. The height of irony!

Anyhow, it sounds like we'll be evacuating again shortly. Most of the other NGOs will likely pull out, too. Another ECOMOG truck attacked by the NPFL, shooting in Totota, a cholera epidemic in Monrovia. What a bloody mess. Another security meeting in the morning. Kathy and Rob from SCF made it back, and Ros never made it out for R&R, so I guess we'll drown our sorrows together. Except I've got giardia, and am on flagyl. No alcohol for me yet. The local staff tried to have a party tonight, but no music, no spirit. I'm too tired for words.

July 27, 1994:

We were confined to the compound for Independence Day. There's no point in trying to stay here if we can't do our work, and they're making that impossible. None of the cars are back, but they've been spotted at some general's place in Gbarnga. Trouble at the Gbarnga gate this morning — they wouldn't let us pass. Charles Taylor is on the road to Margibi and there's a roadblock at Phebe compound, which we are unable to pass. Police, guns, soldiers everywhere! Taylor's losing control and he knows it. His boys are making their own decisions, and they're not listening to their big boss any more.

Lots of fighting in Fenutoli. Nixon Gaye again, the scourge of our existence. It got so bad that Mary cut a hole in the fence of the feeding centre and sneaked everybody out. She heard a rocket blast and the unconfirmed rumour is that it was our feeding centre that was hit. They had to leave behind a couple of disabled people that she couldn't carry out.

Things are escalating rapidly. I don't know how it will end. I saw my EPI team together today and have this sinking feeling it might be for the last time. We leave tomorrow for Man, if we can.

Deb has malaria, but we're trying to have another farewell party for Gert and for Kathy from SCF tonight. Somehow we all seem to be trying hard but not succeeding. I am really scared. I don't want to go, but I don't want to stay. I guess what I really want is peace in Liberia. If we have to leave, I'd like to know everyone behind us is safe.

We didn't end up evacuating that time. Mr. Charles Taylor himself put an end to that security flare-up. Apparently, he drove his nice Mercedes to Margibi, right into the heart of Nixon's territory. He executed some soldiers, flogged several others and sent the cars home. The CRS car had its wheels and doors removed. MSF-Luxembourg had the clutch ruined on their one-week-old landcruiser. ICRC got their stolen vehicle back *washed*, and SCF finally got their number thirteen back, but with the window broken and the radio removed.

We started the program again slowly. MSF had a meeting with Charles Taylor himself. He insisted he was in complete control of the situation and that the persons responsible for the bombing at the Fenutoli feeding centre were captured and punished. Anne had little confidence in his speeches. None of us had much more. We heard that Taylor was busy training 5,000 new recruits with new automatic weapons and rocket-propelled grenades (RPGs).

We enjoyed the illusion of peaceful times and easy access for the few weeks that it lasted. We did have a lovely farewell dinner for Kathy with SCF: roast pig, roasted veggies and potatoes, asparagus in cheese sauce and chocolate cake, all served on china plates with real wine glasses, candles and flowers. It was a beautiful moment of normalcy in the middle of chaos.

Despite the 'break', I was having terrible insomnia. Everybody had been affected by the stress of the last several weeks. People were ill, tired, crabby and sad. Friends were leaving, and the new arrivals were coming in at a very uncertain time. Our energy and enthusiasm were waning, and none of us were certain about how long we could go on.

The stories about random executions continued. Areas that were open one day were closed the next. Our EPI schedule was a joke. We were changing our plans almost daily. Names of new generals and new commanders kept popping up. Then we went back to Fenutoli. The structure was fairly intact, but everything had been stolen, including the furniture from both the health centre and the feeding centre and all the food and medical supplies. Bodies had been thrown into the well. Anthony, our well-digger, started a new one and promptly found an old skull. He tried another place and eventually dug a spot where he happened not to excavate a body. He told me I should try my best to never get thirsty in Fenutoli!

The oranges were in season, and the bush rice was emerald green and almost ready for harvesting. Fenutoli still looked as beautiful as ever, and still felt as dismal. Dozens of new camps for displaced persons appeared.

One day the EPI team and I had set up in a town called Belefuania. A new medical nurse named Josie had joined us for her first day in the field. We'd barely gotten started when I heard shots at the checkpoint nearby. I've never seen a room empty that fast in my life! Within seconds, hundreds of women and children had disappeared, either into the bush or into the fields, as far away from the shooting as possible. The absolute terror in the women's eyes was dreadful to see. How quickly they had become accustomed to running!

I kept my team together and ordered them to start packing up. They were as anxious to flee as all the rest, but I had to see what was going on. Nervously, I went up to the gate to meet the soldiers. There had been some trouble, and two people had been shot in the foot, one quite seriously. I had the local people bring them down to the clinic. Josie dressed their wounds and I called the base. We notified all the other vehicles in the area, and sent everyone home. Even a small incident like that can explode very quickly. As the most senior staff member, I had to wait until all of the cars had passed the checkpoint before I could leave with my staff. I'd already sent Josie in one vehicle with some of my staff and the supplies, to take the two wounded into Phebe Hospital. It seemed like the longest hour of my life! Finally the last of the MSF team was through the gate, and we could join them.

Due to the mounting insecurity, some of my national staff were afraid to stay. Little by little, they began to leave. Some fled to Monrovia, others to the Ivory Coast. I could understand their flight, but it meant I was down five staff members. We managed, however, because many of our plans were cancelled or changed at the last moment, and maintaining a normal work schedule was impossible.

In spite of it all, I was still considering extending my position. Ton didn't think that was the best idea, but in the end it didn't matter. By mid-August, new team members had arrived. They stayed in Man with us while we were on yet another standby for a few days, but they weren't going to get much of a chance to get to know Liberia. Their presence also caused quite a ripple in our previously smooth-flowing team.

For starters, one new woman had some difficulty adjusting to the new culture. She regularly wore tight, short shirts that revealed her abdomen and cut-off blue jeans shorts. Even at official gatherings, where everyone was dressed in their best and certainly expected the expats to dress according to their status, she refused to wear anything else. Several of the national staff came forward, complaining that she didn't respect them. She refused to take them seriously. Warned, as we all had been, not to take the canoe across the river, she insisted on doing so to the dismay and anger of the national staff, who felt she was mocking their beliefs. Despite numerous discussions with her, there was no change in her flamboyant behaviour. It didn't help that within weeks she had started relationships with two different people, which caused a great deal of gossip and hurt feelings.

Two logisticians also arrived in mid-August, causing further problems. One had joined MSF to avoid trouble back home and hadn't really expected to have to work as hard as we expected him to. The other had joined MSF in the hopes of staying in Africa, where he used to work as a safari guide. It became clear that not everybody who joined MSF was working with quite the same level of enthusiasm and dedication as some of us.

Worse, the new members couldn't grasp why the rest of us in Man were not having the same sort of 'fun' as they were. For us, the evacuations had become a sign of the absolute seriousness of the security situation. Our imposed breaks had stopped being restful, enjoyable vacations and were now seen as the forced retreat from a program we had grown to love and care about deeply. The newcomers would have to learn, as I had, the hard way.

Chapter 10

August 18, 1994:

Lots of news these days. Jackta and I finally got to Gbonota to try to do the supplementary feeding program there. It's a ghost town! There was fighting on Saturday, and after a shooting in the street, some soldiers were killed. There are only about thirty people left in town, all old men, no children or women.

The local military commander assures us that he'll kill anyone who disturbs our work. Nice. Made it to Gorkai, too. We've been trying to get in there for ages. There's this one log bridge where I had to get out and walk across, and I swore it wouldn't hold us. It's deadly, and the place is a mess, a displaced camp with some ninety structures holding 1,400 people. Screened seventy people and got thirty-nine into the supplementary feeding program.

Tried to get to Gbalatuah today, too, but got turned back at Belefuania. Saw a truckload of armed soldiers heading up the road. Fighting between LDF and NPFL, and it's going to get worse. New checkpoint in town, and a town-wide curfew has been instated. I saw more armed soldiers in Gbonota than ever before — new RPGs, grenades, AK-47s and loads of ammo. Jackta was pretty nervous the whole time, and I don't exactly blame him. I wasn't that comfortable driving myself there.

We re-opened Fenutoli, but half the town hasn't returned yet. They've either run or are hiding in the bush. We're hearing horrible stories from around there. People having their hands and feet chopped off, people being tortured, having their hearts cut out and eaten. Apparently it's best to use a small child for that, as it makes for very strong ju-ju, or black magic. The soldiers who practise such things believe they will be made invincible, that neither bullets nor machetes can touch them. The whole thing just gives me the creeps!

In Salala, we heard that some thieves were punished by being buried alive for twenty minutes. If they survived, they were considered innocent and released. If they died, they were considered guilty. There are just too many tales like this to doubt them all. I believe that much of what we're hearing is true.

General JR in Margibi is causing problems. He's really hassling the staff, especially the female expats. Anne's had a talk with him. He still tries to get rides all the time and make use of our vehicles as much as he can. He wasn't happy being told to keep his hands off the women, either.

An MSF-Luxembourg national staff member was shot and killed defending their clinic in Gbarnga this last week.

In EPI, I've let Henrietta go as the supervisor. She's going to head a feeding centre for MSF in Monrovia. She's not too pleased, but we could really use her there, and there's some tension among the rest of the team over some minor incidents that happened while I was away on sick leave. I can't really get to the bottom of it, but I hope things work out for everyone.

I heard via a phone call from Abidjan that my uncle Cliff died August 2. I'm two weeks too late to even contact my dad and tell him I'm sorry about his brother. I can hardly believe it. He's gone, and I'm here and it all ended before I even knew.

Denis, Deb and Nikky are all planning a big farewell party tomorrow. I can't get over that they're all going in the next couple weeks. I feel like I've been here so long; Denis showed up after me and now he's leaving. Has it been six months already? Already? I love these people. I don't even want to think about saying goodbye.

And then the country really went to hell. The following passages were taken partially from a summary of events written by the coordinators to show the events leading up to the final evacuation of the team and the end of the project in Greater Liberia.

Saturday, August 20, 1994:
We were supposed to have the big farewell party Friday night, but the curfew on the campus prevented it. We had an expat party, with several people sleeping over. We managed to have a lot of fun, but we missed the staff. Fighting in and around the area continues to worsen. Upper Bong closed. A car to Logotua with Denis, Mary and Jonathan was turned back due to poor road conditions and trucks blocking the route.

Sunday, August 21, 1994:

The trucks were cleared off the road by the Red Cross, and we were told they'd be the last trucks allowed to pass. Gerda hurt her back quite badly. She's completely bedridden, on valium and intramuscular analgesic. She'll have to be medevacked to Abidjan, and I've been asked to escort her. Josie and I went to visit SCF, but were told the curfew had been moved from 6 p.m. to 4 p.m., and we had to get SCF to drive us back to the base. Steph heard on the radio something about all ex-soldiers being asked to return to active duty. This is very, very serious.

Monday, August 22, 1994:

Fighting in Totota. My EPI team was turned back at Suakoko and told that nobody was permitted to use the Gbarnga/Monrovia highway anymore. Fighting intensifies in Upper Bong. The Gbalatuah staff evacuated the feeding centre, and many ran to Gbarnga.

I managed, finally, with much persuasion, to get the UN to medevac Gerda to Monrovia. We flew with their helicopter. Before we took off, I made sure Gerda was sufficiently drugged and informed her that she was now 'officially' paralyzed. The landing strip was surrounded by armed men, but the pilot was able to convince them it was a medical evacuation, and after several searches, we were allowed to leave. Fortunately, they didn't discover the several thousands of dollars under the stretcher of my 'paralyzed' patient. I made my first and final trip to Monrovia. We spent one night there before flying into Abidjan, where an ambulance met us to take Gerda to the hospital. It turned out to be a muscle/nerve problem from which she made a full recovery in a few weeks. My view of the happenings in Gbarnga was limited to radio contacts, which were often poor, and standard-C messages for the next weeks. The standard-C was a sort of telex communication but using a satellite transceiver and a special computer program. I was out. The rest of the team was not.

Loaded into two trucks, several of the team members tried to make it out via the road to Man in the Ivory Coast. They were turned back. The trucks made it as far as Ganta and stayed put. The landcruisers were turned back. A UNOMIL and a World Food Program car were looted in Gbarnga. MSF moved all of their vehicles to the guesthouse and hid them behind the high walls. Local staff were given two months' salary and sent home, and the expats moved together into the guesthouse. Confidential papers were burned. The generals in Gbarnga, normally seen in civilian clothes, showed up in full military uniforms. The soldiers in CUC are walking around with white sheets over their heads, with eyeholes cut out. They are practising their ju-ju again, and it isn't a good sign. Some showed up at the guesthouse, weapons in hand, to loot what they could.

Tuesday, August 23, 1994:

Attempts to meet with the commanding officer, General Carr, in Gbarnga were met with failure. A meeting did occur with those next in command, and the aid organizations were told that each is responsible for its own security. If they happen to be driving a vehicle that a soldier needed, well, that's just too bad for them. The police showed up at the guesthouse asking for radio frequencies and the number of radios per agency.

Wednesday, August 24, 1994:

Two of the team booked to leave by helicopter had their flight cancelled. Two local UN staff were arrested as infiltrators while trying to get on the helicopter. Heavy security on all exits out of Liberia, especially for national Liberians of the wrong tribe. A planned UN/ECOMOG convoy to Monrovia was cancelled. All the agencies can do is stay put.

Thursday, August 25, 1994:

Nikky and Jonathan made it by car to Ganta, picked up the two empty trucks with Francis, and followed Charles Taylor through the border by half an hour. An MSF-Luxembourg car heading in with new expats was warned not to go but refused to listen. Steph was supposed to take the helicopter out, but it was again cancelled. A third attempt to get to the helicopter ended in failure when it left without waiting for the MSF people.

Friday, August 26, 1994:

Gerda was released from the hospital and is being cared for here at the house. I spoke by radio with Nikky in Man, and they might be coming here to Abidjan soon. Tensions are very high. Heavy fighting in Firestone and Compound 2.

Three of the expats finally managed to get the helicopter out to Monrovia in the afternoon. There are still a few people to go. The tension in Man and Abidjan is awful, and we anxiously wait for any news of those we'd left behind.

Saturday, August 27, 1994:

Steph and Jay made it by road to Man with surprisingly little trouble at the border. MSF-Belgium was held at Logotua for four hours before one of their two cars was allowed to pass. However, it is believed that the small boy who dropped the gate for them was later executed for allowing them to pass.

Everyone was very stressed. Arguments and fighting started between a couple of the expats, and Louise was hard-pressed to try to keep us all occupied and out of her way. Nobody is coping well. Steph managed to collect a few of my things that were left behind, bless her, and she did the same for the others. Still, a lot of our possessions have been looted.

Sunday, August 28, 1994:

Iris, Josie and one guy from SCF made it by road to Monrovia, with Iris posing as a patient. Lutheran World Services (LWS) and ICRC also made it through. John Dennis, one of our national staff members and Nikky's boyfriend, made it out with LWS. She's very relieved, of course. Poor Red Cross! They have twenty Ivorian truck drivers and no way to get them safely across the border.

Debbie and Ton are the only ones left. There are reports that Nixon Gaye has been killed by his own men! MSF-Belgium evacuated via Logotua with the loss of another car.

The UN helicopter strip is surrounded by soldiers, and it's unlikely that anyone will be able to travel. Ton hid the radio and antennae in the guesthouse. Everybody was trying to evacuate as quickly as possible. Soldiers arrived at the guesthouse and took one of the cars.

Monday, August 29, 1994:

MSF-Lux fled their compound, and the moment they left, it was completely looted. They went first to the ICRC compound but later ended up with our team at CUC. Soldiers again showed up at the MSF compound to take the vehicles, and they kicked down the front door to get in. Ton hid the standard-C in one of the cupboards. One MSF and one Red Cross car are still hidden in the bush in CUC, and one of the trucks has been left there as well. The soldiers on the road are becoming even more aggressive. Nixon Gaye's death has been confirmed. He was eviscerated by his own men.

The team from Man arrived in Abidjan. Jonathan is ill with typhoid and required hospitalization. The whole thing feels more and more out of control. In Gbarnga, the airstrip is now surrounded by some 300 soldiers wearing wigs, sheets and women's clothes — another bad sign that they were practising their ju-ju. ECOMOG can't and won't assist NGOs in their evacuation.

Tuesday, August 30, 1994:

All the vehicles were taken during the night! The standard-C was taken by the NPFL, but the number was blocked so that they couldn't use it. Ton and Debbie moved into the ICRC compound by Phebe Hospital with MSF-Lux. As they tried to leave the compound, the cars and all their personal belongings were stolen by soldiers. It is impossible to use the helicopter, as it would immediately be shot down. An NGO meeting with Charles Taylor was held in Gbarnga. The NGOs were informed that they will be allowed to leave. Following that, seven vehicles were returned to MSF, painted in camouflage colors. Tomorrow Ton and Debbie will try the road to Monrovia. In spite of repeated attempts, we never managed to make radio contact with the base in Gbarnga today. We later learned from Ton that he overheard death threats made against Debbie on one of the radios, but nothing happened.

Wednesday, August 31, 1994:

Ton and Debbie attempted to leave by road for Monrovia. They were turned back, and anything left of the vehicles was looted. In Amsterdam, MSF is following the situation closely. They've decided that Ton and Debbie might become victims in a hostage-taking situation and MSF will go public if they were not released. They are prepared to put international pressure on the NPFL for the release of the expats. Former U.S. president Jimmy Carter spoke to Taylor, urging the immediate and unconditional release of all the NGOs.

Chapter 11

Sam, the last driver, along with Ton and Debbie, finally made the drive to Monrovia under heavy military escort. Disintegration day! It wasn't until about a week later that ICRC managed to escape. They waited too long, and their compound was overrun. They were forced to flee to the ECOMOG compound outside Gbarnga. They, along with the few remaining UN workers, were escorted by ECOMOG across the frontline at Kakata, but were caught in heavy crossfire and nearly killed. There were heavy casualties in the fighting, and CUC was shelled, along with the town of Gbarnga. All aid agencies left. Nobody went back for nearly a year.

It was over. After days of anxiety and hours of terror, it was over. Deb and Ton arrived in Abidjan, Deb was quite ill with malaria. Anne, who had been out of the country for the last month on holiday or working in the office, arrived from Amsterdam. The decision was made that a skeleton staff would remain behind in Monrovia to do what they could until it was possible to see about returning to Gbarnga. Anne, Josie and a few others stayed. For the rest of us, the Liberia mission was over.

We stayed a few days in Abidjan, to help the others move to the new house and just to be together again. We dined out, we went to the beach, we went swimming, we tried to relax, finally. Those who had been ill slowly recovered. We shed a lot of tears. I went back to Man for a few days with Steph to see the staff there and say our goodbyes. Stephanie and Eddie, one of our national drivers, were married there, and both now live with Eddie's son in Australia.

September 11, 1994:
I couldn't get a flight out Friday night. We went to the beach today with Louise, and it was great. Right now the rest are napping, and I'm packing.

Deb was telling us some things about Gbarnga. A small victory — pouring out all the alcohol in the house before the NPFL could get it! Three of the NPFL generals showed up at the U.S. Embassy in Monrovia claiming to be the people in charge now. Charles Taylor is, of all things, at a *peace* conference in Accra! The place is really falling apart.

Some 80,000 displaced are at Kakata, trying to get to Monrovia, and are being blocked by ECOMOG. We keep hearing that ULIMO has infiltrated Gbarnga, and the civilians will all be considered NPFL supporters. They'll be killed, all of them.

The good news (if anything about this situation can be considered good) is that some of the staff from Jowah and Shankpalai have made it safely across the Guinea border and MSF-Belgium is looking after them. I wish I knew more about my staff and what the hell has happened to them. I hate leaving without knowing.

But I have to let go, and go home. My first mission is over.

I flew home in mid-September, almost exactly seven months from the day I had left. Those who stayed behind began working within and around Monrovia, establishing feeding centres and health clinics. They monitored the ever-changing situation and did what they could when they were able. Nikky later went back to Liberia, as I would myself some three years later, under very different circumstances. Some of the staff were killed. Some escaped to Man, others made it to Monrovia. Some worked with other agencies, and some dropped out of sight forever. It was hard to go home.

Dear Darcy,

We're out. The team is scattered, some here, others in Man, some still in Liberia. But we lost a lot! The NPFL looted twelve vehicles, all our personal belongings, our houses, warehouses, food, medicines, supplies, materials, money, office stuff, everything! Thousands of dollars worth of goods and materials. The project has been completely destroyed.

Nobody knows if or when we'll return to Gbarnga. Man, talk about bad dreams. I'll remember these last two weeks for the rest of my life. I have terrible insomnia and am going to have to start doing something about it soon. I haven't slept in days.

But evacuating is such a shitty way to end a project. It's very depressing — no goodbyes, no chance to leave anything for the staff, no opportunity to end anything properly. It's so very sad. I think it will take a long while to get over this. Does one ever really get over something like this I wonder?

At any rate, I'll be home soon.

Chapter 12 - Home

I was not sorry to be home for awhile, just to have time to absorb everything that had happened. I found this very hard to do. There was so little news about the situation in Liberia, nothing in the papers, nothing on the television. I never knew what was going on, and nobody in North America seemed to care. One more lesson for me to learn. Things that happen in Africa are very far away from my family and friends' world, and what can they do about it anyway? That was the general attitude, and it was clear that I could scream and shout all I wanted, and it wouldn't make a difference. It wasn't perhaps indifference, but it was certainly a lack of will I encountered. Those who think they can do nothing do, in fact, nothing.

I told my story a few times to a few people. Then I shut up and got on with my life. I remember distinctly attending our ten-year nursing reunion. About thirty of my old nursing classmates showed up at a Winnipeg restaurant. Everybody got up to say something about their life and work since graduation. For most, it was pretty straightforward — marriage, kids, places they still worked at. I had to go last, and my story took about ten minutes to relate. Nobody had ever imagined me doing something like that, much less myself. Some of my cohorts congratulated me, a response I didn't quite understand. Others made it clear they thought I was playing fast and loose with my sanity. Most enjoyed the stories I told, and many took an interest in a place they'd never heard of before. For me, that was a great victory, to make people *think*. They kept asking me why I wanted to do this. What could I say? That in spite of the disease, the heat, the struggle, the harassment, the unending problems, I loved it. I loved the work, the staff, my colleagues, the country, I loved it all. I wanted to go back.

But there would be no going back. I waited nearly a month, trying to see if the possibility for returning to Gbarnga was there. It wasn't. In the end, I had to accept that if I wanted to continue with MSF, it wouldn't be in Liberia.

BOSNIA
Chapter 1

My six weeks in Canada flew by. I visited friends, I went to a girlfriend's wedding, life was easy, I was healthy, and things were fine. Then I got a phone call. It was from Ben, the guy who had recruited me in the first place, and with whom I'd had my disastrous interview. The first thing he said was, "What about Bosnia?"

I told him I really wasn't that interested. I had loved Africa and wanted to go back. He told me to think about it, and he'd call me back. A couple of days later, he did. Again, what about Bosnia? And again. Finally I gave in, the ominous phrase "You're going to love it" ringing in my ears. Boy, was he far from the mark!

The truth is, I was probably the only Canadian who didn't really have a clue about what was happening in Bosnia, having been so completely cut off from news and the rest of the world during my time in Liberia. I had a lot to learn. I also had only three days to pack my bags and head for Toronto!

I was to see some incredible differences between a 'front-page live from CNN in Sarajevo' war and an 'ethnic/tribal conflict somewhere in Africa' war. For starters, friends and family who had never heard of Liberia and couldn't find it on a map could hardly avoid the daily coverage of the conflict in Bosnia. Now people *knew* where I was going. They could, if they chose to, follow at least part of what I was doing. It was a much more visible war and therefore far more frightening to my family to have me in Bosnia — though in fact my work in Zaire was to be much, much more dangerous. Despite their coverage, though, CNN made a lot of mistakes and covered primarily only one side of the war, the side seen from Sarajevo. Bosnia is a great deal bigger than one city, and much of the rest was missed.

Also, going to Bosnia meant I was to be a part of a 'real' war, if you will. No barefooted kids with guns manning a frayed rope at a checkpoint. This was a war with professional soldiers and professional weapons, with devastating and incredibly destructive effects.

And while Liberia had been to me a warm and beautiful place, Bosnia would be one of the saddest and coldest. It was not just the weather that changed. To a large extent, the warmth I felt in Liberia was due to the warmth of the people themselves. This is not to say that they suffered any less than the victims in Bosnia, because they did not. But they dealt with their suffering in a different way. Mostly, the civilians of Liberia accepted with grace and good humour the help offered to them. In spite of all they had lost, they somehow managed to continue living. It was never easy for them, but there were so many instances of laughter and singing and dancing, and the continual search for some joy, some happiness in their situation.

In Bosnia, as in Liberia, many people were traumatized by the war. But there I saw far fewer smiles, barely any laughter and a profound suspicion of those of us arriving to offer help. Perhaps it was pride, or fear, or some other age-old emotion that prevented them from accepting the help freely offered to them. Gone were the fun parties with the national staff. Missing was the easy camaraderie, the joking, the singing. These things were so obviously absent during my days in Bosnia that I am hard-pressed to remember much happiness in my job. War is a serious business, and there was no joy in surviving it there, only grim determination and a lasting sadness. It seemed so many people had stopped living. Then again, it was one of the most brutal and despicable wars I've witnessed. Perhaps it will be a long time before there is again singing and dancing in Bosnia.

There seemed to be a prevailing attitude, encouraged by Slobodan Milosevic's propaganda, that the West had turned its back on all Serbs and that there was some sort of international conspiracy out to destroy them. This attitude worked against them far too often. Their aggressive and negative behaviour made working in the Serb-held territory known as Republika Srpska very difficult for us. They did very little to ease the way for aid agencies, to such an extent that in the months I was there, not a single other agency arrived to give a hand. Worse than that, although they definitely needed the aid given to them, the Serbs refused to admit it, even to themselves, and were constantly defensive about the actual situation. They refused to give us accurate information, which made supplying necessary materials next to impossible. It was not going to be an easy job.

At any rate, I arrived in Toronto for my briefing. I was told I would be assisting with a large-scale drug distribution program for numerous hospitals and clinics in two areas. One was in the Republika Srpska, the Serb-held territory of Bosnia. The other was in the UNPAs. These were the United Nations Protected Areas, four patches of land in Croatia that were occupied by the Serbs. UNPA north, south, east and west, were called the 'Krajinas' by the Serbs. In the western part of Srpska were other protected pockets — Srebinica, Zepe and Gorazde. MSF-Belgium had people working there.

I was told that I would be living and working primarily in Zagreb, and occasionally out of Banja Luka, the 'capital' city of the western part of Srpska. I was rather pleased with the thought of living in a city and having access to regular food, restaurants, markets, shops and mail service. After all, Croatia was not at war any more, and at least Zagreb would be safe.

By the time I arrived in Amsterdam for more in-depth briefings, I was told I would be living half of the time in Zagreb and half in Banja Luka.

By the time I arrived in Zagreb, I was told I would be *living* in Banja Luka, and working occasionally out of Zagreb! It was only in Zagreb that I began to get a bit of an understanding about the whole Bosnian conflict.

It remains to me a complex and difficult war to understand. There are ethnic conflicts that date as far back as the fourteenth century, and further internal conflicts arose during the Second World War. But the conflict in Bosnia had less to do with ethnic differences than many assume. Following World War II, Prime Minister Tito became the president and held the various factions together by force if he had to. For a brief time, Yugoslavia managed to build itself up to a fledging democracy. With Tito's death in 1980, things started to deteriorate. The country began to split up, and independence had its price.

In the period of change following Tito's death, Milosevic wanted control of a Greater Serbia, and through the Serbs in Bosnia, he saw his chance for holding on to power. His state-controlled TV and newspapers spewed relentless propaganda that convinced all Bosnian Serbs that they were about to be overrun by the Croats, who were seeking independence. Terrified that Croat forces, backed by the Germans, were about to descend on them, the Serbs began the fight for control of their own nation. Backed by the Serbian army, the Bosnian Serbs began a process of ethnic cleansing before the siege of Sarajevo even began.

The international community mostly ignored the stories of torture and execution, concentration camps and mass rape of Muslim women by the Serbs. They mostly ignored the vast numbers of refugees fleeing the country as the fighting continued. They mostly ignored a lot of things.

Only in the spring of 1994 did the US begin to pay attention to the relentless images on CNN and the horrific tales being told by survivors. After a year of bitter fighting between Croats and Muslims in Bosnia, the two minorities joined forces in a Muslim-Croat federation, in an attempt to halt the continued advance of the Serbs. Covert US assistance to the Bosnian and Croatian government began, and the tide turned with the NATO bombings of key Serb positions in August 1995.

But in the autumn of 1994, the Serbs were a powerful force to contend with, controlling most of Bosnia and ruthlessly determined to take it all. Radoran Karadzic, so his followers believed, was leading his people to victory. He was not about to hand this victory over to Serbia, however. He wanted Republika Srpska for himself.

That's the point at which I entered Zagreb on Tuesday, November 8, 1994. MSF had a large house that also served as an office complex. They had another guesthouse nearby, and the general coordinator, Ruud, lived in a separate house with his wife. I stayed for awhile at the guesthouse with an Irish journalist who had persuaded MSF to provide him with some information in exchange for giving MSF publicity. He and I explored Zagreb together. It was large, crowded and not all that impressive. There were a lot of ugly square buildings and broad roads. But it offered decent markets, shops and the thousand and one conveniences of modern Europe.

One of the more remarkable things we saw in Zagreb was the huge United Nations Protection Force (UNPROFOR) complex. It was entirely surrounded by a waist-high brick monument. Each brick held the name of a different Croat killed in the war, most of them at Vukovar. That town held the dubious honour of being the point of attack by the Serbs and the beginning of Serb occupation in Croatia. It was covered with flowers, wreaths and candles, and it made a very powerful statement.

MSF-Holland had a large team in Bosnia working in different areas. There was one team in Sarajevo, another in Tuzla and Zenica, in the Muslim side of Bosnia; another in Banja Luka, the Serb side of Bosnia, and a convoy team based in Split, who travelled some very twisted roads to get supplies into these areas. The coordinators were based in Zagreb. It took a long time before these teams actually met and got to know each other. Later, yet another team would arrive for Bihać. In essence, each team was independent of the others, and all ran somewhat different programs, depending on the requirements in each area.

Fortunately, I had enough free time when I arrived to do some reading and catch up on events. I was to be working with two logisticians, a Canadian named Aubre in Zagreb, and a Dutch man named Rink, in Banja Luka. Both were away in the field, so I had little to do but get to know the other expat and national staff. One of my best sources of information was Roel, the logistical coordinator who was based in Zagreb. He always used to sign off his messages with the word 'courage', which I thought was terribly appropriate. We needed that. I enjoyed his dry sense of humour and the fact that he was one of the few people who didn't try to convince me I would *love* Banja Luka. Everyone kept telling me that with a funny smile on their face. It kept me wondering.

I finally received my 'blue card', the UN High Commisioner for Refugees (UNHCR) identification pass, without which I would be unable to get into certain areas. Aubrey, my fearless logistician, arrived in Zagreb, and I was ready for the field. Our first visit was to refugee camps in the UN Protected Areas, sector north.

November 14, 1994:

What a day! A beautiful autumn day, sun shining, rolling hills, fields and forests. We went to Batnoga, a Muslim refugee camp in the north of Bihać. This group of Muslims was displaced by fighting between two groups of Muslims in the Bihaćpocket. One group is led by Abdic, a businessman-turned-warlord who had started the fight against the 5th Corps army. He is backed by the Serbs and holds a lot of power over his followers. They call him 'Babu', and see him as their father figure. Anyhow, the displaced ended up in two refugee camps, Batnoga and Turanj.

But the trip there was really something. A lot of wood or brick farmyards, with the barns attached to the houses. Piles of pumpkins, beans, heaps of corn, everything very green and grassy, the leaves changing colors. And then you pass the Croatian police, and then no-man's land — the separation zone between the UN checkpoint and Serb-held areas. Then you *really* see the war.

In the village nearest the frontline, you begin seeing graffiti on the walls, buildings riddled with bullet holes and sandbagged basement windows. As we got closer to the frontline every single building was completely destroyed, shelled, burned, bombed, ruined, empty. It's so devastating to see. A bunch of tanks and APCs (armoured personnel carriers) were at the Serb checkpoint, followed by miles and miles of complete destruction. A few Serbs scattered amongst the ruins surrounded by the ghosts of their neighbours. Every Croat and Muslim gone — dead, exiled, 'ethnically cleansed'. God, I hate that term! Call it what it is: murder. All that emptiness was painful to see. Fields untouched for years, grass growing up to the road, entire areas land-mined and useless.

The few Serb soldiers here are old men; the young have all been sent to the frontline and to Batnoga, up the mountains, 7 kilometres from Bihać. There are twenty-four huge chicken coops with some 800 Muslim refugees housed in each. Along a muddy walkway, crammed in close like the creatures that lived there before them, some 20,000 refugees. Mostly women and children, waiting without running water and with only a few latrines. The UN brings in tankers of water for them, but it's never enough. Everyone who's not in the coops stays in large tents. The refugees try to keep busy chopping wood for fires, washing by the river or collecting water from the river. But in all, it's abject squalor. The Norwegians have a good mobile medical hospital set up, and UNHCR has food and supplies, but the living conditions are still appalling.

A few of the children followed us today, and a few of the old Serb soldiers waved, but there wasn't much of a welcome for us. Abdic has his own police officers at the end of the camps, supposedly to assist the people but actually to keep them from leaving. These refugees are Abdic's power and he's not about to let them go.

Batnoga was one of the saddest things I've seen. The Serbs took that land with such terrible force and destruction. How they can live there after that, I'll never know. To see the trenches, the barbed wire, UNPROFOR everywhere and the scared faces of countless old people and children. This country has been so badly hurt. I don't think anyone will ever forgive the others. I could live here a decade and never understand how it all began, and I see no end in sight.

The Serbs have their own nationalistic graffiti on all the buildings: a cross with four Cs — the equivalent of S in the Cyrillic alphabet — one in each corner, to symbolize that Serbs standing together will be saved. I think it's going to be a long, sad winter.

I later saw a similar situation in Turanj, the second camp. If anything, it was worse than the camp in Batnoga. The amount of destruction was phenomenal. People were living in dreadful conditions, in homes with neither roofs nor walls. Somehow, they had managed to scrape together a way of life that included keeping shops and schools open. There was a good medical clinic, and the doctor there was an amazing woman. They were quite literally within spitting distance of Karlovac, which was bordering Croatia. Had they been able to enter Croatia, they could have applied for refugee status and been safely out of the war zone. But the area was heavily mined, and there would be no leaving. There had been house-to-house combat in the town, and the level of destruction left me speechless. Somehow, I had never expected it. There was serious fighting in Bihać, and the situation there was getting desperate.

Chapter 2

Roel described my logistician in Banja Luka as "a lonely crusader in a dangerous world". I still laugh when I remember that, because I had no concept of the type of trouble my new partner and I would get into. Together, we would become a formidable team. From here on, this story becomes ours.

On Saturday, November 19, 1994, I arrived in Banja Luka, the place that was to be my home for the next six months. Banja Luka had never been shelled. It was the heart of Serb territory, and at that point, the Serbs controlled some seventy percent of Bosnia. The western part had Banja Luka as its capital and was connected to the east by a narrow and heavily fortified corridor, the 'Brcko Corridor'.

I was one of only two expats working for MSF-Holland in Serb territory. MSF-Belgium was working in the eastern section, of which Pale was the proclaimed capital.

There had been a tremendous amount of genocide in the area, and it was near Banja Luka that the infamous concentration camps were discovered. Only one-half to one-third of the original population of 175,000 was still in Banja Luka. The rest had been run off, killed or imprisoned. A few minorities of Croats and Muslims remained in town, but faced a dangerous game of hide-and-seek with the Serb authorities. If found, minorities could be immediately arrested and sent to the frontline for 'work obligation', where they were used as human shields, digging trenches and serving the Serb soldiers at the frontlines. Most of the minorities had had their licences to work revoked. They were hardly considered citizens any more, and had virtually no rights. Somehow, I kept thinking that this was how it must have felt to be in Nazi Germany and see it all from the inside.

Throughout the previous year, MSF-Holland had been running an intermittent drugs distribution program throughout the western part of Republika Srpska. Our task was to supply medicines and medical supplies to the civilian population throughout the region. Since UN forces were not allowed into Serb territory, unlike in the Bosnia-Federation areas, we had no security backup whatsoever. We were on our own and would have to develop our own relationships with the authorities to do our job.

There had been several serious security incidents leading to the latest withdrawal of MSF expats from Banja Luka. Rink, who had been one of the logisticians in Zagreb, volunteered to return in Banja Luka on his own (was this guy nuts?) to re-establish the program. He'd been there for about six weeks, waiting for a medical officer to come and help him out. That would be me...

November 20, 1994:
I hear there have been cluster bombs dropped on Bihać. Shelling

has continued across the frontline in Tuzla for the last five days. A sniper hit the MSF car in Sarajevo, and the driver was slightly injured. Good thing they have an armoured car! I can't believe I now have my own BP (bullet-proof vest) and a helmet with my blood type neatly printed across the top. It seems so bizarre!

I met some people from UNHCR yesterday when I arrived. We went to visit Julian, one of the UNHCR team, and went to a castle that's been turned into a restaurant and bar to play pool. There I met Sanja, one of our national staff, who works as a translator, and a couple of her friends.

I hear that there are only one or two restaurants still open in town due to the fighting. The whole city looks a bit neglected and grubby. We only get water and electricity for a couple hours a day. We've a small generator for the fax and computer. Spent this morning drawing a map. MSF serves fifty-three hospitals/dom zdravjas (DZs) here! It's a far bigger program than I thought. I can't believe Rink's been doing this on his own. Lots of travelling, some of it to several areas near the front.

I sleep upstairs from the office, as do Rink and Sanja. For now it's fine, but it will be awfully cold if my little wood stove stops working. There is a tiny kitchen downstairs next to the office, which serves as the living room, dining room and kitchen table. Not exactly big on space here.

At least there are a few shops in town, and we can usually get some fruits and vegetables around the market. I hear that most of the people in town ignore us. We see the odd dirty look and an occasional sniper, but nothing too aggressive.

The other agencies are on red alert right now. There was an airstrike on Bihać which came from UNPA south. People are expecting some trouble here, but it seems unlikely, since we're so far away. We'll see.

I managed to learn a bit about our '4D' computer program and have done a couple of packing lists myself. I really don't know about the medical system here in Srpska and have no idea if what I'm giving is correct. I've just been following Rink's suggestions so far. It's a good program; you punch in what drugs you want and how many, and the program prints you up a list and automatically subtracts what you've taken from what's in stock.

The day after that journal entry, I took my first field trip with Rink and Sanja. We travelled to Prijedor. As long as I live, I will never forget that trip. A short distance from Banja Luka, I came upon my first close-up view of what ethnic cleansing was all about. There had been a large town with thousands of people living in it; now it was reduced to rubble, a ghost town, one of many I was to encounter. Each house belonging to a Muslim or Croat had been marked with a circle with a cross in it, and each house had then been systematically destroyed by the Serbs. Not a single building had been spared. There had never been a fight there, there was no war. Just the destruction of an entire population by a people determined to make sure that there would be nothing left to return to. I learned that nearly every mosque was also gone. In the entire area of western Srpska, only a single mosque remained intact. The famous mosque in Banja Luka, dating back to the 1500s, had been so thoroughly annihilated that even the bricks had been carted away, leaving only an empty field where the building once stood.

Further along the road, I saw the road sign leading to Omarska, one of the infamous death camps. On the other side of the road was a large factory that had been used as a concentration camp the previous year.

I'm sure I met authorities as I was introduced to people (one of whom was the director of the hospital, who later ended up at the war crimes tribunal in The Hague), but the only thing I truly remember was crying in the back of the car and thinking how I had never expected this, wondering just what I was in for. For the first time, the numbers, the data, the information about ethnic cleansing became real to me. I saw what was really happening in Bosnia, and it hurt to realize how little had been done to stop this.

The following day, the three of us travelled to Doboj. It was, for me, a very memorable trip. We stopped off at a couple of places along the way, Modrica and Jakes (pronounced Yah-kez). Jakes was an institute for handicapped adults, not unlike a facility I had worked in years earlier. It was sad to see the struggle the staff had in maintaining the facility. There was an embargo against Srpska and another against Serbia, which was their biggest supplier. Because of the difficulties with the double embargo, Srpska really had a tough time getting materials in. The previous winter, many people in hospitals and institutions had suffered from the cold. This year, MSF was running a coal program to ensure that facilities at high risk received enough coal to stay alive through the winter, and Jakes was one of the recipients.

We went on to Odzak, a new place on our list, to do an assessment. We had to wait an hour and a half for a police escort but finally managed to get into the area. It had also been a frontline area, and again, the damage was phenomenal. Much of the town was deserted. We went on to Doboj, where I met Mr. Gogic. He was a plump, smiling, balding man, who looked like somebody's grandfather. I believe he used to be a teacher in his other life (before the war), but now he was the liaison officer for all humanitarian agencies in Banja Luka.

It was through his office that all requests for travelling were made. We were not permitted to travel freely but rather were obliged to have a permission letter from Gogic's office before each trip we planned. We would fax him our requests the day before our planned trip, and he was generally very good about sending us permission as quickly as possible. He was a moderate and kind man, and he did his best for us. I grew to respect him enormously. He had a difficult job, trying to provide us with access to the areas we needed to go to while attempting to keep the military satisfied that we were not, in fact, international spies.

We also sent regular reports of our activities to him. Actually, with Rink and me, these reports were a lot more irregular than regular, but Mr. Gogic never really complained and always spoke highly of us to his superiors. Basically, he covered our asses when we needed him to.

While we were on the road to Doboj, the news came over our satellite phone, or capsat, that there had been a NATO airstrike in UNPA south. We were the only one of the teams to have a capsat in our landcruiser because we needed to be able to stay in touch with the base for security reasons, and the radios and phones in Srpska didn't always work, Zagreb sent us a message about the airstrike, ordering us back to our base in Banja Luka. With NATO airstrikes, there is always the fear that the Serbs might retaliate against either UN personnel or international aid workers. Since ther were no UN personnel in Srpska, the aid workers easily became the first target. Unfortunately, we knew we'd never make it back before dark. After a short discussion, Rink and I agreed that we'd have to go on to Doboj and spend the night there.

Perhaps I was just too unaware of the seriousness of the situation, or perhaps Rink had been working with medical staff that were far smarter than me, but at any rate, he was astonished that I agreed to stay. He claims that it was at that moment that he fell in love with me. I think he mistook bravery for something completely different!

It has to be one of the most bizarre war experiences I would ever have. There was only one hotel in town, Hotel Bosna, and it had no windows. They'd been destroyed by shelling ages ago. When we arrived, a formally dressed woman behind the desk asked us for our passports, as if we were tourists in high season and not the first guests they'd had in three years! We couldn't help but laugh.

They managed to find us a heater, since there was no electricity there either, and we dined, still in our jackets, on schnitzel and something remotely resembling french fries. We drank beer and enjoyed our dinner by candlelight. We were asked at what time we would like breakfast, because the entire staff, all five of them, would have to get up in time to feed us the next morning. We agreed that 7 a.m. was a reasonable time.

I'm certain that that night was the longest of my life. Doboj was so close to the frontline that the hotel was practically on it. I shared a freezing room with Sondra, another translator, and listened to the sounds of heavy artillery the entire night. Without windows, the cold was horrible, and the noise even worse. The room was shaking with the heavy shelling, and there wasn't a hope in hell for rest.

The next morning, we awoke to find Rink already up, cheerful and smiling, asking us if we'd slept well! We had eggs and incredibly strong coffee for breakfast. Nobody can make coffee like they do in Bosnia. It can also be used as paint stripper, glue and fertilizer.

The remainder of that day also stands out as being a bit on the weird side. We travelled on to Ozren with a guide that Mr. Gogic had sent us. We were crossing into a frontline area, and the railway that marked it was at most 100 metres from the road we were travelling on! Thank God for fog, because nobody could see us on our way there. We wore our BPs and helmets in the car, and I have to admit I was pretty nervous. Because of the roads, we actually crossed back and forth between the two frontlines a couple of times before reaching the town. It was a strange sensation to be driving in No-Man's Land, where not a soul dared to live, between the two armies.

It was a lovely area, very wooded and hilly, with lots of anti-aircraft guns in people's backyards. There were also several armoured personnel carriers and tanks, numerous bunkers dug into the hillsides and one large ammunition depot. The whole thing felt just a little bit unreal.

The hospital in Ozren served eight ambulantas, or primary health clinics, and covered an area of fifty kilometres. We decided to put them on our list as recipients of our distribution program.

When we returned to Banja Luka, we discovered that we had been very lucky. The International Red Cross had had five people arrested in Glamoc and held for the night. It was a very serious security incident, and the agencies in Banja Luka went on standby for several days until the issue was sorted out.

I had been there for less than one week.

Chapter 3

I began to get the hang of things in Banja Luka, or 'Blue Lagoon', as it was christened. My call sign was 'MSF Green', and our landcruiser's name was Elvis. I know one shouldn't get attached to machines, but Elvis was the best landcruiser I ever knew. He survived the war despite a bullet hole, a couple of minor accidents, and an abduction by the Serbs — who painted him camouflage green but later gave him back. Eventually, he retired as an ambulance service vehicle for a nursing home somewhere in Bosnia.

In Srpska, I met the Minister of Health, and I realized that everything he said would have to be taken with a large grain of salt. However, he did offer some information about the medical system in the region. Each district was headed by a hospital. If there was no hospital in the area, the dom zdravja became the referral centre. The DZs were then responsible for a number of smaller ambulantas. The main referral hospitals for former Yugoslavia had been in Zagreb or Sarajevo, neither of which was accessible to the Serbs. So Banja Luka became the referral centre for the western region of Serb-occupied Bosnia.

Some of the hospitals were like any other large European hospital, capable of admitting and treating most surgical and medical cases.

Some were smaller and had fewer facilities or were not able to handle obstetrical or surgical cases. MSF was trying to supply each centre with enough medicines and materials to last them a month. It was impossible to get to each facility every month, so we prepared their deliveries in the warehouse and phoned them to come and pick up their supplies themselves. In exchange, we received their monthly reports and figures and requisitions for the next month's supplies. It was not an ideal system because we rarely were able to determine if the supplies were sufficient, or being used properly, and it was hard to be accountable for every item.

Another problem was the fluid and ever-changing security situation in the region. There were times when we were denied access for months, yet hospital personnel managed to arrive with a car and collect their supplies. Other times, we knew our supplies were going to the war-wounded, even though ICRC was supplying materials to the same centre specifically for those patients. It was impossible to prove anything, and it became a thorn in my side — how to figure out some system to make the health facility accountable for what they were using and give the right drugs to the right places regularly. This became a challenge that took me months to sort out.

In the meantime, Rink and I got to know each other, and I got to know how things worked in Blue Lagoon. There were only a few staff members there. Sanja was our jack-of-all-trades and chief translator, Tanja was our secretary and Zjelko was our warehouse manager. He was a Croat minority doing his work obligation with us. His wife was Muslim, and his position with MSF was the only thing saving him from work at a frontline. Javanka was our cook/cleaning lady. We hired her for half days to clean and ended up doing most of our cooking ourselves, which was a disaster, because neither Rink nor I could cook. Between the two of us, we managed about three dishes. We got to know the two restaurants in town pretty well.

We had another guest in our house, who was later to become a good friend. As Rink put it, Borislav 'came with the house', and he had a room upstairs where he lived in self-imposed exile. He was the son of the landlord, whose house was directly behind ours. Our landlord and his wife were very good people, and I rather enjoyed their little eccentricities. The owner spoke a little German and chatted with

Rink sometimes. He drank a bottle of vodka and a bottle of slivovitz daily, which accounted for his good health, or so he said. His wife used to make us treats and cakes, and we became regular visitors in their beautiful garden, where we would drink coffee or wine together. They had three sons, two of whom were in the Serb army, and the soldiers' wives and children all lived in the house. Borislav refused to fight in a war he didn't believe in. He spent years hiding from the army, going between our house — where he had a tiny room — and his parents place when it was safe. He never dared go to town, and he lived a lonely life in a very small world. He would have been killed had he been found, but he survived the war without discovery.

We got to know Borislav well and spent many late afternoons and evenings escaping from our job with a glass of wine in his mother's garden. We talked about life and listened to music together, but I know it was a difficult life for him, to be a refugee in his own home.

By the end of the month, I was settling in to the routine of our daily trips to various health facilities. Rink had a 'hospital assessment' form, which we used to upgrade information about each centre: the number of doctors, nurses, patients, wounded and ambulantas being supported; travel distances; road conditions; names of directors, et cetera. It was a handy tool for data collection. Though there were two of us, the work still progressed slowly, as we only had the one vehicle and always had to travel together with Sanja as our interpretor.

Of all the places we served with our drug distribution program, the most vital and important became the work we did with the Merhamets and Caritas.

The Merhamets are Caritas were two local NGO's that supported unofficial and highly illegal medical clinics. These clinics were run by medical staff of the Croat and Muslim minorities in Republika Srpska, the Merhamets served in the Muslim population and the Caritas the Croatians. By law, the minorities had no right to work. Their licences had been revoked, so no medical personnel were legally allowed to carry out their professional duties. To be caught doing so meant punishment by fines, imprisonment or delegation to a frontline.

In private homes, attics and unmarked buildings, the Merhamets and Caritas kept a number of small clinics open for the Croat and Muslim minorities. Unable or unwilling to seek medical care from the Serb facilities, the minority populations were able to receive help from a handful of doctors and nurses who were determined to provide access to health care for their own people, at great risk to themselves. It was a daring and courageous act on behalf of these people, and MSF was the only NGO in Srpska who was able to provide the illegal clinics with supplies and materials.

A few Merhamets had a good working relationship with the local hospital or DZ and were able to have their serious cases cared for there. But more often, the hospital refused to look after their patients. More than once, we had to threaten a hospital director that unless he or she allowed access to the minorities, MSF would stop supplying their facility. It was a discouraging thing to have to ask my colleagues, as diplomatically as possible, if they were treating minorities in their centres. I kept stressing the fact that they were professionals, and as such had taken the same oath as I had to care for patients. I hated having to look through the admissions chart to check if the names included those of Croats or Muslims.

The staff of the Merhamets were amazing people. They diligently supplied me with all their information and were always honest about their situations. Of course, they had nothing to lose. Without us, there would have been no supplies whatsoever, except for the few that were smuggled in on rare occasions. They also shared some tragic and heartbreaking stories with us. One doctor told us a story about the funeral of a man who was killed in a fight by some of the Serb military. His sister came for the funeral and afterwards went upstairs in her brother's house for a rest. While she was there, the same soldiers came back to the house to rob it, and when she caught them, they shot her as well. We heard many similar stories of intimidation, robbery and physical violence by the Serbs against the minorities. Some of these reports we could do nothing about, but many we brought to the attention of the UNHCR staff, whose legal team would then investigate the happenings.

Our trips to the Merhamets had to be done cautiously and discreetly. We often parked our car quite a distance from our actual destination and walked to the place. We brought our supplies in quickly, and usually the windows were shut and the door locked until we announced ourselves. It was the stuff of cloak-and-dagger novels, but it was not at all amusing.

The authorities were well aware that MSF was supporting the Merhamets, and we made no attempt to cover up our work. But in order to protect the Merhamets, we tried not to bring too much attention to them. Our approach was that in matters of health, all people would be treated equally, and MSF would support whomever we wanted, regardless of the approval of the Ministry of Health. The Serbian officials might not have liked our policy, but it was the only way we would assist their own centres, so it never became an issue.

In fact, most of the Serbs working in the hospitals and DZs were fairly moderate people. They appreciated the help we could give them, and most behaved in a professional manner. Unfortunately, there were always exceptions.

Chapter 4

December 1, 1994:

I suppose you could say I'm getting used to the place, but it seems a lot to get used to. Bosnia is a beautiful country, especially around Jajce, which is simply gorgeous, with its dams, high hills and waterfalls. We went to Sipovo and there are about 2,000 refugees from Kupres living in a school and a hotel there. It's not a bad set-up, but they aren't too happy about it.

The farewell party for Leanne, the outgoing medical coordinator was great. I finally met a lot of the team members from other towns, and had great fun with Sherri, who is across the frontline from me in Tuzla. Her Muslims and my Serbs are busy trying to kill each other. Weird.

Zagreb has asked Rink and me to try to get into Bihać! We leave tomorrow to see how far we can get. We'll be taking Tom-Tom, the armoured car, and the standard-M (satellite phone) with us. I barely got started on UNPA north and south, but I guess they're going to have to wait.

There's heavy shelling in Bihać, and lots of artillery. No one has been able to get in with supplies for ages, so I don't know if we'll have any luck, but we'll see. We're heading for Topusko tomorrow, in

UNPA north, and we'll see how far we get from there. It could take a week or two.

I called Mom and told her the news. She's not too happy. We've bought our supplies, so I hope tomorrow goes well.

Rink and I spent the next two days at the Mosenica checkpoint, the last checkpoint before UNPA north. We got to know a couple of the soldiers there. I chatted up 'Curly', a rather good-looking young fellow, and Rink worked on their nice female interpreter. After a wasted day, we returned again with no success. Other than sharing coffee with the Danish guys at the UN checkpoint near Mosenica, we didn't get far.

It was cold, and the days were long, and no matter who we spoke with, there was always somebody above them that had to give us permisssion. It was a couple hours' drive each way, and we started very early. Rink, ever the optimist, was determined we would succeed. After two days, I realized this was going to be a slow process, and the waiting game was just beginning. We did a great deal of smiling, nudging, smiling, pushing and smiling on our quest to enter Bihać.

We made a plan that Roel and Aubrey would try from the administrative side in Knin, in UNPA south, while Rink and I would keep trying from Mosenica.

December 5, 1994:

Unbelievably, we made it to Topusko today. They even let us through with our useless MSF papers. Spent a wasted day meeting Major T (convoys), UNHCR people, some Danish UN guys and G., a Canadian engineer, who was very helpful.

Spent the night in the Hotel Tropicana (shades of Hotel Bosna in Doboj) and drank with the guys in the UNPROFOR bar. They have no plans to cross into Bihać, and we've been told we'd have to go in with the next UN convoy.

The UN are supposed to be ensuring the delivery of humanitarian aid in Bosnia. What a joke! They might get lucky occasionally, but all they do is bring supplies into their own UN bases for their own staff, and certainly nothing gets to the population.

Shelling all day. But the hotel is fine. You can have water or electricity, just not both at the same time. What a grim and dreary place. I hate this waiting, and I find the whole business discouraging. These empty houses in empty towns, in places that have lost their history, their stories, their past, their future. Buildings shelled, the names of towns changed, an entire population gone. It's the most heartbreaking thing I've ever known. Are these people so evil, or are they just misled? Mistaken? Is this human nature or human tragedy? How did it start, and who can stop it now? And what am I doing here? Nobody wants us, nobody trusts us, and nobody cares what we do because it's never enough anyhow. I'm so tired tonight. I shouldn't be drinking. I should go to bed and not think any more. I could learn to hate Topusko.

The next two days were not a lot of fun. We took the advice of G. and went to Komoro, a small village near the frontline, where we had hoped to be able to cross. Instead, we were stopped by the Serbs at the checkpoint and had all our equipment confiscated, including our $30,000 satellite phone and handsets. We spent *four* hours in the freezing rain trying to negotiate for the return of our stuff. We had to follow one guy into his home to try to get him to speak with us. We were two kilometres from the frontline, but these guys made it clear that we weren't about to get past it. We tried to call Banja Luka on the radio and tell them our whereabouts, to no avail, and it wasn't until about 8 that night that we were able to get away. By that time, one of the soldiers had started taking a more personal interest in me, asking Rink if I was married or had a boyfriend. Rink was getting worried, and we both felt it was time to go.

We made it back in the fog and rain to the Hotel Tropicana. Nobody was supposed to be on the road after dark, and I'm certain only the fog and miserable weather kept us from getting shot at. Back at the hotel, we finally managed to phone Zagreb, and though they were glad we were still alive, they were not pleased that we'd been missing the whole day. They weren't too happy about the stolen satellite phone either. The guys in the UNPROFOR bar thought we were nuts, and everyone was saying the road was mined and dangerous (as if we didn't know), but they had a grudging respect for us for trying.

The next day was a nightmare! We were up and on the road at 4:30 a.m. in order to meet our truck full of medical supplies. However, the

UNPROFOR convoy that it had been travelling with was cancelled. We borrowed one handset from the truck, to replace the ones we'd had stolen the day before, and headed back to Topusko. We made a stop at Glina at the military headquarters to try to lodge a complaint about our confiscated equipment. At the checkpoint the night before, we'd also met one lunatic who was trying to get his convoy into Bihać without any papers! He asked us to intervene by collecting doctors at the hospital to escort him through. We passed the message on to the hospitals, but as far as I know, not a single doctor showed up to give him a hand.

On our way back to Topusko, we finally made radio contact with Zagreb. This was such a rarity that I told Rink to stop the car so I could speak with Vera, the new medical coordinator. Big mistake! We'd barely stopped when two cars loaded with Serb police and several military pulled up, one behind us and one in front. My only words to Rink were, "Are they all for us?"

They were, and they did not seem friendly. We had just heard the day before about a bunch of Italian journalists who had been arrested and tossed in prison. I had visions of losing the armoured car, which would make the satellite phone seem like small potatoes, and I really didn't like the prospect of jail again.

About twelve well-armed soldiers surrounded the car, and motioned for us to get out. I was a bit too slow for them, and one started tapping the window with his gun. I kept thinking, "Please don't shoot, it's an armoured car and you'll kill yourself, and if you die, we are in *serious* trouble!"

Rink and I stumbled out of our respective doors without having a chance to speak to each other. For some reason however, we both reacted in what turned out to be the best possible way. We played stupid.

We found one guy who spoke English, so we explained to him what we were trying to do. He informed us we should go back to Topusko because "there's a war on, you know". We smiled a lot and explained politely that that was the very reason we were trying to get across the frontline. He must have thought we were mad! He told us repeatedly that it was dangerous, and that we should go. We kept explaining the position of humanitarian aid, with a smile on our faces the whole time. He didn't seem to grasp the concept of neutrality very well, but he finally seemed to understand that we were actually just doing our job. He had his men search the car thoroughly, but since there was nothing to steal anymore, they took the one handset we had and let us leave. They obviously thought we were too stupid to be dangerous.

Rink took a little run after their car to try to get our handset back, but considering the circumstances, it wasn't a big deal to me. A UN jeep carrying two soldiers drove right by during our hijacking. They didn't bother to help us. They didn't even slow down.

My legs were shaking by the time we got back to the hotel. It was clear that we weren't going to succeed this time. We returned to Zagreb a couple of days later, as did Roel and Aubrey. Our first real attempt to cross the frontline was a failure.

December 8, 1994:
Dear Darcy,

I'm back in Zagreb after five unsuccessful days of trying to get into the Bihać pocket. Spent a lot of time chatting up UNPROFOR guys, especially those Jordanians. Also spent a lot of time listening to the sounds of heavy shelling eight kilometres away. Had two security incidents in two days, one of which scared the shit out of me. If my life gets any more interesting, I'll have to get a new one!

We'll try again tomorrow to hook up with a UNPROFOR convoy, since that seems to be the only way in as the roads are all mined and both sides have to agree to lift them and stop shelling each other for an hour while the convoy passes. This is such an interesting job. So what about yourself? Had any life-threatening incidents lately? Want one of mine? I can hardly wait for next week. And I've only been here a month.

The rest of December was spent running between Banja Luka and Zagreb. Rink and I were driving back and forth every couple of days, trying to hook up with a UN convoy that could take us into Bihać. In the meantime, I was trying to deal with Srpska, UNPA north, UNPA south, and an unexpected new romance with Rink. Not that I didn't have enough on my hands!

In Srpska, the frontlines were changing rapidly. Fighting around Doboj increased. Thousands of refugees arrived in Glamoc and Grahovo, fleeing from the fighting. Over 400 minorities, mostly men, were abducted in Banja Luka over three nights and sent to the frontline. Zjelko was terrified and spent his evenings hiding in his blacked-out apartment, refusing to answer the door.

There were usually two or three UNMOs (United Nations Military Observers) at the airport in Banja Luka, but they were more often than not either under house arrest or kicked out of the country. They were the only UN personnel in the entire region. We started getting messages on our satellite phone to please try to contact these poor guys and have them report back to their commanders, who had no idea where they were or when they might be released. It became a bit of a game for us, trying to determine when the next message would arrive requesting information about the missing UNMOs.

Bernie, one of the MSF doctors in Sarajevo, apparently couldn't wait for the UN flight — fondly known as 'Maybe Airlines' — any longer. He actually sneaked out via the tunnel that ran under the airport. He made it up Mount Igman, crossed the frontline and caught a bus to Split. And they thought we were crazy!

It was a long month. The convoys that we worked so hard to get on were frequently cancelled at the last moment, and our trips to Zagreb were a waste of time, except for the fact that I got to know the city quite well and found Rink's favourite pizza place not a bad spot. We also stocked up on food. As winter was setting in, the produce available in Banja Luka was reduced to onions, garlic, potatoes, and cabbage — not an appetizing selection to choose from.

One day in Zagreb, we played hooky and took a drive up the mountain. We sat on a terrace where there was a ski resort and wasted the afternoon drinking beer. Sometimes we went to Dutchbat, the Dutch battalion in Zagreb, to buy stroopwaffels and eat french fries. We'd go to the odd movie, or out with Bianca to the bars in town. The next day I'd be back in Blue Lagoon counting war-wounded in the hospitals. I felt a bit like a yo-yo.

In the towns near the frontlines in Srpska we started seeing more and more sophisticated weapons. As Rink said, some people just have a car in their backyard — these guys had anti-aircraft guns, tanks, mortars, heavy artillery of all sorts, and a few items I couldn't even guess at!

December 20:

It's my birthday. Sherri, Vera and the Banja Luka gang sent me satellite messages. I wonder if Sherri knows how right she is with her horoscope: "You will find yourself falling in love with a co-worker. He is tall, dark, and Dutch".

Nicolein and Sherri even sang me "Happy Birthday" on the radio. After dinner, Roel, Aubrey and I went to a show. It snowed today as we walked to town, beautiful, thick, heavy white stuff. It was great, feels like Christmas. Mom phoned, and I had a lovely glass of good wine tonight, and I laughed. It was a fine birthday.

Chapter 5

On Christmas Eve Rink and I drove to Teslić, along a mountain road that had not yet been plowed. We listened to Wim Merten on the tape Rink gave me for my birthday, and it was gray, misty and silent. The day seemed so beautiful. Then we arrived at our destination and remembered all about the war. The hospital was close to a frontline and had been shelled before. Though primarily a military hospital now, it was the only show in town, and the staff there were terrific. One more assessment complete, and only twenty-five more to go before I had seen them all.

Aubrey and Ardi, a new logistician working for MSF in Sarajevo, showed up for Christmas. Not that Banja Luka had a lot to offer, but we went to the castle for dinner and played a little pool before the guys left for Puerto Rico, the local disco. When they returned, they each contributed to a hysterical letter that I sent to my Mom. I have no idea what they said, but I don't think she was reassured that my life was in capable hands.

On Christmas day, we were invited to dinner with some UNHCR people. The electricity came on just in time for us to put together a makeshift meal. We dined on potatoes and mushroom gravy, egg and salmon salad, bread and fruit salad, and we enjoyed good wine and companionship. It was an unusual Christmas.

Afterwards, we joined Zjelko and his wife, Daniela, who made us lovely cake and coffee and brandy and lemonade. It was very special but sad to see how they were forced to live in the dark, without a friend, constantly hiding from the authorities. We were very worried about Zjelko's safety those days.

On December 30, we left again for Zagreb to try once more to get into Bihać. This time we succeeded.

Rink and I travelled in Tom-Tom, the armoured landcruiser, and Aubrey drove the truck behind us, with it's nine tons of medical supplies and materials. For a change, we passed Mosenica with no trouble. Poor Curly had a terrible sinus infection, and I promised him something for it when I returned. We made it as far as Polbat, the Polish UN battalion just at the Bihać border. The road was crowded with refugees from Batnoga and Turanj returning home to Velika Kladusa on Abdic's orders. It was slow going, with hundreds of tractors and trucks on the road.

We spent the evening drinking with a dreadful Polish doctor. He wasn't expecting guests, and we told him we'd be happy to sleep in our cruiser if there was no room. He kept saying, "My men will sleep in the snow. *You* will sleep in a bed. My men swim freezing river, but *you* will sleep in a bed…" I was offered a room of my own but took Rink in with me for security reasons. I didn't trust our good friend the doctor as far as I could spit! He did, however, give me some medication for the respiratory infection I had developed. I couldn't read the instructions (they were in the Cyrillic alphabet), so I kept it for future use.

We joined up with a woman named Hannelore, from the Marie Stopes Foundation. She, too, was trying to get into Bihać and back to her team.

Our first move was to try to get past the next checkpoint and into Velika Kladusa. That was Abdic's town, and located there was the last UN base before the frontline, the Bangladeshi Battalion. There was no way to send a message to the battalion in Velika Kladusa, so they had no way of expecting us and no means of intervening on our behalf from their side. We were on our own.

The day started out with a terrible storm, and between the wet snow, the lightning and the shelling, it was pretty noisy. We put on our bullet-proof vests and helmets and made our way to the first checkpoint. The lone soldier agreed that we could pass if the guys at the next checkpoint would allow it. Without really discussing it, Rink did the most daring and outrageous thing I've ever seen. He drove, alone, through no-man's land to the next checkpoint and dragged one of the soldier's *back* with him to give verbal permission to the first guy for MSF to cross! Aubrey and I waited in the truck, convinced we were working with a madman and wondering how on earth we'd tell Zagreb about losing Rink somewhere in the Bihać pocket.

I think the guy from the second checkpoint was too shocked to do anything but agree. And the fellow from the first checkpoint picked up Rink's ID card, which he had dropped in the snow, and returned it to him with a rather dazed expression. I don't think he had any idea of what had just happened. After weeks of effort, Rink managed in a matter of minutes to get us farther than we'd ever been before.

We waited at the second checkpoint for hours in the freezing snow while soldiers searched the truck and landcruiser several times. In the end, a military escort drove us to the gates of the UN Bangladeshi battalion, and we were in the Bihać pocket. Now, we just had to cross the frontline.

The Bangladeshis were wonderful people. There hadn't been any aid agencies able to cross into their area for months, and they were happy to see us. They hadn't received proper supplies for their own people in ages but willingly shared what they could with us. We were put up in a container that had four bunks and a little stove, and we were invited to dine at the officer's table. We met the commander and his officers, and everyone did their best to assist us. Aside from four female translators, there were some 200 UN troops that had been unable to leave their posts for the last couple of months. Their building had been shelled in the fighting, and they were short of everything: food, water, electricity, medical supplies, et cetera.

The next day, New Year's Eve, we went to town with one of the UN men, a fellow who happened to speak some Serbo-Croatian. We met the local authority, a Mr. Dolic, in Velika Kladusa, and expressed our desire to cross the frontline and get into the town of Bihać to deliver our supplies. Both ICRC and UNHCR were working in Velika Kladusa, but neither group had received permission yet to cross the frontline. They had their doubts that we'd succeed where they had failed. Frankly, so did I.

Hannnelore was refused permission, but we were told to return the next day. There had been some incident in Velika Kladusa earlier with people from Hannelore's organization, and Dolic refused to allow her to stay. Before she left, she gave us some materials, money and supplies for her people in Bihać, in case we succeeded.

I have to say at this point that we did not in fact deliver everything she left us. She had a supply of vegetables and food items for her team, but we knew there was no way we could get it across the frontline without it causing big problems. That night we donated some of her perishable vegetables and fruits, along with a bottle of our whiskey, to the Bangladeshis for their New Year's Eve party. Dinner was a veritable feast, and they were grateful for our 'donation'. I must thank Hannelore for her contribution.

That was by far the most memorable New Year's Eve I've ever had. The translators did what they could with the few food items from the army rations that they'd been living on for weeks and prepared a little party. It was held in a small room by candlelight, so as not to draw attention from the two warring factions sitting 200 metres away at the frontline. Regardless, there was music, dancing and drinking, and everyone enjoyed the evening.

Just before midnight, Rink and I went outside together. Standing in the snow behind the sandbagged containers, we popped open the champagne. At midnight, the heavy artillery started, and it went on for about half an hour. We stood there in the snow, wearing our bulletproofs and drinking champagne to the sounds of shelling a few hundred metres away. I cannot adequately describe my feelings at that moment, but the whole thing seemed unreal. Most guys I know have taken me on pretty routine dates. You know, dinner and dancing, maybe the movies. Nobody but Rink took me to drink champagne at a frontline on a first date! I knew then that this guy was exceptional. It was the most original way to bring in the new year that I've ever experienced. And if ever there was a time I would like to have had other people looking through my eyes for a moment, that was it.

Over the next couple of days we were back and forth from the 'Bangbat' base to town to see Dolic and seek permission to cross. Velika Kladusa was a grim town. Most of the buildings had been damaged in the fighting, and there was a lot of destruction. We saw several prisoners of war shuffling from their prison, one of Abdic's factories, to town, where they were forced labourers. In town there was no food, poor water supplies and lots of wounded in the hospital. The hospital was filthy, and the used materials had been thrown in a heap just outside the building, which was crawling with rats.

I asked the hospital to supply us with a list of the materials they needed, and promised to return as soon as possible with supplies. However, the director had other ideas — he thought that about sixty percent of the supplies we were carrying to Bihać should be left with him. More negotiations. It seemed that the person able to give us permission couldn't quite make up his mind. Or, as Aubrey said, "The man with the key is not available".

We spent the rest of the time at Bangbat. I got to be quite friendly with the guys and talked with quite a few of them. I chatted with the UN Military Observers and spent a little time watching them monitor the 'ceasefire violations'. Basically, all they did was count how many rounds of shelling there were each day. The day I was there, there were almost a thousand rounds of shelling, mostly outgoing.

One day, in the middle of a blizzard, Rink and Aubrey went up on the roof to try to repair the antenna so the guys could watch CNN on the TV. They could have been killed on the ice up there, but both managed to live through it. I began to think that neither one of my logisticians was exactly normal. Another day we asked the interpreters if we could manage a bath of some sort. The entire battalion joined in on the mission. Snow had to be collected, water heated with the one and only electric heater — which meant that the generator had to be turned on — and arrangements made for an empty shower stall for us. It took a whole afternoon to prepare, but it was bliss. That evening at dinner, every officer inquired about my state of cleanliness, and all were truly delighted that I was so pleased. I was touched by their effort.

The day we finally received our permission to cross, Rink and Aubrey went alone to town to negotiate. As they had taken the cruiser, I had to sit in the freezing truck to have access to the radio. The UN guys were great, bringing me tea and waiting to hear any news. It was hours later, getting dark and close to curfew, and they still hadn't returned. The UN were about to send a rescue party to get them when Aubrey called on the radio to say they were returning — and with permission!

I found out from Aubrey that Dolic spoke a little German, as did Rink, so most of the discussion was between the two of them. Dolic had demanded again that we give half of our medical supplies to the hospital, and Rink apparently lost his temper and started yelling at him. I guess his German improved when he got mad, or maybe he actually frightened Dolic, but Dolic backed down and actually agreed to sign our permission papers. We could go in with our full truck.

We went to town the next day to receive our permission, which turned out to be half a page of thin paper with one stamp and one signature from the 'Newly Liberated Territory of Western Bosnia'. You should have seen the faces of the ICRC and UNHCR people that day. We were going across.

Chapter 6

We were now allowed to cross the frontline, but only on the condition that we travel with a UN convoy. The Bangladeshis made arrangements with both sides to allow the next UN convoy through. We put the snow chains on the truck and got ourselves ready. On Thursday, January 6, the French battalion passed by. We joined in but, again, communication had been poor and nobody knew we were coming. We switched to their radio frequency in time to hear the convoy leader say, "It looks like we've just been joined by an MSF truck and a second vehicle. Welcome."

It was 6 p.m. when we joined the convoy, and we had a long and daunting drive ahead of us. It was dark, deserted, very icy and snowing steadily. We came to the actual confrontation line at 8 p.m., which was marked with a big log and a police stop sign. The entire convoy stopped, expecting an ambush. I held my breath and prayed. A couple of UN soldiers from the lead vehicle finally got out and removed the log, and the rest of us followed across. Suddenly, we heard gunshots, very loud and very close. Aubrey swears they almost hit the truck. He was in a more precarious situation than Rink and I, who were driving an armoured vehicle. His soft-skinned truck offered no protection against bullets.

But we made it across, and I could breathe again. The entire trip, a mere thirty-eight kilometres, took a total of five hours. At one point a tanker truck in the convoy slipped on the icy road and got stuck in the snow. Then we were stopped by the 5th Corps at their checkpoint, and the vehicles were searched. Our two vehicles weren't on their list, of course, so we were delayed an extra hour while they checked us out. The rest of the convoy went ahead, but one of the UN fellows was very kind and agreed to wait with us. By 11 p.m. we finally arrived at the UN base in Coralici. The tanker was emptied, and electricity resumed for the first time in days. We were put up in what used to be an isolation container.

The next day, we started a whirlwind delivery/assessment tour of the Bihać pocket. We'd been told that the convoy would leave a couple days hence and we were strongly advised to leave with them. Otherwise, we could be stuck in the pocket for heaven knows how long. After some discussion, we put it to a vote. Rink lost, and Aubrey and I agreed that the best plan would be to go out together with the convoy.

We made it to Cazin and Bihać to deliver our supplies. Both hospitals were very relieved to see us. Cazin especially had had a difficult time. The place was crowded with stretchers, the wounded lying on mattresses on the floor, dressings being re-washed and used again. The staff was coping, but just. With our supplies, they were a bit more hopeful. Their biggest concern was the food and water situation.

In Bihać, they had some stock left, and the situation wasn't quite as desperate as we'd been led to believe. Still, everyone was overworked and pretty stressed. I gathered as much information as I could from the director while Aubrey unloaded our last supplies.

The area was quiet, and we had no trouble on the roads. But the markets and shops were empty, and the food situation seemed to be everyone's chief concern.

We made it back to Coralici before dark. I was asked to dine with the officers, as I was one of the medical personnel. It wasn't nearly as much fun as when we'd been together in Velika Kladusa.

The next day was the Orthodox Christmas. We rejoined the UNPROFOR convoy and headed back to Velika Kladusa.

While we were stopped at one of the checkpoints, a bunch of children gathered around the vehicles and started asking for candy.

One little girl, about seven years of age, was standing there in her boots and sweater and, unlike her friends, was asking for nothing. I called her over and gave her a box of our army rations. She gave me a huge grin and ran off for home.

I thought that would be the last of it, but a few minutes later she returned with a big bag full of walnuts. I was so moved I could hardly speak to thank her. How could this girl from this family, who could hardly afford to share food — much less give it away — offer us this gift? That was easily the greatest Christmas present I ever received.

We got back to Bangbat and spent a final night with our friends. The next day we headed home for Zagreb, mission accomplished.

To be honest, I was a bit disappointed when we returned to Zagreb. Not a soul was waiting to congratulate us or welcome us home. Nothing. Just empty champagne bottles on the table and no food in the house. Fortunately, my Christmas parcel from home had arrived, with chocolate, cookies, toiletries and plenty of cards and letters from loved ones, including the news that my sister was engaged. After a hot shower and some sustenance, we worked on our reports.

Being the first NGO to get into the Bihać pocket was a real coup for MSF. It was great publicity but, more importantly, our crossing paved the way for the other NGOs to do it. Slowly, Bihać became more accessible.

I was, however, very disappointed by the reaction I received from the coordinators. I felt that my assessment, though done in a short time, was quite accurate. It seemed to me that the biggest concern was for regular medical supplies and for adequate food and water. I did not get the impression that the assistance of a surgical team was necessary. I thought that the national staff could handle things pretty well. MSF had other ideas. A surgeon arrived to do a more thorough assessment and came to the same conclusion that I had: a surgical team was not necessary. Still, a team was standing by, and it was decided that they be sent in. I felt that all the risks I had taken were not worth it in the end if nobody was going to listen to me anyway. But the powers that be had made up their minds. The Bihać team was formed.

At any rate, we spent the next few days discussing the issues. We did some shopping for the translators at Bangbat and returned a couple of days later with supplies for the hospital in Velika Kladusa, and some materials for the UNPROFOR doctor at the Bangbat base. We also gave the girls their treats: clothes, magazines, toiletries, chocolates, et cetera. Rink and I spent our field allowances buying everyone something. We wrote a letter of appreciation to the commander, and that was my last trip to Bihać.

Rink and I took another trip up the mountain for a bit of a break one afternoon. As we sat drinking hot wine, the Croatian owner arrived, asking us where we were from and what we were doing there. Usually, we never mentioned to the Croats that we were working with the Serbs; all that did was start arguments and useless discussions. For some reason, we told this guy we were working in Banja Luka. He told us he thought we were doing a good and difficult job, and gave us the next glass of wine for free. During all the time I spent in Zagreb, that was the kindest thing anyone ever did for me.

We returned to Banja Luka in time for the Orthodox New Year's Eve party at the castle. We had a great evening dancing and playing pool and enjoying our friends again. At our second New Year's Eve, we stood out on the bridge at midnight watching the soldiers fire off their tracer bullets, leaving red trails in the air. It was a good deal quieter than our first New Year's Eve, but it was good to be back.

Chapter 7

January 17, 1995:
Dear Darcy,

Thanks for the Christmas package, I was delighted to hear from you. What can I say? I'm back in Banja Luka. It's a bit of an adrenaline letdown, but I'm glad to get on with the job. It's cold here (-17° C), and with no central heating, it's like working in a freezer. Fortunately we get electricity now for about twenty hours instead of two per day. Don't know how long it will last.

I'm still having a hard time with the program. Vera, my medical coordinator, tells me I have to start getting more accurate numbers from these centres, and I'm working on a big medical report for her. It's hard here, because nobody wants to tell me the truth. She also says I have to stop doing these 'charity runs' for every individual who asks me and start focussing on the big picture. I know she's right, but the big picture seems just a bit blurry and out of my grasp.

I'm finished with Bihać. They're sending in a separate medical officer for the area and giving us a second cruiser for our program here, so I'm free to focus on Srpska, which I enjoy. We have our little community here of MSF, ICRC and UNHCR, so it's nice to be back in my little family again.

Our financial controller from Zagreb, Bianca, came for three days and rearranged our bookkeeping. She told us to stop living in this little office and get a real house, which is something we could use. There's no space and no privacy here, and you never escape from work.

I was still having a bit of trouble getting a grasp of the whole program. It was such a big project, and we had tons of material and more than 160 different items in our warehouse. Zjelko had his own system of organizing the warehouse, but it wasn't methodical. We were having staff troubles, with one of our secretaries performing poorly and the other threatening to quit. Rink and I had enormous arguments over the program and how to manage it. He lived in a disorganized chaos, which worked well for him, but I needed more structure. We both had different ideas about what the priorities should be for the program, but with only one vehicle, we were limited as to how many places we could see, and how often. I always felt at least one step behind, and I couldn't seem to catch up. It didn't help that most of the population didn't have a clue about what we were doing, so we weren't exactly supported in our efforts.

Partly because neither of us cared in the least about public relations, we didn't write articles for the local newspaper or radio explaining our work, as the other agencies did. We were lucky to get our monthly reports in to Vera, let alone anything extra. All those people receiving treatment at their local hospitals usually had no idea that their prescription was filled with medicine that had been donated by MSF.

I was also discouraged by the lack of interest other NGOs showed for working in Republika Srpska. There was so much to do and such a lack of materials. In Sarajevo, the population of a couple hundred thousand was served by almost 200 agencies! In Srpska, the population of about one million was served by three agencies. Our pleas fell on deaf ears. Nobody wanted to work with the Serbs. They had heard too many stories, and they didn't trust them. One American Christian agency offered a significant amount of help if we could assist them with getting settled in Banja Luka. I agreed, only to have them call the next day and withdraw their offer. They hadn't realized Banja Luka was in Serb territory, and they wouldn't help the Serbs. So much for Christian charity!

Even within the MSF team, the country coordinator had never been to Banja Luka. Even Vera had never made a trip yet. I felt pretty much on my own out there and didn't find that I was receiving a lot of support from the Zagreb office.

Still, I was starting to get a feel for the place. We did a great many assessments in the next weeks, and I became familiar with the roads and the hospitals and DZs in our program. We had frequent problems with our coal program; the delivery was late, the coal was stolen, the payment was overdue, the trucks were broken, and it was always — or so they said — too little, too late. For most people, though, the situation was a great improvement over what they had had the year before, which was nothing.

January 23, 1995:

Today we went to Kotor Varos through this 'shortcut'. Rink is famous for his shortcuts. Once, he drove right through the middle of an army barracks that had been off limits for ages! The guys were so amazed to see him that when he waved at them, they just let him pass. I don't know how he gets away with it! It must be those dimples and that charming smile. That does it for me, anyway.

Anyhow, we took this beautiful snowy mountain road that *nobody* takes. Even the locals said it couldn't be done. We drove past this utterly destroyed village, practically through the river, until we had to stop and put the snow chains on. Unfortunately, in the end, we turned back.

Poor Little Gordana! She's the new translator we hired. She's such a sweet little thing and looks about fourteen years old. But she has spunk. Too bad she gets carsick. Her first day was a bit of a waste.

We always set off with fresh bakery bread and Rink's peanut butter for breakfast, good music in the tape deck, army rations, water and paracetamol in the back, with our packing list and permission papers close at hand. Some days it seems as if we're just going for a little visit for the day, a holiday almost. But the first checkpoint usually brings us back to reality in a hurry.

A couple of days ago, Rink and I were invited to the ICRC house for dinner. I really like the new team: an Australian and a Brit. We had a great laugh together, but when we came out, our car battery had been stolen, right from their backyard! We had a hysterical drive back to our office to pick up a new battery for Elvis. I think I'm going to like these two.

Rink left for Egypt for holidays, and I had the place to myself. I reviewed my medical report with Vera, and she came up with some good suggestions, which started me working on a plan. It took another several months to sort it all out, but in the end I developed a survey for each facility to help me select the appropriate types and amounts of drugs for the individual centres. There were months of work ahead for me, but it was a start.

The Bihać team was still working in the pocket. Rink and I had gone with them to Mosenica checkpoint the first time to try to get them and their thousands of dollars worth of equipment across. They were refused. In fact, Curly warned us that he had orders to confiscate all our material! Because he knew us, he turned his back on us and went inside with his friends, leaving us alone to re-pack our stuff and get out. He could then honestly say to his superiors that he hadn't seen us go. Sometimes it helps to be owed a favour; the respiratory medication that had been given to me ages ago by the Polish doctor had worked well on Curly's sinus problem, and now, he'd just saved us from losing some very expensive equipment.

One day, I joined a convoy of UNHCR and ICRC and we travelled to Krupa at long last. I enjoyed driving Elvis on my own for a change. It was an area that had seen heavy fighting, and we'd been denied access for a long time. There was still quite a bit of shelling, and one person was actually killed while we were at the meeting, but the trip was a success. We were finally able to see the situation for ourselves, and were pleased to be able to begin supplying them with materials for their hospital.

Sanja and I did fifteen assessments in the next two weeks. I also made a new schedule for visits and a list of places that needed to be seen next. We worked on a lot of packing lists for the hospitals and generally had a chance to catch up on things. The field trips through the mountains and rolling hills were beautiful.

We received a visit from a man I was surprised to see still in town. He was a Croatian who had come to our office quite a while ago, during the day, which was a very risky thing for any minority to do. He told us his wife was ill with a treatable cancer, and he wanted her to be taken to Zagreb. We told him it wasn't possible. There was an NGO that would accept 'treatable but life-threatening' cases, but only for children. He was the most determined man I'd ever met. He kept telling Rink and me that we were humanitarians and that it was our job to find a way. He insisted that we could do it, and he had so much confidence in us. He adored his wife, and he simply kept coming to all the agencies week after week to insist his wife be sent out. We tried everything, but it was very difficult for the minorities to get permission to leave the country at that time, in spite of UNHCR's attempt to help. Somehow he finally managed it. We'd all written letters explaining the situation to the NGO in Zagreb, and something must have hit home, because they accepted her at last. The man came by to thank us for doing our job.

Vera said I had to stop getting involved with these individual cases. She might have been right, but the smile on that man's face was payment for any amount of trouble I might have gotten into.

February 9, 1995:

Little Gordana is still carsick. But I've gotten heaps done. Have been to Kljuc, Srbobran, Ripac, Doboj (to meet with the various directors who are combining their requests for us), Derventa and Prnjavor.

Spent one day playing hooky and shopping with Sanja. We went for cakes and coffee and a trek through the market. I had dinner with her at her mother's. I got Francesco from ICRC to give Elvis a free wheel alignment and wash. He looks great!

A couple of nights ago, Julian, our UNHCR friend, got held up in their parking lot by three guys, two in military uniform. They threatened to shoot him, then stole his car. We took Julian to the police station to make a report and brought him home afterwards for dinner. It was pretty scary.

I also had a good meeting with the WHO rep who was in town for the first time today. They seem surprised at the problems — minorities paying huge sums for health care or being denied access altogether; no medevacs out of the country for anyone over the age of sixteen years; people being charged for health services, even if the aid has been donated by an NGO; the lack of materials in the region, the lack of agencies working here. Maybe they'll finally do something.

Rink and I had a lovely, romantic reunion when he returned from holidays, but it wasn't to be for long. Just after he arrived, I left for an assessment to UNPA south, an area that hadn't been checked in ages. Aubrey had left, and I was to go with Paul, my new logistician for the Krajinas, and Nicolein, a logistician from Zagreb.

The drive was lovely, through the national park and waterfalls, then along a very hilly and forested road to Knin. We stayed there at the Canbat, the Canadian UNPROFOR base, for the next few days. Canadian beer, Canadian flags, voices from home. It was nice for a while. My UNHCR 'blue card' had expired, so I hid the date from the soldiers at the gate and bluffed my way in. I was getting good at it.

We travelled with Branko, a UNHCR national staff, who agreed to show us the ropes. He was terrific, helping us plan our route and even coming along as a translator. I made deliveries at Knin, which had a central warehouse for the whole area and seemed to be functioning quite well. Over the next four days, I did assessments at six or seven places. They were long and busy days, but I was pleased with the result. I was finally getting a picture of UNPA south.

We drove several times right along the frontline, and I could see the trenches from the road. Some of the villages were ghost towns, completely shelled, with just a handful of people left. All the Croats and Muslims had fled, leaving behind thousands of empty farms and houses.

During lunch with Branko and his wife one day, he spoke to me of his dream to work on one of the oil rigs and make enough money to join his brother at his medical practice in Serbia. He also told some incredible stories about the war. He was convinced it was all economically based. He said that each side would 'hire' soldiers from the other side, arranging to be fired upon at certain times, enough to convince their commanders that they shouldn't be moved from their present positions to where the *real* fighting was. A hundred thousand dollars would buy some soldiers, a tank and an 'understanding'. He claimed there was a trade route into Bihać where two to three million dollars' worth of supplies and equipment regularly went. Busloads of Croat soldiers had passed through Knin into the Federation area.

Chapter 8

February 28, 1995:

Well, I'm sort of recovering. I had a dreadful head cold and was forbidden to work for the last two days. I think I needed the rest, and I do believe I need a holiday! Sherri and I are headed for Greece, and it can't be soon enough for me.

Meeting with Mr. Gogic today. MSF-Belgium is having problems in eastern Srpska, Pale and the enclaves. Ruud went and threatened to terminate *our* program here if MSF-Belgium isn't allowed access. I'm glad he's supporting our colleagues, but to terminate this project without even discussing it? I am *not* a happy person!

These people drive me nuts! The Sarajevo team can't get their supplies out of the airport. The Serbs won't allow the supplies to pass, even though MSF is one of the few agencies working in the Serb-controlled side of the city. In Tuzla, they have more drugs than they know what to do with and are even supplying some to the UN bases! Here, we keep struggling and arguing and fighting for more.

We did finally get a truckload in the other day. Roel's replacement, John, arrived with supplies. His wife, Moniek, is also in the project as a logistician for Zagreb. I'll really miss Roel. Bianca is also leaving, and so is Nicolein.

There are about 1,000 refugees in Knezevo. There was a big offensive, and four villages were attacked. One woman kept saying her husband had stayed behind with the cattle, but the Commissioner for Refugees says they found him with his throat slit. Everyone's been put up in the hotel, so they're okay for the time being.

We took a two-day trip past Doboj into the Ozren pocket. It was a stunning drive, very mountainous and high. We spent one night in the

Ozren DZ, and made it to Vozuca, the farthest Serb position in this region. Military everywhere! Trucks, tanks, field guns, grenade launchers (we saw one in use — the most obvious ceasefire violation I've seen to date!). There are bunkers everywhere in the sides of the hills, and the army is living in the woods now. They've seen aircraft — which are of course not permitted in this no-fly zone — and about forty trucks of men across the frontline, so a big offensive is expected any day. It's a military hospital, but there are still a few scattered civilians around, so they're on our list — if they can ever make it to Blue Lagoon to pick up their supplies.

On our way back, we were stopped at a checkpoint. Rink had been seen taking pictures. He agreed to hand over his film to the soldier as long as he could keep his camera. Of course, the guy didn't know the film was blank and had just been put into the camera. The photos were all on *my* camera, which I hid in my pocket while Rink negotiated his way out. We're getting good at this.

March 6, 1995:

On Friday, the Bihać team was stuck in the pocket due to fighting., and they asked us to help them out. We spoke with the highest authorities in Pale to see if we could arrange permission for the team to come out via Srpska. A daring plan if there ever was one, but it didn't quite work out.

The second Krajina Corps, the Serb army, heard our request and used it for their own propaganda purposes. Suddenly, the radio, the TV and the front page of the papers, were all saying, "MSF team held hostage by the evil Muslims," and the like. It took us four hours, endless communications between us, Zagreb and the local authorities, and a press release to the paper before we resolved it. Maarten, a logistician with the Bihać team, was totally pissed off, and blamed us for making their situation worse. Of course the Muslims in Bihać also heard that MSF was being held captive and were furious, because it wasn't true. Anyhow, we put a stop to it as soon as we could.

Then we had this sad case where we received a phone call from a man asking us to come to his apartment. He was a Croatian fellow who had been badly beaten up by some Serb police officers. They'd stolen his ID papers, and he'd just made it to his sister's place. The poor guy had a punctured lung and was quite distressed. We took him to the Danish mobile hospital, hoping he would get seen more quickly, but it still took them another day or two to get a chest tube put in. I was furious with the slow reaction, but there wasn't a thing I could do.

I just finished reading Roy Gutman's book *Witness to Genocide*, one of the most chilling books I've ever read. There are times it would be very easy to hate this place and everyone in it.

The good news is that we moved to our new house, and finally have a little privacy and freedom from the office. The other good news is that in a few days, Sherri and I are leaving for Greece.

March 8, 1995:
Dear Darcy,

Well, just when I thought life couldn't get worse, God starts laughing. Our team is stuck in the Bihać pocket. It's been days since anyone could get in or out. Rink and I came up from Blue Lagoon to try to get the new surgical team in and the other guys out, but no luck. Poor team in the pocket. All their contracts are finished this week, but like it or not, they've just extended. Such loyalty to this organization!

The other shitty news is that our work in Banja Luka just got ten times harder. Every time we want to bring in aid supplies, we now have to go through the worst bureaucratic bullshit you have ever heard of! First, we have to get authorization from the 'Bosnian' authorities, meaning the Croat-Muslim Federation. Then we have to ask the Croatian officials in Zagreb for approval. Only with their approval are we permitted to ask the UN sanctions commission in New York to *allow* us to bring in some medicines and supplies to those 'nasty' Serbs. (I've heard this UN guy refer to them exactly that way!) The entire process takes three to four weeks, and if anyone along the way says no, we have to start all over again. This means that the refugees will have to warn us how many of them are going to arrive, and when and where, so we have lots of time to get ready for them. Heaven forbid we should need anything on an emergency basis (even if it is a war, you know!). I do hope the military will inform us ahead of time where they are going to attack and how many they intend to wound, so that we can arrange some extra stuff when they need it!

Do I sound just a little bit frustrated, fed up, pissed off, irritated and annoyed? Well, you got it. At this point, I just want to tell the useless UN to leave and that we should all go with them and let the country fight it out themselves. Believe me when I say I need a holiday. Greece in two days! I have never had to work this hard for this many ungrateful people in my life. I am coming home in June, and anyone there who wants to risk their life is cordially invited to discuss politics with me.

To top it off, I just found out from my sister that I haven't been paid my thousand dollars a month since November. Well, this is a rather pessimistic note, isn't it? I'm giving up optimism for awhile. It just doesn't work here. Reality is much more fun.

Chapter 9

To say that my two-week vacation in the Greek islands was a lifesaver would not be an exaggeration.

I loved every minute of it! Sherri and I spent our days doing amazing things like taking walks along nearly empty beaches, watching sunsets, eating gorgeous food, drinking wine and just relaxing. The luxurious silence! Greece was clean and fresh, white and quiet. No soldiers, no shelling, no checkpoints, no handsets, no people. We browsed the shops, read mindless books and sunbathed on the terrace of our beautiful apartment. We wandered through villages, took the standard tourist photos, and watched the fishing boats come in. We strolled through vineyards, dined in small restaurants, chatted with shopkeepers and picked wildflowers. We even watched the moon rise.

In Athens, we visited the museums, got our hair cut, bought magazines and souvenirs and dreaded our return, which, alas, arrived far too soon. It had been a touch of paradise. And then it was over.

Chapter 10

I'd like to say I eased back into work, but that would be a lie. I was plunged back into the chaos almost immediately. In Srpska, there was growing concern over the minorities. Both Rink and I, along with our national staff, had always been given monthly crossing papers from the Serb authorities, which allowed us to travel from Srpska to Croatia without trouble. We heard that those papers were about to be revoked. Zjelko was terrified and spent a couple of nights sleeping in our office because he was afraid to go home. Finally, he reluctantly agreed to let us take him to Zagreb. Unfortunately, we couldn't bring his wife out at the same time, but we promised to try later. On March 27, Rink drove him across the border into Croatia. Zjelko became a refugee.

A couple of days later we travelled for Grahovo. I had prepared my hospital survey and begun handing them out to all the centres. We ran into a horrendous snowstorm and got stuck behind a Danish convoy. One of their trucks was disabled in an accident and a driver wounded, whom I had to attend to. The mountain roads were extremely treacherous, and we could hardly see the sides of the road. It was with tremendous relief that we returned to base. The next day, the snow was gone as if it had never happened.

It was fortunate that we got Zjelko out when we did, because the Serbs changed the rules only days later. Monthly crossing papers were forbidden to all Serb nationals, and try as we might for the next few months, we were unable to get Daniela out to join her husband. We passed messages and money between the two of them, but it was so depressing to be unable to do more. It wasn't until July that she was able to escape on her own and join Zjelko in Croatia. Ultimately, they managed to emigrate with their children to Sweden.

With Zjelko gone, we gave some attention to reorganizing the warehouse in Banja Luka. It was a long process, but I was justifiably proud when we had finished our inventory and everything was alphabetized and rearranged. As Rink said, "A blind horse could find his way around in here now." We also had to go through several candidates to find a new warehouse manager. The problem was that there were few available men in Srpska, as they'd all been sent to the frontline. That was also the only reason why Rink and I were allowed to drive ourselves. Normally, national staff are hired as drivers, but none were available in Srpska at that time. As for the warehouse, we finally hired Dolibar, whose call sign became, to our amusement, 'MSF Pink'.

Due to the relatively small number of aid agencies working in

Srpska, all of us were inundated with endless requests for assistance. As a consequence, Rink and I became quite famous for scrounging materials from whomever we could. We weren't above sneaking a little something from the main MSF warehouse in Zagreb, even if it was meant for UNPA north or Tuzla or Sarajevo. Roel had christened us 'the vultures', and the name stuck. My natural talents expanded in unusual ways; I learned to lie with impunity, cheat, steal, negotiate with and manipulate anyone, to beg, borrow, stretch facts, bend truths and get what I needed by any means necessary. I worked hard to earn Roel's nickname.

We started out with World Health Organization (WHO). They had heaps of materials but no office in Srpska. So we agreed to do their deliveries for them. The Marie Stopes Foundation had women's health kits for everywhere else in the country, so why not Banja Luka? We arranged to take the kits in for them. We needed insulin for the country; if CARE Austria could donate the drug, we said we'd be happy to deliver it for them. Heparin for the dialysis machines? We would find someone who could help. Doctor's kits for the Merhamets? We'd be happy to take them off WHO's hands. Stuffed toys for the kids? Sarajevo didn't really need all those boxes. We developed quite a ruthless reputation but, considering the circumstances, one could say that necessity drove us to it.

We got so good at scrounging that at one point a large UNHCR convoy arrived in Banja Luka with two trucks loaded with MSF supplies that WHO had arranged for us. The UNHCR staff unloaded it for us, and stored it for us, free of charge, in *their* warehouse! But it was never enough.

April 6, 1995:

Meeting today with Merhamets, Caritas and the humanitarian apoteka, a makeshift pharmacy run by a woman doctor to provide drugs — from any agency that will donate them — to the entire population. So tiresome and frustrating. Everyone wants more, more, more. No one understands what we have to go through to try to get even the minimum supplies in here, and they all want these expensive IV drugs. They want parts for the CAT scanner, for God's sake! They already overtreat everybody. When Michael was helping in the warehouse and cut his arm, all he needed was about twenty-five stitches, but they gave him a prescription for two kinds of antibiotics and painkillers!

It's just Rink and me here, but they seem to think we have endless supplies and nothing but time on our hands. I'm fed up, worn out, completely frustrated. I am so *tired* of this. Right now, I just want to give up and go home. None of this matters. What are we doing it for? Today, all six people at the meeting told us how small and insignificant MSF was, and I just felt like saying, "Fuck you, we can leave!"

I don't feel I'm getting any support from Vera — though I can see how overworked she is — and no support from anyone else either, except Rink, of course. And we keep fighting all the time. Maybe a war is not a good place to start a new relationship. None of the recipients of our program give a rat's ass about how hard we're trying. It just isn't worth it. Vera plans on sending Rebecca into Blue Lagoon soon. She's doing an evaluation of the whole program. Good idea, let's shut the damn thing down. It seems to be what everybody else wants, except maybe Rink and I, and I don't know why we keep trying so hard.

And the bloody army is now demanding more information about our program, how much we're delivering, what it all costs, all this shit. We still can't get Daniela out. We're not getting permission to go in where we want. There's more fighting. The minorities in town are really scared.

The doctor at the Nepalese UNPROFOR base in Okucani is also getting worried. He says there are new troop movements and fresh fighting in UNPA east and west. His base is the only UN base we will ever see in our region, a tiny corner of UNPA west that we have to cross to reach the highway to Zagreb. We've delivered medical supplies to him before, and he's always such an easygoing and relaxed fellow. If he's starting to worry, the situation is getting serious.

Though I may not have been loving every moment, we did manage to have some fun. On April Fool's Day, Zagreb sent a capsat saying that the UN was pulling out that very day. (Well, their mandate had expired, so it could have been possible.) They said we could get some great deals on the Dutchbat trucks. Sanja called us urgently back from the market, only to discover it was all a joke. We wrote back saying things were already out of control, and that we'd seen a mujahidin in Banja Luka. Sherri from Tuzla replied by saying there was a chetnik on her side. The jokes got passed from station to station, and all the bases joined in. It was a short, but fun, respite.

We also had an enjoyable social life with the other agencies in Banja Luka. While I was away, Rink had gone for another dinner with ICRC. Yet again, the battery from Elvis was stolen while he was there. When I returned, and they invited us again, Rink asked them, "Why? Do you need another battery?" When we went back the next time, we decided to walk.

We had some great pool tournaments at Kula's, the bar above the castle. And Rink and I became regular customers at the two restaurants in town, the castle and the fish restaurant. The latter was a bit of a joke, because there hadn't been fish on the menu for ages. In fact, both places served the same thing: a piece of well-done beef, greasy fries and pickled sweet peppers, cabbage or onions. It was almost laughable when the waiter showed up with the menu in his suit and tie, since there were only one or two things available, and they never changed throughout the war.

Our trips to Zagreb were also fun. We got to know the Bihać team quite well. I became friends with Sidne, a Canadian nurse who had taken over my position in UNPA north and south, as well as the Bihać pocket. She couldn't believe I'd once done the whole thing on my own. It was a great relief to hand that job over to her. We also got to know the new coordinator and his wife, John and Moniek, who were both helpful and easy to talk to. We nicknamed John 'Frankenstein' because of his large size. Really, though, he was a marshmallow. Very sweet and only as tough as he had to be.

Once, Moniek sent us the following message in an effort to sort out where all the bulletproof vests had disappeared to:

Dear Family,
The following differences have been noted. Please inform me:
11	*Tuzla says 11 went to Split, Split says they gave 11 to Guus for Sarajevo.*
35	*Sarajevo says Guus has 35, Tuzla says Haris has 35. My list says 35 has always been in Tuzla. Sarajevo, pls check.*
15	*Sarajevo says Helen has 15, Zenica says Sanja has 15. My list says 15 was always in Sarajevo, and Sanja used to have number 14, Zenica, pls check*

14   *Was on my list for Zenica/Sanja, where now?*

20   *My list says for Boris in Zenica, Split says used to belong to*
        Boran. He left, so where is it now?

37   *Was lost? Found in Zenica for Boris. Boris used to have*
        number 20, is this now changed?

79   *Zenica says it has this number, but it does not exist. Could this*
        be 19?

48   *Rink (of course, who else) had one without a number. Pls*
        note, yours is now number 48.

It was hard not to share a laugh in the midst of such craziness. We also became good friends with Pierre, from MSF-France. He was working in Croatia but trying to expand the project a bit and get involved in UNPA west. He wasn't having much success persuading his boss to expand, but we used to see him quite a bit, and MSF-Holland sort of adopted him.

Best of all, the head office decided to take a good, hard look at the program in Bosnia. Rebecca, who was to become a very good friend, was sent into Bosnia to do a drug consumption survey. In the end, she ended up doing a program evaluation on the entire project. When she finally arrived in Banja Luka, she asked about a million questions about our program, as she did with every team. In the end, her input was invaluable in arranging a workshop that helped get the entire team together for the first time since I'd arrived.

We were also enjoying our new house. The landlady was great, and we actually hired her daughter as MSF staff. We occasionally had a barbecue or shared a meal with them, and I really appreciated being able to leave the office when the day was done. The warehouse was sorted, my survey had been sent, and things were under control.

We spent Easter Sunday with Borislav and his family in their garden, drinking wine, eating his mother's famous cheese pies and enjoying the flowers in bloom. It felt like spring, and I was happy I had only a couple more months to go.

At the end of April, the entire team was ordered to Zagreb for a three-day workshop. It was the first time I actually met some of the team members. Rebecca had discovered in her evaluation that there were several problems within the program, and people were having trouble prioritizing their goals. Each program was so different from the others that none of us knew precisely what the rest were doing! The workshop was a great idea and got the whole team discussing some important issues. At the end of three days, plans had been made about which projects required more support, which ones were essentially closed or could be closed, and how we could all work better in the future. On the last day, we had a wonderful brunch together at a restaurant before each team started for home. Rink and I went for a few nice rides on his motorbike, and things between us seemed better.

A member of the mental health team arrived from Amsterdam and spoke with all of us individually, and for the first time in ages, the team *felt* like a team. The capsat messages became more personal, and there was a connection between us that had been missing before. Best of all, people were finally sold on the project in Banja Luka. Until that time, there was not much support for the Serbs, even from our colleagues. They finally realized that the minority population MSF served in Srpska was not going to be helped by anybody else. They also realized just how huge our project was. It was by far the largest area being covered, and with the smallest staff. The fame of the 'vultures' was spreading.

When we returned to Blue Lagoon, it was with an invitation to visit Sarajevo and with some new friends in our lives. Maarten, from the Bihać team, decided to join us for a visit to Srpska and on our trip to Sarajevo.

Chapter 11

Sarajevo was a bit of a holiday for me and Rink, which illustrates the state of things in Srpska those days! It was unforgettable. We had been invited to attend a big NGO meeting in Pale, and Helen and Ardi, the team from Sarajevo, invited us to drive home with them for the weekend.

The trip itself was extraordinary. We set off through the Brcko corridor, the famous narrow stretch of land connecting the eastern and western parts of Srpska. It was through that narrow road that most of the supplies from Serbia arrived. As such, it had been fiercely fought over, and the destruction in that area was enormous. The Serbs clung ferociously to this little stretch, but the shelling was fairly regular. There were no road signs to show us the way, and it was a dangerous ride. There were burned and abandoned tanks and a wide variety of weapons in the fields and along the road. In spite of the shelling, the only time I worried was when we came upon a sign reading Rata Zona, meaning 'war zone'. At that point, I assumed Rink had once again taken the wrong shortcut! We managed to turn back and find another road out. For a change, I really didn't mind how fast Rink was driving.

We got through the corridor and arrived at the MSF-Belgium office in Pale. Pale used to be a ski resort and wasn't much of a capital city, with one restaurant and an 8 p.m. curfew. It was, however, close to Sarajevo, and Pale was to be the Serbs' capital when they won the war. We spent the night there with our colleagues and joined up with the other NGOs the next day at the meeting.

The NGO meeting was well attended, presided over by Professor Kolnevic, the vice president of the so-called Republika Srpska. After the war, the professor committed suicide. As I write this, his boss, Mr. Karadzic, is still at large.

The main point of concern was the issue of the Pharmacies Sans Frontieres (PSF) people who had been arrested and imprisoned two months earlier. Apparently, five members of PSF, a French NGO, had taken the wrong road while leaving Sarajevo and ended up at a Serbian checkpoint. They were promptly arrested and imprisoned without trial or appropriate legal representation. All the NGOs present were outraged and insisted the people be released. Kolnevic seemed surprised by the reaction and was visibly shaken by the outspoken support PSF was receiving. A few weeks later, the group was released.

Our input was limited to Mr. Gogic speaking very kindly on our behalf and some words of high praise from Kolnevic about the amount of support MSF was giving the Serbs.

After the meeting, we followed Helen and Ardi's vehicle into Sarajevo, giving us a unique experience, one that very few expats have had.

Throughout the siege of Sarajevo, there were only two routes in and out of the city. One was via the tunnel under the airport, through which almost all the supplies arrived and through which most of the people travelled if they dared. This route involved a trip up and over

Mount Igman, which meant one became a very visible target for the Serbian snipers surrounding the city. It was a very dangerous route but essential for the survival of the population.

The second way into Sarajevo, the one that the UN and NGOs used, was to fly 'Maybe Airlines', the UN-brokered flights in and out of Sarajevo. The problem with this method of transportation was that the Serbs controlled the airport, so all flights depended entirely on the whims of the commanders. The plane rarely, if ever, flew on schedule, and was routinely cancelled at the last moment. All supplies that did arrive at the airport were again scrutinized by the Serbs, who determined just what could be released and when. Like dozens of other NGOs, MSF had tons of supplies sitting in the airport, which they were unable to move for months.

We arrived via the little-used third way. We *drove* into Sarajevo in the middle of the war, in Elvis, the only vehicle in the city that wasn't an armoured car! As we drove the winding hills above the city, it was easy to see how the Serbs held Sarajevo under siege. Dozens of sniper and heavy artillery positions were clearly visible along the road. The Serb military manned each position, and they could pick and choose their next victims at will. In front of the sniper's position, a long wall had been erected, virtually overnight, in 1992. Safe behind it, the Serbs managed to completely control the city. They cut off water and electricity at their leisure, targeting the population as they pleased. The UNPROFOR armoured tanks drove up and down sniper alley every day, and the Serbs above the city watched them and laughed. The UN did not do a single thing to stop them. Nor did they have a mandate to do so.

The sensation of being that closely watched made my skin crawl. I remember sitting in the back of the cruiser, and as we descended into the city, Maarten reached back and held my hand. He must have felt as I did, the sense of horror, the shame. I wanted nothing more than to sob my heart out for all those people below me, who were helpless and forgotten, at the mercy of the same people I struggled every day to assist.

At some of the checkpoints, we had to make certain that the soldiers were aware we were from Banja Luka. Then, two blocks further on, we would claim to be MSF colleagues in Sarajevo for an assessment, being careful *not* to mention Banja Luka. Rink said at the end of the weekend that working like that could really twist a person. He was absolutely right.

The destruction in Sarajevo, considering the size of the city, surpassed anything I had seen so far. Entire city blocks had been reduced to rubble, and there was scarcely a single building left unmarked. Every structure was pockmarked with holes from bullets, shrapnel and artillery. We entered along sniper alley, but Helen and Ardi avoided the major intersections, since we didn't have an armoured car. Along the way, huge metal containers used for transporting goods offered the only protection to pedestrians, and little of it. The containers had been shelled so heavily that some of them were nearly shredded.

Helen took us on a daring tour of the city, and we saw first hand what the war had done. So much of what had been old and treasured and beautiful was now utterly and completely destroyed in the city. Fresh graveyards had cropped up throughout the city as the old ones filled up, and nobody dared establish new ones outside the city limits. Every spare inch of land that wasn't a graveyard had been converted to vegetable gardens to enable the residents to eke out a living somehow.

Yet the people hung on with a tenacity and courage I could only marvel at. They opened schools, gave concerts, worked in their shops and opened their terraces, in full view of the snipers. The newspaper remained open, though the entire building was destroyed; the staff continued working out of the basement. A solitary restaurant remained open throughout the war, and clients dined in their basement. Illicit films arrived, and clubs opened for the desperate few. The city closed down with the midnight curfew, but every morning the people rose and began their daily routine.

Rink and I went to the marketplace, where a few weeks earlier shelling had killed about seventy people. The shops were better stocked than in Banja Luka, and we were happy to dole out our money, as the prices were better too. It was a strange and bewildering experience, but the atmosphere in the city was somehow considerably lighter than the atmosphere in Srpska. Perhaps these people had found something worth living for.

Helen took us to one shop where we were able to purchase the famous Sarajevo postcards. Printed by *Trio*, the cards were wonderfully sarcastic reprints of famous scenes. For example, the 'Twilight Zone', with its starry background had been replaced with the 'Sarajevo Zone'. On the back, the cards said, "This document has been printed in war circumstances. (No paper, no inks, no electricity, no water. Just good will.)"

We left Maarten there to help out the Sarajevo team and headed for home. As usual, we managed to get ourselves lost in a Serb-occupied area. We found a few men drinking at a café, who, when they heard we were headed home to Banja Luka, were happy to give us directions. Twisted. Really twisted.

Chapter 12

May 1, 1995:

Today the ceasefire officially ended. Now there's lots of fighting — shelling in Okucani, Gradiska, and Dubica. Gradiska could be very serious. That's our one and only escape route, across the bridge, through UNPA west, and on to Croatia. That highway has been closed, and there's no way to get Rebecca in — or ourselves out! I'm not too happy being stuck here.

We've heard the Croatians have a thousand men, tanks, guns. I guess they want their land back, and they intend to take it. They've taken fifteen UN checkpoints so far. And the Serbs have taken Nepbat and are holding fifteen UNPROFOR men there hostage. I hope our doctor isn't one of them. I wonder if the refugees there all got out, or what?

On the humorous side (since I could use a laugh) I can't believe what Rink and I did. On our way to the workshop in Zagreb, we accidentally drove over our new computer with Jabba, our new landcruiser! When we got back to Blue Lagoon, we saw the tire tracks still on the case and one side of it completely crushed. We thought up about a dozen possible excuses, but I finally convinced Rink to tell John the truth. They thought it was another April Fool's Day joke and didn't even believe us! I think our reputation as liars and thieves might be going just a bit too far.

The following week marked a turning point in the war. UNPA west, the Serb-occupied area, was re-taken by the Croats. It was done in a matter of days, resulting in hundreds of deaths and thousands of refugees. In retaliation, the Serbs shelled Zagreb twice, leaving several dead and many wounded. The agencies in Banja Luka were incredibly busy for the next couple of weeks, setting up refugee collective centres around Banja Luka. For the first time, public sympathies ran with the Serbs, but it was too little, too late. We heard there were pockets of Serbs trapped across the Sava River, in what was now Croatian land.

One tearful soldier arrived in our office claiming to have seen Croatian tanks mowing down children and civilians in the streets. Like his comrades, he kept waiting for reinforcements that never arrived. Rumours of human right violations abounded, but the UN was not permitted access to the area.

The International Red Cross had two vehicles taken from them. The cars were used to transport nine Roman Catholic nuns across the river and into Croatia and were later returned. The church was taken over as a military headquarters. The refugees in the new centres reported incidents of being shot at by snipers, civilians being shelled, and buses of civilians being attacked.

One night at 4 a.m., I woke to a tremendous explosion. Rink reassured me that it was outgoing shelling, and I somehow got back to sleep. In the morning, we found out that a Catholic church in Banja Luka had been bombed and the priest had died of a heart attack. Rink had been very reassuring in the middle of the night, but when we heard what had happened, I found out he remembered nothing of what he said to me and had in fact been fast asleep the whole time!

The situation was deteriorating, and none of the aid workers were permitted to leave Srpska. We were all getting tired, stressed and irritable. All we could do was wait and see what would happen. Every single night we held meetings with the three agencies and the refugee commission to discuss who would bring what supplies and where the next assessments would be.

On May 12, we were finally able to get Rebecca in via another route, the Mosenica-Kostanjica checkpoint. We got there hours early to wait for her and ran into a couple of police officers from Prijedor. We ended up sitting in the café and drinking beer and coffee with them for a couple of hours. I managed to steal one of their police stop signs, which I had been coveting for some time. Sanja thought I was losing my mind — stealing from the Serbian police! I did have the courtesy to return it when Rebecca finally arrived with a UN convoy, though and fortunately, the officers had a sense of humour about it. In retrospect, I almost wish I'd kept it. It would have made a great souvenir.

We made it back to Banja Luka in time to attend a cocktail party that ICRC was holding at the Hotel Bosna for their fiftieth anniversary. We had dinner at the castle and went to Keitel's house to watch a movie. A nice, normal day in the middle of a war.

I realize now how easy it becomes to accept things as 'normal' when you work in such abnormal situations. The destroyed towns, the soldiers on the streets, the shelling every day, the regular evening gunfire from trigger-happy soldiers who are just having fun, the parties you have while under house arrest. These things must be accepted as a part of normal life, or you couldn't cope. I look back now and am amazed at how bizarre my times there were, but 'normal' had taken on totally different meanings. I remember that one set of instructions in case of shelling was to go into the cellar and stay put until reinforcements arrived — or the beer ran out.

I had developed quite a bad eye infection that no amount of drops seemed to be helping. I decided I'd better go to Zagreb and have it checked out. Getting permission to travel in or out of Srpska had become increasingly difficult, but I needed the break, and I took a chance. Fortunately again I ran in to my friend Curly at Mosenica, who allowed me to pass even though I didn't have the correct papers. I stayed put for several days, enjoying the peace and quiet and relishing the few free days.

May 17, 1995:
It turned out to be a simple ingrown eyelash, for all the irritation it caused me. I really enjoyed my days off. I finally called home. My sister, Marna, had called Zagreb when she heard about the shelling. Little does she know it's more dangerous to be in Banja Luka than in Zagreb! I've spent a couple of very leisurely days here, getting my hair cut, sending mail, visiting with Pierre, shopping in the markets and generally having a very nice time.

However, some things haven't changed. They are shelling the shit out of Sarajevo. No ODPR clearance for Bihać, so nothing can go in. ODRP, the council caring for Croation refugees from Krajina, has been assigned by the government to check on humanitarian shipments brought into Serb-controlled areas via Croatin-controlled routes. They do everything they can to block aid to the Serbs, even though they're bound by security council resolutions not to. Since the fighting has increased, we're practically guaranteed to have clearance denied or at least a hundred administrative irregularities to hold up delivery of our shipments. Maarten is stuck in Slunj, Sidne in Velika Kladusa and Cheik in Coralici! The whole Bihaćteam is separated and not able to move. Ripac used to be in Srpska but has just been taken by the Muslim fifth Corps. I can't get my clearance papers from Mr. Gogic yet, so no going back today. Tomorrow I'll try with Win Win from WHO. Nigel, Rink's replacement, arrives tomorrow, and the nurse for me, Marijke, has agreed to take the job. Hallelujah!

I heard from Rink that he found a bullet hole in Elvis today, from where and when he doesn't know. I'm just glad I wasn't in the car when it happened. I need to get back because Rink also needs to get out for a break. The last few weeks have not been easy.

I did make it back with WHO, and Rink made it out for a few days' break. We were coming to the end of our assignment. Our replacements were on the way, and I could finally think about going home.

Chapter 13

Julian of UNHCR came by one day to inform us of another security situation. Their safe, with quite a sum of money in it, had been stolen from their office. Around town, tensions were running high. The Croat minorities were being pressured to hand over their land and goods in exchange for Serb-held land in Croatia. Permission for the minorities to leave the country had been revoked.

May 25, 1995:

Last night we had dinner with Rade, our Serbian military spy whose job is to report on our activities. He's quite open about it, and I rather like the guy. He once phoned Rink to congratulate him on being the only expat brave enough to be travelling in the field that day. Apparently, there had been threats against the expats in retaliation for airstrikes, and Rink was supposed to stay home. Since when does Rink listen to reason? Away he went, unknowingly, and luckily nothing happened. Since that feat, Rink and Rade have got on quite well. We don't see Rade very often, but I like him.

We ate at the castle, and a very odd incident occurred. We were out on the terrace and heard shooting down by the river. It was some idiot, just firing off his gun for fun. A soldier eating at a table near us was getting tired of the noise. Suddenly he stood up, fired off several rounds with his gun and sat back down. We were just sitting there, wine glasses in hand, and none of us even jumped! I think I've been here too long. We didn't even blink. The waiter came over to apologize. All we could do was laugh.

After dinner, we went to Rade's house to share a bottle of very old, very good French wine. I also had to try numerous glasses of slivovitz and plum brandy. A nice evening indeed.

The only problem is that Rink's replacement isn't really getting into things here. He refuses to follow the way we've set things up and won't do any hospital assessments, claiming it's not his job. I hope he and Marijke can work it out, because this is a job that really needs two people. At any rate, it will be out of my hands soon.

I'm off to Split now for a few days of medical meetings. I'm looking forward to the sea, decent food and a little relaxation. And working, of course.

There's been heavy shelling in Sarajevo all last week, and NATO airstrikes against Pale today, which could be very bad news for everyone in Srpska. UNHCR in Banja Luka is on standby. It's a good thing I got out for this trip to split when I did.

May 28, 1995:

Where to begin? Split was wonderful. We toured the old city and had a great time. Got lots done with the medical team, and my survey is being picked up by the others as a guideline. Even the Amsterdam office will receive a copy. All that work actually was for something, I guess.

But the security situation is increasingly dreadful. There's heavy shelling in Sarajevo. The Serbs have taken 140 UNPROFOR soldiers hostage. In Pale, the Canadians have been chained to bridges and ammunition dumps. It's getting very scary. Helen can't get back to Sarajevo, and I can't get back into Banja Luka.

I phoned home and heard that Ed, my grandmother's partner, had died while on a medevac flight from northern Manitoba to Winnipeg. It so upset my grandma that she ended up having a heart attack. She's in the hospital now, and I just wish I was there. I can't do anything, and I'm so far away. God, I miss my family right now. I want to go home. Rink has his own concerns, and he's not giving me any support in this. I don't know what's going to happen with us, but it doesn't seem to be working out these days. Everything feels like it's falling apart.

May 30, 1995:

Things are just getting worse and worse. UNHCR pulled out of Sarajevo, leaving just five expat staff in place. They left via Mount Igman at 4 a.m. Tomorrow, some of the other agencies are following suit.

In Mostar some madman broke in to the Medecins du Monde (MDM) office and killed five people: one expat and four national staff. Another staff member escaped through the window. Unbelievable! Rink and I will try to get into Banja Luka again tomorrow. I can't help but feel that things are really taking a turn for the worse, and I dread what's going to happen next.

Theo from the Human Rights department in Amsterdam is here, but the security is so bad that I really don't think this is the time for him to come in with us.

June 5, 1995:

What a week! We finally got in to Banja Luka to find that all the other agencies have been trying to get out. They think we're crazed for returning. It was a bit odd driving into the region, as nobody else was on the road. The guys at the checkpoint gave us the strangest looks. But we were warmly welcomed back. Borislav had us and UNHCR over for a barbecue. We made it to Doboj to introduce Nigel and

Marijke to Mr. Gogic. He took us for lunch and was actually very generous with his praise. We must have done some good work here, because we seem to have earned a measure of respect I hadn't expected. The mayor also prepared a thank-you card for us, which really surprised me.

On Friday, we had a farewell party here at the house. The staff brought us presents and beautiful roses. Everyone had a very nice time, and I'm sad at the thought of saying good-bye to these wonderful people. I don't think I could have survived it here without them. On the other hand, if I never come back to this country, it will be fine by me!

John called an evacuation of the Blue Lagoon team because of the deteriorating security situation here. UNHCR and the Danish mobile hospital received their clearance papers the day after us and also made their way to Zagreb. We take the long way now, since the bridge over the Sava River at Gradiska has been blown up. I wasn't very happy with the way Nigel handled the request from John, because he didn't even bother discussing it with us. Anyhow, we were able to speak with John and he explained his reasons. We had no choice but to leave.

In Zagreb, I had a good evaluation with Vera. Funny that I had such a hard time with her at first, and now we've turned out to be good mates.

We finished our final handover to Marijke and Nigel, and after a few days they were able to return to Banja Luka and carry on the program.

In the meantime, Pierre of MSF-France invited us to have a farewell party at his house. It was a total disaster because Rink acted like a complete fool. Particularly with a good-looking blond that wasn't me! I'm just about ready to give up on him. All I want to do right now is go home. The problem is, I don't even know where that is any more.

June 7, 1995:

Today I am leaving for Amsterdam. Exactly seven months since I arrived in this godforsaken place. I feel so discouraged. I look back, and all I can think of is, what was it all for? What good did we do? None of it will last, and none of it matters. I wept like a baby when I left Liberia. I'm not shedding a single tear for Bosnia. Maybe I will at some other time, but not right now.

Rink spent a long time apologizing before he left for the

Netherlands yesterday. He came here on his motorbike, and it will take him a couple of days to get home. I don't know about us. We had a lot of problems, and a lot of arguments, and I just don't know if I have the energy to work this out. Right now, I don't have a lot of energy for anything. All I know is that I'm leaving. End of story.

Chapter 14 - Home Again

I may have left Bosnia, but it didn't leave me. After my debriefing in Amsterdam, I agreed to spend some time with Rink at his home in Vlissingen, a town in the southwestern tip of the Netherlands. We wanted to see if we could get along without being constantly in the middle of a crisis.

I had never lived by the sea, and I loved it there. I met Rink's friends and family, and we travelled around the countryside. I helped him do some renovations on his house and generally enjoyed the peace and quiet. Mostly, we took the time to get to know one another. We had started this relationship in the midst of a war, and I had no confidence that it would last outside of it.

We were two very different people, from two very different backgrounds, and the only connection we really had was our work. I doubted then that that would be enough. Besides, the fact that Rink had gone through enough girlfriends to fill the local phone book did nothing to reassure me!

However, in spite of our constant bickering during the program, the arguments had never been personal, only about professional matters. When we fought about our work, we were both stubborn, and we were usually both right. Of course, I was more right than him. I had found someone who, like me, could work with a passion and a dedication that few others understood. Rink was a risk-taker. He would not stand by if he could make a difference. He was always prepared to go the extra mile if it would benefit the population. I admired his courage and envied his optimism. Somehow, we might be able to make this work.

In the meantime, Bosnia stayed on the front page, and it wouldn't go away for some time. Within weeks of our departure, UNPA north and south fell into the hands of the Croatians. Thousands of Serbs fled to Banja Luka. Nearly 200,000 refugees filled the roads for miles. The same three agencies were there to receive them: MSF, ICRC, and UNHCR. Our little team of two quickly expanded to fifteen expats at its peak. The 'Blue Lagoon' had become flooded with refugees.

During that time, Rink would glue himself to the television to watch the coverage, and I would do what I could to avoid it. I spent my time worrying. About Borislav, about Sanja, about the program, about Daniela, about a thousand other things that ruined my sleep and interrupted my days.

For that was the turning point of the war. With NATO taking the initiative with the airstrikes, the Serbs lost nearly one-third of the land they had occupied. They were not going to be able to win the war. By the time the Dayton Accord was reached late in the year, the country was divided almost 50/50. It was the beginning of the end of Serbian domination in former Yugoslavia.

For me, the memories of my work there are bittersweet. I had met some wonderful people and made some dear friends. But I didn't leave, as I had in Liberia, feeling that I had done a good job, or that my work had been a success. I felt that I had failed, that we of the international community had failed to act, failed to respond and failed to do enough. It was not a job I looked back on with pride.

After my stay in Holland, I returned to Canada. I did some newspaper and TV interviews on behalf of the Toronto office. I had a good debriefing in Toronto, and then I flew home.

I appreciated the peace and quiet, but not as much as I appreciated the attitude of the people I found myself with. For the first time in ages I was around people who were friendly, laughing, pleasant, helpful and kind. Gone was the constant suspicion, the underlying tension, the distrust and the fear. I could finally relax. I was not obliged to defend my position, or fight for supplies, or argue for the extra materials I had to have.

A lot had changed. My grandma was much better and out of the hospital. My sister had a new diamond engagement ring, and my brother had another child, a boy. My first nephew!

I reacquainted myself with my friends, but there, too, much had changed. There were new marriages, new children, new cars and jobs and plans. Everyone wanted to hear my stories and see my photos —

for about five minutes. Then I'd see the look in their eyes and I'd change the subject to their children, their jobs, their new cars. It just became easier that way. I didn't have as many funny stories this time around, stories of parties and laughs. Bosnia wasn't warm and friendly and fun; this time the photos were grim and depressing and ugly.

I was a little bit removed from everyone, and had just a little less to say. Their lives had moved on, and all their memories of the last year did not include me. And mine, well, mine were of Rink and me.

He surprised me with a visit to Canada that summer — shocked would be a better word, actually. I was grateful for his familiar face among my suddenly unfamiliar friends and family, and the visit brought us closer together.

After that, MSF arranged for me to take a tropical medicine course in Liverpool. It was a three-month course starting in September, and both Rebecca and Vera would be there with me. I was looking forward to the study. Rink, meanwhile, would be heading back to the field.

Dear Darcy,

Have found out where our next assignment is. Burundi! Not the part of Africa I had in mind. Rink just accepted a nine-month position there as logistical coordinator, on the provision that I join him in December or January. Small problem is that I don't speak French. Rink's going for a two-week crash course, so maybe I can do the same.

The way things are going there, by the time I arrive, they'll probably all be evacuated. You've got your Hutu government and your Tutsi army, each with their own hired gang of thugs, killing each other off. In the last year, ten expats (that's me!) have been killed. Security-wise, this could make Bosnia look safe. Just when I thought it couldn't get worse...

LIVERPOOL

It was sad to say goodbye to Rink in September. I was truly going to miss him. We'd been together day and night for so many months that it felt strange going off to England without him. But the separation did us good. I made him write me wonderfully romantic letters (which he hated), and I got to anticipate phone calls from somebody I was fast falling in love with, which was a first for me.

Rebecca, Vera and I were living in a boarding house away from the school, and our landlady was terrific. She used to lend us her cat, Fred, whenever we needed some warm company. Rebecca and I were taking the certificate program designed for nurses, and Vera was taking the doctor's diploma course. It turned out to be rather therapeutic for the three of us. We did a lot of talking about Bosnia, and after three months I was finally able to sort out some of the mental garbage I'd collected and put the whole experience into a better perspective. The BBC aired a series called *The Death of Yugoslavia*, and every Sunday night we'd get together in front of the TV, whiskey in hand and tissues on the table. There came a time when I could finally both cry *and* laugh about it all.

But I had become much more cynical about the aid business. I asked a lot more questions, and I questioned a lot more decisions, and my generally positive attitude towards people had taken quite a blow. I had always believed in the intrinsic goodness of man, but now I had my doubts. I was much better acquainted with the evil in men, and I didn't appreciate the negative response we'd received while trying to help. I had changed, and I would never look at things as simply as I had before. I believed now that goodness was learned, not automatic, not intrinsic to all men. Which meant evil could be learned just as easily, and by anyone, given the right circumstances. Not such a pleasant revelation.

But the course and the break from work served me well. The classes were challenging, and there were people from all over the world taking the course. I made, again, some terrific friends, and I learned a lot. I loved the people in Liverpool. I'd never met a friendlier bunch, and we had a lot of fun. We got to know the city well, especially Keith's wine bar in Lark Lane. One weekend, Vera and I travelled to a cozy bed and breakfast in Wales, and another time, a group of us went up to the Lake District to do some hiking. The entire class got together for dinners and hikes in the hills, and the time flew by.

I also managed a trip to Cambridge to visit Nikky, my colleague from Liberia. She had been able to return to Liberia, but it was not an easy experience for her. She wasn't able to continue her relationship with John Dennis, and things hadn't worked out for them. So much had changed in Liberia, and the program had headed in a very different direction. Still, we enjoyed sharing recollections for a time. Nikky was soon leaving for an assignment with MSF in Sudan.

My biggest disappointment during that time was the fact that I couldn't make it home for my sister Marna's wedding. I hadn't the money and couldn't afford to miss the time in school. Although Marna was very understanding, I hated to miss such an important day in her life. It was one more memory I wouldn't be a part of.

While studying for the final exams, I was able to practise French for a few weeks. My instructor, a little old lady from France, was able to get some of the basics through my thick skull. Rebecca graduated first in the class, and I received an honourable mention. She was off to Sri Lanka to join her boyfriend Ardi, the logistician from Sarajevo whom she'd met in Bosnia. What was it with these Dutch logisticians? To date, I know of at least three couples who met in Bosnia and are now married. Must have been something in the water.

I was able to return to Winnipeg for five days, which turned out to be the coldest days of the entire year, with temperatures of -37° C! I wasn't that disappointed to be leaving for Africa.

BURUNDI
Chapter 1

This time I skipped Toronto on the way out. I flew overnight and arrived, sleepless and miserable, in Amsterdam early in the morning. I spent the entire day in the office for my briefing and then flew out again that night for Bujumbura, the capital of Burundi. After a lengthy stay in the airport in Nairobi, I finally arrived, late in the afternoon of December 12, in Bujumbura. I had been awake for over forty-eight hours and was never in my life as happy to see Rink waiting for me as I was that day.

Completely done in by the flight, I had just enough time for a long-awaited reunion with my beloved before falling immediately asleep.

December 13, 1995:

Arrived yesterday in Bujumbura. Hot, hilly, green. The capital sits right on the lake. A nice view from the house. Briefings with Rink and James, the medical coordinator, who seems like a very nice guy. I'll be working in Musema Hospital, and from what I've heard, I'm the only expat with any MSF experience. Sounds like they are all a bit nervous there. Should be a challenge for sure.

It's so good to see Rink again. I didn't realize how much I've missed him. But he's not liking it here that much. He's tired and frustrated. The project seems to lack strong direction, with too many inexperienced people here in a very uncertain security situation.

Funny place, Burundi. All the schools and universities are open, but the health sector seems to have gone to hell. There are constant stories of massacres on a small scale of ten, twenty, forty people. Tonight in Gitega there were grenades thrown at Action Contre la Faime, the International Red Cross and the Belgian Red Cross. The president of the moderate Hutu government doesn't get on well with the Tutsi army. The Hutus have infiltrated from Rwanda to the northwest of the country, around Cibitoke, and are causing all sorts of trouble. The prevailing feeling is that the capital will soon be surrounded. The people are nervous and paranoid. Lots of fun.

We're off to Ngozi tomorrow, the base from which most of the MSF projects are running. I guess every time there's a problem, the Musema team gets terrified and runs away, which makes it a bit difficult for us to get any work done. Well, I'll see how it goes.

How can I describe what the situation in Burundi was like? To begin with, MSF was working in the entire Great Lakes region, meaning all the countries surrounding Lake Victoria: Burundi, Rwanda, Zaire, Uganda, Kenya and Tanzania. Even before the April 1994 massacres began in Rwanda, there had been years of civil unrest in Burundi. The same systematic barrage of racist propaganda used in Rwanda to pit neighbour against neighbour was used in Burundi earlier.

In June 1993, a Hutu president, Melchoir Ndadaye, took power in Burundi for the first time, leaving the Tutsi-dominated Union for National Progress (UNPRONA) as an opposition party. This was the first time a Hutu had been elected president, and for a short time, the Tutsi army seemed to support him, even foiling an early coup attempt.

Refugees returned home then, and changes occurred in a school system long dominated by Tutsis and about to be joined by Hutus. A move towards equality and the end of 'tribalism' seemed underway. It all ended with the assassination of the new president in October of 1993.

The death of the first president who appeared to support democratic change led to a killing frenzy that set Tutsis against Hutus, resulting in the death of 50,000 to 80,000 people in just a few weeks. Those massacres went largely unnoticed in the West. Some 700,000 people fled Burundi to Rwanda, Tanzania and Zaire. The international community was slow to respond, and thousands died of hunger and dysentery within weeks.

By early March 1994, most of the Burundian refugees who had fled to Tanzania returned home. In late April, almost 200,000 *new* refugees arrived in the country, fleeing the genocide in Rwanda. Within the country, thousands of people were seeking shelter in the capital or in camps protected by the armed forces.

With the death of the newly elected President Nytaryamira, along with his Rwandan counterpart, in a missile attack over Kigali on April 6, 1994, the country was plunged into a precarious situation. The arrival of thousands of Rwandan refugees added to the civil unrest.

By the time I arrived in December 1995, not much had improved. There were numerous 'manifestations', the local word for demonstrations, in the streets of Bujumbura, and several stay-at-home strikes by students and workers. The influx of Rwandan refugees, including some who were responsible for the genocide, made matters worse. Extremists on all sides were armed, and there were regular attacks and provocations against each ethnic group by the opposing militia or rebels. Massacres occurred regularly in villages and towns, against both Hutus and Tutsis, and the presence of international aid workers did nothing to deter the attacks.

The genocide of Rwanda had an enormous impact on the surrounding regions as well, and the borders between the Great Lakes countries remained unstable and insecure.

Chapter 2

I made a quick start to my project by spending the first weekend in Ngozi to meet the rest of the team. I visited Musema hospital, where I would be working. It was a seventy-bed hospital in the country's isolated north, a Hutu hospital in a mostly Tutsi-controlled area, and MSF had taken over complete control of the hospital in an effort to start an enormous renovation project and to supervise the management of the hospital. The big problem was, I just wasn't sure why. I discovered that MSF was running a variety of different programs in Burundi, but the overall direction of the agency remained unclear to me. MSF was carrying out water and sanitation programs in certain camps, feeding programs in some areas, a hospital rehab and supervision program for one hospital, some primary health care clinics and a few other projects in the capital. I felt, however, that the whole program lacked vision from the start. MSF seemed to be present more for advocacy purposes than for responding directly to the emergency needs of the population. They had been asked by other agencies to take on this region, as it was felt to be lacking in health care services. The program just didn't seem to be organized in a systematic way.

I also discovered that Musema hospital had a few difficulties of its own. My colleagues there were not getting along too well, and there had been tension between them. Most of the team members were new to MSF, and everyone was quite nervous about the security situation. The Belgian Red Cross, who had been working there, had left the region due to a security incident. Apparently, they had picked up a wounded soldier, and he had later been taken out of their car by the opposing militia and killed. Also, ICRC had left the region and were on standby in Bujumbura, which indicated that the security was pretty uncertain.

Nevertheless, I did my rounds, met the hospital's national staff and began to get a picture of what needed to be done in Musema Hospital over the next few months.

December 22, 1995:

Well, the boys were nice enough to make me a cake for my birthday, and we even shared a bottle of wine that evening. It looks like my first week in Musema is about to come to a fast end.

I've gotten to know John, the Zairean doctor working for MSF, quite well. He and Isaac, the director of the hospital, seem to be managing things nicely, but I get the feeling that Isaac intends to depart pretty soon, which leaves us without a doctor for the hospital. John and our Russian surgeon, Yuri, are probably leaving next month, when their contracts expire. Of course there are no replacements yet. This could pose a problem.

Yuri is an interesting case. How he ended up in Burundi from Russia I'll never know! He's all right, but I've seen a lot of post-op infections in his patients and don't know if it's him or the nursing care. I also suspect he might be hitting the bottle a bit too much, although I've never seen him drunk on the job. He's really a loner and has nothing to do with the rest of the team. All he says to me all the time is "C'est grave, c'est grave", so I gather he's not really enjoying himself here.

Daniel, the logistician here, is from Quebec, so his French is significantly better than mine. He's getting lots done on the house, so there's a hundred men in and out all day, but I still don't have a bedroom!

I'm back in Ngozi now because we were ordered to come out last night. It looks like my first week will end with an evacuation to Bujumbura some time today. Last night a couple of grenades were thrown in the compounds of the aid agencies here in Ngozi, one at the Red Cross Federation, another near the UNHCR building. Apparently, one guy was slightly injured. I spent the night with a mattress against the window, but no explosions here so far.

The good news is I'll get to spend Christmas with Rink. The bad news is that this is the fastest evacuation I've ever done, barely a week in the field. All that rushing around to hurry up and arrive early in Burundi, and then this happens! Figures. I probably could have spent Christmas in Canada for all the work I'm *not* getting done here. Well, I think the plane leaves in an hour, so that's it for week one.

The Ngozi and Musema teams evacuated to Bujumbura. The day after we left, another grenade was thrown at the MSF-Belgium house in Ngozi, and their team also evacuated. We also learned that the governor of Ngozi was killed the night of the first grenade launch. Not a very good beginning to my third MSF mission.

The country coordinator for MSF held a big meeting with James, the medical coordinator, and Rink and me to discuss the situation. It became clear that we wouldn't be returning to the field any time in the next couple of weeks, so we spent the day lounging by the pool (yes, the house in Bujumbura actually had a small pool in front of it!) and planning our Christmas dinner.

Most of the team decided to use this respite as an opportunity to get away for a holiday, and shortly after Christmas, most of the team left for parts elsewhere. Ton, the temporary country coordinator, stayed behind with myself, Rink and Erwin, one of the Ngozi team members. The four of us brought in 1996 together, drinking wine, playing cards and listening to the sounds of shelling and gunfire in the city.

I enjoyed being back in Africa after my time in Bosnia; the red dusty roads, the markets, the traffic, the noise, the sweet-smelling flowers everywhere and the smiles of the people. The Africa that I knew was such a mess politically, but it was always so beautiful to me, and I was glad to be back.

By January 7, some of the team started to return from holidays. The house was dreadfully crowded, and unfortunately a Hutu extremist group chose that time to blow up electricity generators in the city, leaving us without electricity or water.

Poor Bonaventure, the cook. He was a lovely man, neither Hutu nor Tutsi, but a Twa, one of the pygmy tribes. Rink is a pretty tall guy, and Bonaventure came up to his waist! Bonaventure was terribly busy with a house full of guests, and with the lack of water, things became quite hard for him. We hired some extra help, but clothes, floors and dishes had a hard time getting washed in those days. We used the swimming pool water for bathing and flushing toilets, and soon everyone got pretty sick of our imposed 'vacation'.

With the team back, Rink and I were able to make our own escape for a quick but more satisfying vacation. I hardly felt that I needed one, but Rink had been working for almost four months, and he was more than ready for a break.

Chapter 3

January 10, 1996:

Yesterday we flew into Nairobi and shared the evening with Tom, the head of the logistics department here in Kenya. We had worked with him in Bosnia, too. He'd just returned from a great safari, and we enjoyed a nice evening with him and a friend over dinner at a terrific Chinese restaurant.

Today we flew Air Kenya to Lamu, a gorgeous island off the African coast. It's a strictly Muslim area, with no alcohol. There are no roads on the island, so the primary means of transportaion are donkeys and one old government jeep. We found a nice guesthouse to stay in, and the beaches look fantastic. I think I'm going to enjoy it here.

We did indeed enjoy our visit. Lamu was a beautiful island, both quiet and restful. We dined on lobster and fresh crab, went on a fishing trip in an old dhow, lazed on the beaches, shopped, visited the museum, strolled through the town and took a sunset boat trip to the mangrove swamps. Every day we would try one of the wonderful fruit drinks that the locals made in their stands, and each concoction was delicious. The beaches were great, and there were not too many tourists at that time, so we had plenty of privacy if we wanted it.

While there, Rink and I also had the first serious discussion about our future together. Rink was, in principle, totally opposed to the idea of marriage, while I took it as an accepted part of a permanent relationship. To me, only that type of commitment would make me leave my home and move to Holland to start a new life in a land I didn't know. I sure didn't intend to do all that for a boyfriend. He didn't see any difference, and I think he was a bit surprised to hear that I had no intention of moving to Holland with him. We dropped the subject then and I figured we'd be better off just enjoying the time we spent together and not worrying too much about what might lie ahead.

Before we knew it, the week was over, and we were headed back to Burundi. We were tanned and relaxed, and not too unhappy to get back to work.

Chapter 4

January 18, 1996:

Rink and I left Lamu on Monday and had to take a hotel room for one night in Nairobi. We actually went to the movie theatre to see the new James Bond film, and I couldn't even remember the last time I had gone to the movies. It was fun, but I think I had a bit of food poisoning from dinner the night before and had terrible cramps the whole night.

We arrived in Bujumbura to find there had been another big general strike, with roadblocks up all over the place and no offices or shops open. Threats were made against the local staff warning them not to try to go in to work that day, so the office is basically shut down.

That same day two MSF cars attempted to drive to Ngozi. They felt that it would be less of a risk by then as the security situation had improved. Bad decision! The team came upon a robbery on the road, and I guess the robbers panicked and shot at the cars several times. No one was hurt, thank God, but the team was pretty shaken up. There were several shots through the landcruisers. Talk about being in the wrong place at the wrong time!

Yuri wants to quit immediately, and personally, I think he should.

He's got financial troubles of his own, and there is some suspicion — although no proof — that he's responsible for some MSF property going missing. The coordinator would rather have a bad surgeon than no surgeon, but I don't think Yuri can do a good job in this condition. How can he work if he's so anxious about every little thing? His drinking doesn't help, either.

John is also leaving soon, but they have found a replacement, a doctor from Afghanistan who has worked with MSF as a local counterpart. This is his first job as an expat, so I hope this works out.

Right now, I can't help but be somewhat pessimistic about the future of this project. Things aren't going well in Bujumbura. The national staff are difficult to manage. Any move against them is seen as a racist reaction. MSF is accused of being for or against either the Tutsis or the Hutus, depending on who happens to be in trouble. It's difficult to fire anyone, even if they aren't doing their work, because it could pose a security risk to the team.

Rink really doesn't like his job. He's limited strictly to logistics, and he'd rather concentrate on other priorities and become more involved in the whole picture. This just isn't working out for him. And I still haven't had a chance to get my hands on the hospital, though I've been here for a month now! I'm getting very frustrated.

Today Daniel and I returned to Musema. Everyone seemed happy to have us back. Isaac, as I suspected, has left, so the hospital is without a doctor now. This is not going to be easy.

From then on the road to Ngozi was off-limits. The only way in was to fly with the World Food Program plane. The pilots were a strange pair. One was so frightened, he carried a gun with him on the journey. The other was an Italian daredevil who made the flights rather entertaining. The landing strip in Ngozi was a gravel strip cut into the side of the hill. The pilot practically took the tops off the banana trees on his approach. Once, James and I flew to Ngozi in a storm, and we very nearly missed the runway altogether. Another time, Rink and I flew into a storm, but the high cumulus clouds around us on the way in were a dazzling orange and gold as the sun set between mile-high mountains of clouds. It was a fantastic view, which vanished after a few minutes into black clouds and lightning.

I finally began slowly settling in to life at Musema hospital. We were back for just one day when Yuri and John heard rumours of soldiers in the area arresting people and fled to Ngozi. Daniel and I had little choice but to follow. The two of us returned alone. Our feeling was that if we left every time there was a rumour, we'd never spend a day in Musema. Burundi is the most rumour-riddled country I've ever worked in. Every day there was a new story of yet another imminent attack. The stories never ended, and it was impossible to know with any certainty what was really going on.

John and Yuri finally left the program, and the new doctor, Khaled, arrived. He was a devout Muslim who had been a national staff member with MSF in Afghanistan. He was a good doctor, and we were able to sit together and discuss the whole situation honestly. I tended to agree with much of what he said.

The main problem was that MSF had assumed full responsibility of the hospital when it really wasn't necessary. John and Yuri had fostered a dependency on MSF that was not productive for the hospital. With no national counterpart, whatever we did in the hospital could not be sustained after we left. As well, the national staff made it clear that they would only stay as long as MSF was present. If we were forced to leave because of security reasons, they'd leave as well.

Khaled refused to stay overnight with Daniel and me in Musema. He was fearful of security incidents, and as the only doctor, was afraid he might be targeted. Daniel and I by this time were completely frustrated. Khaled even refused to do rounds and check on patients, and the national staff in the hospital couldn't understand his reluctance. I did a lot of talking to try to smooth things over, and assured them all that it would be sorted out. But we were stuck doing expensive rehabilitation on a hospital full of patients that weren't being seen by the one available doctor.

I felt torn between the needs of the patients and the reality of what Khaled said. He wanted a Burundian doctor working with him, and he didn't want to assume full responsibility of the hospital himself. I just wanted the patients to receive the best care they could under the circumstances.

After numerous lengthy meetings with everyone, Khaled made a compromise. He agreed to stay in Ngozi and travel every day to

Musema. He would do rounds on the in-patients, and he would do consultations for the most serious of the out-patients. But he would not live in Musema, and he stubbornly refused to give an inch on the matter. Nobody was happy with the solution, but it was all we were going to get.

Meanwhile, I had my own set of headaches. Zachary, the pharmacist, had taken over temporary directorship of the hospital. He spoke English well, which was a blessing for me, and we managed to get along quite well. However, Musema was meant to have a team of seven persons, and there was only Daniel and myself. I gave up any thought of doing teaching sessions, partly because the staff were pretty well trained already, and mainly because I just didn't have the time.

I had to set up a laboratory in the hospital, establish an ambulance service with a donated vehicle and supervise rounds with the nurses and Khaled daily. I also planned to open a pediatric ward, with eight beds that were yet to be made by Daniel's team, and a new feeding centre on the hospital grounds, which meant I needed staff, cooks, cleaners and a kitchen somewhere. I had to totally reorganize the dysentery unit, which was isolated up on a hill and in dreadful condition, with no water, no decent shelters and no separate staff to care for patients. I also had to hand out proper guidelines for treatment to the nurses running the outpatient department and to arrange for a separate room for an MSF pharmacy so we wouldn't have to rely so heavily on supplies from Ngozi, which was an hour's drive away.

The pharmacy in the hospital was pretty disorganized, with poor record-keeping and no proper consumption records. Zachary and I started working on improving the situation. I soon received complaints from the staff about payment. Some nurses had been hired by MSF and others were paid by the state. The state nurses rarely received their money on time, if at all, but they did have permanent jobs, whereas MSF staff were all temporary. Iris, the financial controller from Bujumbura, had to come up to meet with everyone.

To say Daniel and I were kept busy would be an understatement. My daily notebook was full of problems. Here's an example of an entry for one day:

June 2, 1996

—gloves, 510 pairs/week; syringes and needles, 750/week; per month need 2,000 pairs of gloves, 3,000 needles and syringes

syringe and needles — 750/week

per month need 2,000 gloves, 3,000 needles and syringes

—need inventory by Khaled of OR supplies and needs

—check pharmacy list from Zachary, does MSF supply everything, what proportion from MOH (Ministry of Health)? Regular delivery? Cost?

—call Christine to bring routine feeding centre meds, these are not to come from our hospital stock

—order dry skim milk powder for the malnourished inpatients, make recipe for staff

—collect drug requisitions from each service, don't forget maternity!!

—ambulance meeting tomorrow 0900

—they are not going to Muyaga, why??

—need private room for TB patient? where?? NO IDEA!

—clean stock room, move feeding centre food in

—Daniel and Zachary to discuss local purchase of food for TFC, how much weekly, and at what cost?

—staff changes, James needs list

—Christine needs TFC med list for Ngozi

—tents for TFC, how many, where? Ask Zachary.

—need lab supplies, list from Vanetie

—need enough plastic sheeting to cover 48 mattresses. Daniel?

—beds for pediatric ward, 8-12? How big, what size, when is the room ready?

—emergency preparedness list to James — is this possible without a doctor?? Revise list for nursing care, decrease OR supplies, expect no MD around for emergencies

—houses for staff, relocation costs 5,000 Franc Burundian (FBU)?

—charge patients for meals in hospital? 10 FBU — discuss with James

—need for TFC: 2 cooking pots, 2 large spoons, 3 ladles, 4 aprons

—need pharmacy key from Celestine!

—check with Daniel, water supply for dysentery ward, how soon?

Still, Daniel and I managed. The hospital was set up on a slope, and every day on the walk from the house, I could look down into the valley between the hospital compound and the college across the way.

It was cool up in the mountains, and Daniel had done a great job with the house. We had a fireplace, which was necessary in the evenings, and a terrific cook. We couldn't get the kerosene fridge to work for ages, but we finally stood it on its head for a day or two, and things went fine after that. We had a generator for electricity so we could enjoy the luxury of a hot shower, and we could listen to music when we wanted. Every weekend, Daniel and I would go to town, visit the clinic of the Catholic nuns, shop in the market, eat brochettes of goat meat in the cafe and drink beer with the local people. We got on well together. The only thing I really suffered from was the bedbugs! No matter what I did —buying a new mattress, spraying the sheets, et cetera — I continued itching from the bites for three months. A minor but constant irritation.

I found Burundi to be a beautiful country, hilly and green and lush. We had a pet goat, named Bequette, and the neighbour girl used to come by to see her, to show us her baby brother that she cared for, and to bring me flowers. I found living in Musema quite peaceful and easy.

Though my French still wasn't that great, enough people spoke English that I managed. After the night report, we waited for Khaled to arrive and do rounds. Then he started his consultations, and I made my own rounds to check up on the lab, the ambulance service, the pharmacy, the maternity and outpatient wards, the operating room, the dysentery unit, the sterilizer for used needles and syringes, the cleaning staff and much more. Though the new feeding centre was not officially my responsibility, I checked up on it daily to sort out problems with food and supplies.

Daniel was responsible for the security, and he and I made several visits to people and places that were useful to us. We visited the displaced persons camp nearby and met the military commanders. We went to the college to meet the directors and were then able to share electricity with them sometimes — theirs during the day, and ours in the evenings. We met the local police chief, the director of the local health department and numerous other people who were useful for collecting information.

Once, after we'd been asking for ages for a new and more powerful generator to service the hospital, one finally arrived via a very twisted route that somehow included Uvira, Zaire and a few other areas. It weighed about two tons, and the roads were precarious, so it had to take the long way around to reach us. Rink accompanied the generator, and we were very excited to see the truck finally pull into the hospital compound. However, about twenty-five metres from its final resting place, the truck lunged into a deep ditch. The entire village came to help out, and with much singing, sweating and maneuvering, they got the generator out of the truck and the truck out of the ditch. The entire episode lasted for hours, but we got our generator in the end!

I was beginning to feel a real bond with the people and the place and, somehow, since nobody else was available, I ended up as the person in charge of the hospital. It was to me that all complaints, concerns and requests arrived, so naturally, I was seen as the person responsible in Musema. However, that wasn't how it was on paper, and that wasn't how it turned out in the end.

Chapter 5

February 16, 1996:
Dear Darcy,

Greetings from the jungle! I've been in Burundi for two months, and am just starting to get to work. For nearly a month, the whole team was on standby in Bujumbura because of security incidents.

I'm currently in charge of some forty nurses in a seventy-bed hospital in the north of the country. It's a pretty isolated place, and so far it's just me and Daniel, my logistician, working here. We hope the team will expand soon, since it's pretty quiet here. There is a lot of work that can be done, but the doctor only comes for a couple of hours a day from Monday to Friday, and the rest of the time it's up to the nurses to handle things. Alas, they aren't the most motivated bunch.

Not that I really blame them. Every day you hear of massacres nearby, of bandits and gangs throwing grenades, of violence by extremist groups against half of the patients here. The wards are full of people who don't need to be here, but are too afraid to leave. It's difficult to comprehend the level of anxiety these people constantly live with.

As for myself, this job has become very frustrating in many ways. The coordinator has made several changes in the management structure without consulting those of us involved in the field. The result is the loss of several positions, including mine. Not to mention that MSF has found itself in the unfortunate position of having taken over complete responsibility of the hospital, as there is no Burundian medical doctor working there. Essentially, MSF has taken charge of a Hutu hospital in a Tutsi area, which means their neutrality could be in jeopardy. That's something that can get you killed in this country.

There have been numerous discussions about our work here and whether or not we should even stay. I am still undecided, but I won't be surprised if we end up resigning. There have already been about four or five people who have left the project, so clearly something isn't working here. I don't know exactly what it is or if it can be fixed. For now, I am settled in Musema and getting on with the work, but it's not a very comfortable situation, and the security is poor. We're always trying to keep good contacts with all the factions while really only working in one area. Tricky!

Rink is also pretty fed up with things. He's had a run-in with the coordinator and refused to even sign his evaluation. He just doesn't agree with what the coordinator said, and he doesn't agree to the type of changes he's being asked to make. I don't know that much about the situation, since he won't really discuss it, and it's not up to me to make a judgment. But we both might be leaving here sooner than we expected.

At any rate, it's been an interesting experience, quite a challenge working with such unclear guidelines and knowing that nothing we do here will be at all sustainable without a local doctor involved. Can you believe there are thirty-five hospitals in this country without a doctor? Though we do some essential work now, the minute we leave it will all fall apart. We saw it happen when we evacuated before. So, do we put a band-aid on this gaping wound, or do we wait for someone else to actually stitch it up? To what extent should we foster this dependency? And at what risk to ourselves do we remain in this situation? Do we stay, accepting that we are no longer seen as neutral or impartial, words that MSF lives by? But then how can we practice advocacy, how can we speak for the people, if we aren't present at all?

Anyone who can answer these questions can come and have my job and the headaches that go with it! If I ever get out of this mess, I'll let you know!

After many discussions and many tears, Rink and I handed in our resignations. My position was to be handed over to another expat, who had been in the country for slightly longer and whose own job was redundant. There just wasn't anything left for me. Two supervisors would be too many in Musema, especially when the rest of the team was finally arriving. I also didn't feel it was fair for me to stick around with another person in charge, for fear that it might undermine her authority. I didn't want people to keep coming to me for assistance when it was no longer my responsibility.

Rink, James and I discussed all aspects of the coordinator's undiplomatic decision to replace me without consultation, but in the end I just didn't see what my position would be, and I was sick and tired of already struggling with such uncertainty.

Wouter, the desk officer in charge of all of the Great Lakes region, arrived in Bujumbura from Amsterdam and tried to persuade us to stay. We agreed to wait, but within a week it was clear that no real changes would happen, and with a heavy heart I resigned from the Burundi project. The coordinator apologized, not realizing what effect his changes would have on the project, but by then I was pretty sick of the whole thing. I was hurt by the way things had been handled and felt that I had done the best job I could with such limited resources. I was angry, upset and depressed. I'd never imagined resigning from MSF and was very sorry to have things end this way. James was almost ready to resign himself because of the ways things turned out!

A new couple, Piet and Karen, arrived to take over our positions. Piet would be replacing Rink, and Karen would be replacing me in the hospital until the role of the other expat could be determined. Karen's position would likely be changed later, when the more senior expat took over the management position. Musema saw the addition of a surgeon and a nurse anesthetist. Finally the hospital would have a team, and hopefully things could really get going. I gave Karen a full handover. The surgeon, Angie, and the new nurse, Kate, got settled in the Musema house.

On her second day, Angie performed an amputation on a young

fellow with tetanus. There were complications, and he never awoke from the anesthesia the whole night. But with the MSF pharmacy in place, we had enough supplies and materials to manage. We never got any sleep, but he slowly came around by the morning. It was good to see Musema Hospital actually *work* before I left.

But just as I was preparing to leave for the Netherlands, Rink accepted a job offer for the both of us in Zaire! Our reputation as *'the vultures'* had preceded us, and somebody had plans.

Shortly after we left, the project in Burundi ran into some problems. James was in a serious car accident and had to be medevacked to England, where, fortunately he made a full recovery. Poor Piet was beaten up in a robbery of the MSF house, and the whole program had to be suspended for awhile. But the work went on without us.

Years later, I heard that Musema hospital had been burned to the ground in the continued fighting. A lasting peace remains as elusive as ever in Burundi.

March 6, 1996:

What a mess! Roel, our good friend from Bosnia, is working now in Goma. Apparently he needs a team to set up a base somewhere in Masisi in Zaire, where nobody in their right mind wants to work. He spoke with Wouter and even Jacques de Milliano, the president of MSF, and somehow they all think we'll be perfect for the job! How did this happen?

Rink took me to Kasuku's for lunch, and he actually proposed! Marriage, that is. My head is spinning, and I'm totally exhausted. I even think I said yes! Yesterday we were supposed to be going home, and now we're flying to Goma in a couple of days, and I still have no clue what we'll be doing! Rink got the fax, but I didn't, so I'm basically just going along with him. God, I hope he knows what we're doing, because right now, I don't. I think the marriage proposal was enough for one day, but now I have to get my hands on this fax and find out just what sort of a mess Rink's gotten us into this time.

It was a strange ending to the project. I had been in the country only three months and had found a lot of problems with the design of the program. I had received a marriage proposal, handed in my resignation and accepted a new job within days. I was a bit overwhelmed by all the turmoil, and I would have liked a little time to sort things out and talk with Rink. But time, in MSF, is of the essence. We didn't have that luxury.

I had my fears that our resignation would not go down well with MSF, but the coordinators seemed quite understanding. Rink had a harder time afterwards than I did, but I think we were both relieved to be offered a new job so quickly. I was quite looking forward to a change. We had both encountered personal problems with other expats in Burundi, and we both had concerns about the program itself. The experience had been valuable, but we were hoping things would be different in Zaire. And were they!

ZAIRE
Chapter 1

Rink once described Zaire as 'a cruel paradise'. He was right. It was one of the most beautiful regions I had ever worked in, and one of the most tragic. Goma was situated just across the border from Rwanda, literally a stone's throw from Gisenyi, the exit port for more than a million refugees who fled the devastating genocide in Rwanda in 1994. They arrived by the hundreds of thousands over the course of a few days, a humanitarian crisis on a scale the world had never seen before. The largest refugee camps in the world were created, but the sheer number of people was overwhelming. Thousands died of cholera and related problems before the aid agencies could get a handle on the situation.

By the time Rink and I arrived, in the spring of 1996, the situation was well under control. There were several enormous camps outside of Goma that housed up to 300,000 people each, and there were numerous aid agencies managing them. Houses, schools, even a movie theatre and a hotel had cropped up in the camps. The streets of Goma were crowded with people, and they moved like ants on the road to and from the camps, seeking work, working on their small garden plots and scavenging for a meagre existence.

One notable problem was that the camps were largely controlled by the Hutu ex-military from Rwanda. The camps served as a training centre for new soldiers, and the military kept a tight grip on the civilian population. They continued to poison the refugees with endless propaganda about what would happen to them if they dared return home to Rwanda. The camps had been in existence for two years, but efforts by UNHCR to return people home were met mostly with failure. To complicate matters, many people who were responsible for the genocide were hiding out in the camps, side by side with the survivors. The civilians were too afraid or intimidated to leave, and the situation remained uneasy.

Naturally, the Zairean people resented so much attention being paid to the refugees, especially since they themselves lived in one of the poorest nations on earth. They were receiving only limited assistance of their own, in spite of the fact there were serious problems in the country.

Escalating ethnic clashes in the east of the country, mostly between Hutus and Hundes, were causing the displacement of thousands of people. Afraid of the possibility of a civil war in Zaire (which did begin in autumn that year), many people — mostly the Tutsis, who in this case were bystanders and not participants in the fighting — were trying to cross the border into Rwanda. Rwanda did not want to accept them. The conflict was influenced by armed forces of the Zairean government and by input from the Rwandan Hutu militia in the surrounding camps.

The health infrastructure, which had been running on a cost-recovery system supported by the European community, had started to crumble. The usual endemics and epidemics of malaria, dysentery, cholera and measles were affecting more and more of the population, who had less and less access to health clinics because of the security situation. As usual, when fighting broke out, people fled, leaving behind empty health clinics, abandoned schools and burning homes. What had started out as sporadic fighting between the Hutus and Hundes had turned into a constant battle. Few agencies seemed aware of the seriousness of the incidents, and fewer still seemed prepared to do something to help the increasing numbers of displaced people. MSF was one of a handful of agencies trying to assist the Zairean population in the region.

Rink and I were being asked to set up a base in Mweso, a village of a few thousand residents, including hundreds of displaced people. It was in the province of Masisi in eastern Zaire — basically in the middle of the fighting — about a hundred kilometres north of Goma, a five-hour drive for us on appalling roads. No other agency had a team living anywhere near where we were planning to go. We would be well and truly on our own.

Our goal was to establish a base from which we could supply medicines and materials to the population through existing structures. As well, we had to monitor the movement of the displaced and the security situation. We would start by finding ourselves a home from which to do our exploratory missions, and then bring supplies to those clinics still functioning in the region. It all seemed straightforward. I didn't guess then that our mission would end in disaster.

Chapter 2

Goma was a bustling city like Bujumbura, but with a completely different character. It was a lot more grubby and run down. Our project was also completely different from the one in Burundi. For one thing, the coordinators of the project were terrific. Roel was managing the logistics and a woman named Lisette was the medical coordinator. She was extremely knowledgeable about the whole area and was a valuable source of information. She also gave us the freedom to establish ourselves in our own way, provided we discussed the guidelines of the set-up with her.

There was a team in Goma of ten or twelve people, living in two houses outside of the city centre. The main house and office were situated on Lake Kivu, which became a great recreational spot for us. Just further down the road was a house called 'Hotel India', which belonged to a man named Ed and his wife, Deirdre, better known as Didi. Ed managed ASRAMES, a cost-recovery drugs distribution program used throughout Masisi. The name was an acronym that used a letter from every agency that had helped to establish it. The "M" in ASRAMES stood for MSF. MSF had helped to create ASRAMES and was now one of several agencies that supported it, both financially and by encouraging their own clinics to purchase supplies through the ASRAMES distribution program. Ed had spent years getting the program up and running, but the recent fighting was threatening his entire project. Rink and I stayed with them when we first arrived, and they were kind enough to allow us to return and make it our second home whenever we were back in Goma.

Our colleagues included another Canadian named Roy, a physician who was based in Goma and working in the southern area of Masisi. We would be living and working in the north. He, too, faced some serious security incidents in his area and was very helpful with information and suggestions. Then there was Solly, a South African expat doing water and sanitation in the project, and, of course, the country coordinator, administrators and loads of national staff. Everyone helped us get settled in Goma, and before we knew it we were off on our first assessment trip with Lisette, heading for Mweso.

March 10, 1996:

Mweso, it turns out, is a five- or six-hour drive from Goma on roads from hell! I thought Burundi's roads were bad, and Liberia's worse, but *nothing* comes close to these. The countryside, however, is absolutely gorgeous. There's a tarmac road from Goma to Sake, or about the first thirty kilometres. Then it's hard, rough, mostly volcanic track to Mweso. The sight of the camps simply took my breath away. I have never in my life seen anything like it! Thousands of people living shoulder-to-shoulder in homes made of blue and green plastic sheeting that stretches for miles! Someone told me that to walk around the perimeter of one of these camps would take eight hours. Just amazing! I've heard so much about these camps, but the sheer number of people living in them is staggering. It seems that such a number would be totally unmanageable, but I guess they know what they're doing by now.

There is a stretch of road, after you turn off at Sake that leads up the mountainside to reveal a stunning view of the volcanoes that surround Goma, about fourteen in total. The roads used to be maintained by the owners of the big farms and the lumber companies, but by now almost everyone has fled, leaving only one tea plantation that is still operational. The roads are so bad, we never got out of second gear the entire trip.

At one village still in flames, we ran into Hutu combatants, some in army gear. We also encountered the Hunde villagers, who were fleeing their burning homes. Some members of the Zairean army were sent in by Mobutu (who is pro-Hutu) to maintain the peace. I'm not sure whose side they're on, but they don't seem to provide much comfort to the fleeing Hundes.

There are a few areas of concern for us here. This region is almost entirely populated with Hutus. There are two Hunde strongholds among them: Kichanga, a village about half way between Goma and Mweso, and Kalembe, a village north of Mweso. In both these villages reside a group of very fierce fighters called the 'Mai-Mai', which means 'water'. These combatants have the reputation of being invincible.

Bullets fired at them reputedly turn to water, or bounce back to kill the person who fired the shot. They seem to be protected by special magic, and though the Hutu outnumber them and have far more weapons (and, apparently, governmental support through the Zairean army), the Hundes are greatly feared.

Then there's Mokoto. This is a Trappist monastery not too far from Kichanga, where a group of monks still live and work. They are supporting a camp of about 1,000 displaced Tutsis. No agency is really looking after this group of civilians, who come under regular attack from the surrounding Hutus. It's quite dangerous for the Tutsis, and they'd like to leave the country, but nobody seems able or prepared to help them. Apparently, the monastery is situated on a lake, and the location is beautiful. Many expats have taken sabbaticals there. The monks have a herd of cattle, make their own cheese, keep hives of bees for honey, operate their own wells and water-pumping system and are entirely self-sufficient.

We met the Mwami, the leader of the Hundes in Kichanga, in town where MSF has a clinic and feeding centre. We also met his wife, the Mama Mwami, toured the clinic and feeding centre and met several of the staff before heading on to Mweso. There is a stretch of road between Kichanga and Mweso that is unbelievably bad. It runs about fourteen kilometres and takes about an hour to drive!

In Mweso, we met the two Catholic nuns who manage the hospital. We were told that the only doctor in the hospital has recently left because of fighting in the area, but the nuns are still hanging in. The hospital seems to be in good condition, and the sisters are living in a pleasant house nearby. There is also a large church and parish in Mweso, still tended to by the parish priest. We stayed there during our trip. Many other parishes in Masisi have closed because of the insecurity.

We met Marc, the director of Zairean Tea Management (ZTM), on the tea plantation that he manages. He's a very nice guy, about fifty years old, and speaks both English and French fluently. The plantation is a beautiful place off the road from Mweso, with miles of wonderful green fields of tea. Marc said we might have a house available for us on the plantation.

When we left Mweso, we drove home another way, via Tongo, which also provides a spectacular view of the camps at the foot of the volcanoes. I can't get over the scenery here, it's just so beautiful. There are several roads that lead to Mweso, and I guess we'll have to learn them all.

Anyway, we're back in Goma, at the Hotel India, and excited about this new project. We'll be really on our own out there, but it's quite a challenge and I think we can do this.

Chapter 3

March 13, 1996:

We're back in the parish in Mweso. Problems galore! There was some shooting in Sake on Saturday between the Hundes and the Hutus. The orphanage in Sake was evacuated. One of the monks tried to drive to the monastery in Mokoto but was attacked on the road and had the window of his car broken. Lisette and Vincent, the country coordinator, went to talk to the combatant leaders in Sake to check out the security situation and ran into a group of about 100 spear-wielding Hutus. In Kichanga, the Hundes are fearing an attack today.

On a positive note, we've found a nice little house to live in on the tea plantation. We need to make a plan to get started there. The house is not bad; small, but sufficient for us. It has a fridge, shower (with cold water of course, and I am sick to death of cold showers!), and a toilet. What luxury! There is a generator on the plantation so we have electricity in the house for part of the time.

The house sits on a hill overlooking the tea workers' village. It gets a bit noisy because they wake the workers at 6 a.m. with this horrible air-raid siren, some ancient thing from God knows when! And then there are the spiders. The house is literally crawling with them. We actually saw a fight between a cockroach and a spider, and the spider won! They are big, big, ugly things. I am sleeping under a net.

There is a little store for the workers where we can buy soap, sugar and, most importantly, beer. We might be able to get diesel if we need it in an emergency, but most of our supplies will come from Goma. Some of the markets have shut down, and there's hardly any meat available. This whole area used to be a big cattle raising region, with thousands of cattle, but they've all been stolen and/or eaten, and there's just a couple hundred left, mostly around Mokoto, that the monks look after.

Yesterday, while we were driving, we came upon three men wearing nothing but grass skirts, all Hunde combatants. One had a machete, one had a spear, and one had a Kalashnikov! What a photo that would have made! The evolution of an African combatant. I expect we'll be seeing more of them in the near future.

The other night in Goma, we had a lovely barbecue at Alif, the neighbour's house. He even had a piano that I could play on for a bit. It's been a long time since I've played. We had quite a lazy weekend, which is good, because from now on I think we'll be working our asses off.

Rink and I even talked about getting married here in Zaire or perhaps in Kampala, Uganda. It might be a bit complicated, but it would be neat if we could pull it off. The problem is that the only people who can marry us in Zaire are either Catholic priests or warlords. Not our ideal wedding.

Within weeks, we had set up our 'Vulture Base' in Mweso, on the ZTM plantation. The first weeks were difficult, as there was much we had forgotten and no way to go next door and pick up supplies. Everything had to come from Goma, which was hours away. We did our cooking on a charcoal burner, as we didn't have a stove. There were few markets and little food available. We ate a lot of canned goods, some of which had arrived in the first emergency shipments for the refugee camps two years earlier, and had by now expired. We didn't have much choice, as even within Goma supplies were not that plentiful.

We managed to create a sort of hot shower by heating water over our little kerosene cooker or the charcoal and runing it through a plastic jerrycan we'd rigged up. It wasn't great, but it worked. Later, Rink devised a system where we could heat water outside for washing, but we only got to enjoy it for a few days before we evacuated.

We eventually found a cook/cleaner named Didas, who spoke neither French nor English, only a smattering of Swahili. Somehow, we managed to communicate. One day, Didas brought us a barefoot old man dressed in a ragged jacket, carrying an ancient spear. He, too, spoke only Swahili and greeted us with "Jambo, Mama, jambo, Papa".

He was to become our night guard. It was a bit of a joke. He'd go around the house two or three times in the evening and spend the rest of the night snoring in the small shed outside the house. We gave him blankets and a flashlight whose batteries miraculously ran out every night. I have no idea what he ever protected us from, but we were happy to have him, and he enjoyed his new status.

When we began our program in Masisi, we had one of the national staff from Goma act as our translator, but after a couple of weeks we were doing alright on our own. We had our own landcruiser, Bravo, and our own driver, Kambale. He wasn't the greatest driver when we started, but he learned those roads quickly, and although he was a very quiet and soft-spoken fellow, he was loyal and hard-working.

While we got our house and base set up, we started off on our rounds of the area and got to know the villages and the people in the region. We began checking out which clinics were working and who required supplies, how many patients they were seeing, how many refugees and displaced were arriving, and where the fighting was happening.

By the time the translator left, we had our little base pretty much set up, complete with radios in the landcruiser and our home/office, a satellite computer link-up, handsets, computers and a warehouse full of medical supplies.

Our warehouse was located just down the hill from our house. In practically no time, we organized the warehouse, alphabetized our pharmacy and devised our drug consumption records for the clinics. Our experience in Bosnia held us in good stead, and it didn't take us long to be up and operational. Soon, we had fifteen clinics on our supply list, then twenty-five. We were back in business!

The first few weeks went fairly smoothly. There was a great deal of travel involved, hours on the road every day. The health centres in the area, unable to maintain their cost-recovery programs, were running out of drugs, money and staff. They were delighted to see MSF in their area and relieved that we were able to provide medicines and materials for the displaced people in their villages. We began to get a much clearer picture of the situation in Masisi, and it was not pretty.

Security in the region was totally unpredictable. From one day to the next, things could change dramatically. As no other agencies were present in the region, we couldn't rely on the rumours and usually had to investigate the situation ourselves. It was risky business, with Goma so far away in case we ran into trouble. Nevertheless, we enjoyed the challenge and found the work both exciting and exhausting.

As usual, we rarely had a moment's privacy. Though we tried in principle not to work on the weekends, we couldn't avoid it. In the evenings, the senior workers from the plantation would come to visit, drink beer and share the latest rumours. On the weekends, nurses from clinics miles away would arrive, asking for supplies. They would stand outside our bedroom window from dawn, patiently waiting for us to get up and speak to them. It was impossible to say no. And every day at 6 A.M. the stupid alarm went off, calling the tea pickers to work. The only other agency we ever saw or worked with in Masisi was ICRC, and then not often. We did have a good working relationship with Jean Luc from ICRC, and when he was in the area, he'd often drop by for a drink and a chat. But in reality, we were the only show in town.

Situation Report, March 24, 1996:
Been here a week, and the tam-tam works well. Everybody knows we are here, and we've had several visitors already. In general, the situation remains tense in Mweso, with people fearing attacks. The hospital is nearly empty, the market deserted and the *chef de localité* (local leader) has been trying to solve the recent trouble without success. Recent trouble includes:
19 March — Hunde combatants stole a Hutu truck outside Kalembe, killing eight people from Mweso in the process. The Hundes claim the truck was carrying weapons. During ICRC food distribution the next day in Mweso, a shooting occurred, related to the truck theft, which made ICRC stop distribution. The nuns from Mweso brought their car to the tea plantation for security.
22 March — The Hundes attacked a village north of Kalembe and burned the huts. The military is in Mweso. Hundes attacked a second village between Mweso and Kichanga, six people killed. Two corpses arrived in Mweso hospital a day later, one had been disemboweled. Part of the Mweso population is now sleeping in the surrounding hills, as it is not safe to stay in town.

Medical:

Assessments done at ZTM, Bushumba, Kichanga and Mokoto. Kichanga is using too many drugs, and I suspect some are ending up in the private pharmacy in town. Anyone coming from Goma, could you check this out?

In Mokoto, there are some 900 displaced Tutsis who badly want to go to Rwanda. The monastery is looking after them now but can't manage for long, as they are out of food and out of money. Living in one big shelter in terrible conditions, lots of scabies, bronchitis, et cetera. The biggest problem is food, as ICRC already did a non-food distribution. Can UNHCR be contacted about these people, and can some arrangement be made for them? There is no food nearby to forage any longer, and they can't even go to market because of the security situation. Access to the health centre is still okay, and a third of Joseph's patients are from the camp.

Water/sanitation:

In Kichanga, Rink found that almost nothing has been done to prepare for the installation of a second water bladder. Can Solly look into some teaching or something there? The Mwami says nobody will work without pay, but they need this bladder, even as a temporary solution.

I should add that the incident with the stolen truck spiralled completely out of control. One of the commanders came to use our radio to try to negotiate for the truck's return. It didn't happen. Both sides made weak attempts to negotiate but ended up retaliating. The attacks went back and forth until more than thirty-five people had been killed and numerous huts burned. Neither the Hundes nor the Hutus would stop things. Finally, in despair, the Hundes who had stolen the truck in the first place stripped it of any valuables and burned it to the ground. They left it standing on the road leading to their village as a sign that the fight was over. Unfortunately, it wasn't.

The truck was just one of several incidents. From the moment the base opened on the ZTM planatation, the security situation was precarious, and we had numerous encounters with combatants, both Hutu and Hunde, some of which were more than a little frightening. We did our best to remain neutral and made sure villages from both sides were recipients of our medical supplies. The trouble was that the attacks were so sporadic we could never predict where or when the next incident would occur. Fighting in one village could lead to repercussions miles away and days later.

In the beginning of April, there was another incident with one of the monks. Father Pierre from Mokoto monastery had a rather serious incident where his car was attacked on the road near the Mokoto turnoff. He managed to escape and drove to Kichanga, where he picked up a DSP soldier who was based there. The DSP were the special presidential army forces who had been sent out by Mobutu to handle the situation in Masisi. They were poorly paid and sometimes undisciplined. Nevertheless, they did represent the government of Zaire and provided some security for the population.

Apparently, the soldier didn't see anybody at the turnoff, so he returned to Kichanga. Pierre continued along the road to Mokoto, and was attacked again just 300 metres down the road! A lot of money and supplies were taken from him.

As a result of this incident, the two remaining nuns in Mweso were evacuated, taking all but a couple of the hospital staff with them. First, no doctor and now, no nurses. The priest from the parish left with them, as did the paramilitary forces in Mweso. Most of the Tutsis and Hundes who were living around Mweso wanted to leave as soon as the paramilitary did, feeling it was far too insecure to remain in the area. A crowd of people made their way to the tea plantation, seeking some safe place to stay.

Literally in front of our house in the plantation, some 500 Hunde refugees gathered in the market square. There was a small contingent of DSP soldiers present on the plantation, and they intended to send the displaced away immediately, forcing them to travel at night to Nyanzale, which at the time offered better security. But travelling at night presented some big risks. After a lengthy discussion with Rink and a lot of persuasion, the DSP commander agreed to escort the displaced to a safe area the following day. The next morning, we met the whole group on the road under military escort to Nyanzale. We dropped off some medical supplies at the clinic there and hoped for the best.

In Mweso, the Hutu combatants started plundering the houses that had recently been evacuated. We met with Erasto, the Hutu combatant leader, and urged him to keep his men away from the hospital, the house of the sisters, and the parish. He promised to protect them as best he could. We wanted to re-open the hospital as soon as we could, but the staff situation was not too promising.

Rink and I continued our assessments in the area, urging the clinic staff to stay open to provide care for the population and trying to determine the truth behind the endless rumours.

There were a string of Catholic parishes throughout the Masisi region, and the nuns and priests working in them were amazing people. When we travelled, we often ended up spending the night with them at their parishes. They were always friendly, helpful and available. However, they were also often the first targets of the combatants of both sides. They had built numerous schools, hospitals and clinics, and now so many were being destroyed.

One of my cherished memories occurred when we spent the night with the nuns in their house in Birambizo. We awakened to the sound of the sisters singing in the church just down the road, as the sun came up over the hills. All I could hear through the mist was harmonious voices raised in prayer and the early morning sounds of the people waking in the village. There was beauty in Birambizo for a moment.

Chapter 4

Usually every two or three weeks, Rink and I would return to Goma for meetings, supplies, debriefings and a bit of a break. We were working in a very isolated area, and we needed some time away to rest, relax and discuss further plans with either Lisette or Rachel, the new country coordinator. We also needed to spend some time with the rest of the team.

Often we would go to town for dinner, usually a place where the expats hung out, called 'No-No's'. We also went dancing sometimes, or shopping. Or we would take the zodiac, a motorized rubber boat, out on Lake Kivu for a day trip to one of the nearby islands. I always enjoyed our time on the lake, except for one incident that I still laugh about.

The zodiac was actually part of the emergency evacuation plan, in case there was a need to leave Goma by boat. Boats operated by the NGOs weren't normally allowed on the lake, so we needed special permission and papers to use it. It took ages to procure them, but eventually we received our papers and carried them in the boat at all times. Once, we spotted a second zodiac following us. It turned out to be 'SNIP', the special police force. Three soldiers came up to us, with their guns pointed at us, demanding to see our papers. They were fairly disappointed when we could actually produce them. One of the soldiers even had the audacity to ask us for fuel, since we had, in his mind, made them drive all that way after us, so the *least* we could do was replace their fuel for them! We told them there was only enough for ourselves and tried not to laugh until they were out of sight.

The level of corruption in the area was legendary. Another time, Rink, Didi and I were in the car returning to Hotel India. We were stopped by two police officers who demanded to see Rink's papers, since he was driving. He could only produce a photocopy, which wasn't good enough. Fortunately, I was carrying the original. That still wasn't good enough. They wanted to see the car registration papers next, so Rink obliged. The pair became more frustrated as they realized they would be unable to catch us on some minor infringement. Finally, they demanded to see special insurance papers that all the agencies had applied for but which they knew had yet to be issued. Unfazed, we called the base, and the temporary permit was soon on its way. The police, frustrated and annoyed, then asked us to simply pay them twenty dollars, so we could all get on with our busy lives and not have to sit and wait for the papers. We told them we really didn't mind sitting and waiting. They dropped their price to ten dollars, but we said we'd wait for Solly to come with the papers. When he arrived with the documents, they asked us to buy them each a Fanta, since they were parched from having to talk to us for so long! This kind of nonsense could drive you crazy, but it was part of the game in Zaire, and everyone had to play along.

When not in Goma, we were back in the thick of things in Mweso. I really liked the nurses we were working with, and we did our best to try to support them. The plan was to ensure there were enough supplies from MSF so that the displaced and refugees wouldn't have to pay for their drugs. But we found out that, in reality, almost nobody could afford to pay for their drugs, and maintaining the cost-recovery drug distribution program was increasingly impossible. Either ASRAMES couldn't deliver because of the insecurity or the clinics didn't have enough paying patients to be able to afford new supplies. We were soon supplying what we could to cover the whole population, regardless of whether they were local people or displaced.

The state of most of the clinics was poor, usually just a dirt hut with no access to water or latrines. Many of the so-called nurses were mere assistants and even required basic training in treatment protocols and correct use of drugs. All of them had to be shown how to collect data for us, and all of them were required to show us their patient logs and pharmacy records. Those who had none were given instructions on how to get started, but in some clinics, the care was so basic that I couldn't allow more than simple painkillers or malaria drugs in, for fear they'd never be properly used. It was a sad state of affairs. Yet the workers had the courage to stay in difficult times, and they were extremely grateful for the support MSF provided. I was constantly amazed by their bravery and resourcefulness. Some of them would walk for days, often risking harassment or attack by the opposing faction, just to pick up a box or two of medical supplies. They never once forgot to bring along their patient records or pharmacy data.

Meanwhile the DSP and the regular Zairean army had a plan to get the combatants to disarm, called 'Operation Kimya'. It was a quick and easy solution: just ask the combatants nicely to hand in their guns. Nice try. It lasted for about a month. A group of Zairean army soldiers set up base in Mweso. Nobody handed in their weapons. Nothing changed. The army started stealing supplies from the local population to feed their men, and the fighting throughout the region continued.

We did have one funny incident during Operation Kimya. Erasto, the local rebel leader, gave our driver, Kambale, a message to take to another local militia leader in a village we were heading for. The note instructed the local commander to hand in one, and just one, of his machine guns to the DSP when they arrived. Beyond that, they could hand in their spears or machetes, but no other weapons. Kambale knew that as a humanitarian organization we could not be responsible for delivering any sort of military information. He wisely left the note on the dashboard so that the wind could just 'accidentally' blow it out the window. As he said, papers do get blown away in the wind. Shame.

In the meantime, Lisette had managed to get a donation of several tons of food for the Tutsis in the displaced camp in Mokoto. She sent a truck to deliver the goods to Mokoto, so the camp had food again, albeit for a short time. But nobody addressed the main issue of this terrible predicament. The refugees were trapped between two warring factions with no way out, and UNHCR wouldn't consider evacuating them out of the country. They lived in fear for their lives in the camp. There had already been more than one attack against them, and several people had been killed. Everyone was aware of the situation, but no one seemed to have any solution to offer. All we could do was ensure that the nearby clinic had enough supplies to care for them all and put some pressure on the other agencies in Goma to respond to their predicament.

Rumours of another attack in Birambizo sent us off on yet another fact-finding mission. We were quickly learning that there wouldn't be many peaceful moments in Masisi.

April 10 Update:

In Mweso, the situation is calm, but thirty houses were burned yesterday by Hutus. Hospital to re-open as health centre tomorrow. Found Valentine, one nurse, who will stay and manage things. To be paid by MSF for now. Hospital still, fortunately, not touched by the soldiers.

There was an attack the day before yesterday in Kichanga. DSP there used some of their artillery, two wounded. The feeding centre was closed for the last two days. Met Colonel Lasisa of DSP, who has just arrived from Goma, in Kichanga. He saw a group of Hutus on the road before he arrived, so the Mwami sent out some of his Mai-Mai to find them. Lots of naked men in town, preparing their ju-ju. It's bad luck for them to be seen by a woman (oops!), so I was obliged to hide behind a building while they marched off to battle wearing their grass skirts and carrying spears. Well, they all had spears, but the grass skirts were sort of optional.

On the road to Bishusha, we saw evidence of people who had fled in a great hurry; baskets dropped in a pile, some fallen clothing. We ran into some Hutus just before Bishusha, who fled the minute they heard the Mai-Mai singing as they came to battle. They were all killed later, though the Mai-Mai had spears and these Hutus had guns. Go figure.

In Bishusha, we saw a few more Hutus, who said the fight with the Hundes had been going for three days. Five people dead, many wounded and sent to Birambizo hospital.

Driving towards Tongo, we ran into about 200 *very* agitated Hutus, who had blocked the road with felled trees and were very nervously waiting for an attack by the Hundes. They surrounded the car, and one madman thrust a landmine in my face, which he later tried to place under the car. Others had their spears or machetes pointed at us. They were extremely jumpy, and only when Rink stepped out of the car did they calm down somewhat. They had an improvised health post for the wounded, and I saw one patient with shrapnel wounds. I thought it wise to leave some supplies and talk our way out, which we somehow managed to do. But it was rather tense there for a moment.

We continued to Rushekera, then on to Tongo. Mr. Kazuku, who owns the big farms and the hotel up around Tongo, was kind enough to let us stay for the night, since the road behind us was full of fighters. We did an assessment there, as he has several refugees arriving in the area. We found one small clinic we may be able to support.

The next day, we went to Bambu and Mushebabwe for assessments. Lots of displaced arriving in Tongo and Rushekera, and about 5,000 displaced in Mushebabwe.

Meanwhile Dr. Muke in Birmabizo has sent his wife and kids to Goma for safety, and it's not looking good there.

The incident with the Hutus on the road to Tongo indicated just how unstable the situation was becoming. There was a real battle going on, and we had not intended to end up in the middle of it. Rink and I, following the flow of refugees from town to town, had landed ourselves in the midst of the two warring parties. Many of the civilians were getting involved in the fighting now; it was no longer just rebels and combatants. In principle, we tried not to be away from the base at night unless arrangements had been made with Goma. This time, the circumstances had been such that we were forced to take refuge in the hotel unexpectedly, leaving our base unattended. It was not a great position to be in, but with fighting going on just behind us, there was no way to return. The number of displaced people leaving the area was on the rise, and there seemed to be no end in sight.

The next day, we did an assessment in the hospital in Birambizo. We found only two of the nuns remaining. After the trouble with the Mai-Mai, most of the parish had evacuated. The abbé had taken a group of Tutsis with him to Tongo, hoping that they would be safer there, and he had not yet returned to Birambizo. Meanwhile, the fighting around Kichanga continued. We were shown the body of a woman, apparently a Hunde, who had been hacked to death with a machete. Emotions were running high throughout the area. At least Valentine was able to keep the hospital in Mweso open and had done forty consultations that day, with three inpatients.

I was asked to assist with one of his patients, a Hutu soldier who had been shot at a checkpoint. With Rink helping, we performed very rough surgery to treat his gunshot wounds and set his leg in traction. There was very little in the way of anesthesia for the poor guy, and it was no easy task to go after bullets with no x-rays, blood, or intravenous fluids available. Setting a fractured femur without a proper set-up was also a challenge. With some rocks, rope, MSF tape and a few planks, we managed a reasonable imitation of a traction set-up for his fractured leg. The entire process took about two hours. Talk about frontline surgery! I wouldn't want to repeat that performance. I don't know what we would have done without Valentine. It was an obvious example of how essential it was that the hospital remain open for the population.

Just a few days after our encounter with the Hutus, Rink and I had yet another argument over the management of our project. We heard there had been another attack, this time in the village of Katwe. There was regular contact between the parishes, and on April 15, Katwe parish reported that their radio had been stolen, along with some cattle. The thieves were reportedly the Hundes, which meant that they were on the move, far outside of their stongholds now.

I agreed with Rink that we should go as far as Nyanzale, a mid-way point, to check out the situation. But I was firmly against travelling further into what was now apparently Hunde territory. I knew the area would be extremely tense, as it always is following an attack. Rink insisted we travel as far as possible to check out the validity of the stories. I insisted there was no need, that we'd find out all the pertinent information by doing our usual assessments on the way to

Nyanzale. I warned him that we were heading for a serious security incident if we continued this way. He was convinced we'd manage, as we had so far, and that there was no need for me to worry. I was furious, but that didn't dissuade him. In the end, he overruled my objections. The next day, we headed for Katwe.

In Nyanzale, we encountered several people on the run from the recent attack in Katwe. Sure enough, the Hundes had attacked the parish and stolen the radio and seven cows. The local people were heading steadily westward, away from the fighting. In Katwe, we found one worker left in the parish, who asked that a car be sent so he could evacuate with all the belongings of the monks and nuns in tow. We agreed to pass the message on. The village was quiet, as most of the population had already left.

We continued on to Kikuku, another small village further west. There we found that, again, most of the population had fled. We had a close encounter with the Hundes, who had now taken over the town. They were fighters who had come all the way from Kalembe, and were now 'guarding' (read: terrorizing) the town. Fortunately, they let us deliver our supplies to the clinic, which was still open, and didn't give us too much trouble. It was obvious now that the Hundes really had moved out of their stronghold and were taking over more territory. I figured we had enough information to know the rumours were true. Rink figured we'd better move on.

On route to the next village, Kibirizi, we passed through no-man's land, a totally empty stretch of road dividing the Hundes, who had taken over the town from the fleeing Hutu population. I'd never seen the road so silent and empty. It was eerie.

Soon we came upon thousands of refugees on the road to Kibirizi. For miles, we passed groups and individuals, women, children, old people and young, all fleeing the fighting and on their way to what they hoped would be safety.

Kibirizi was crowded with displaced people, with more arriving by the minute. The health centre seemed to be managing the increased load, but there were concerns about sufficient water supplies. We agreed to contact Goma and have one of the water and sanitation boys check it out. Many of the displaced were already integrated in private homes, schools and churches. Most of the Tutsis did not want to stay and intended to travel farther west towards Rutshuru. By the time we arrived, 720 families had been registered.

After doing our assessment, we turned around and headed home to Mweso and finally ran into the trouble I'd been expecting all along. We arrived in Katwe to find a number of large trucks stopped in the road, on their way to ZTM to pick up the tea for shipping. We were instantly stopped by the Hunde combatants and told we had to wait. One of the truck drivers, who seemed quite upset, came out of his truck to speak to us. I heard the word 'Hutu', and before we knew what was happening, we saw a man run from a hut. Not ten metres from our car, he was shot in the head and killed. He was a Hutu who had refused to leave his home when the Hundes arrived.

The fact that we had witnessed this atrocity was extremely dangerous to us. If they didn't want witnesses, the only solution would be to kill us, too. We were in a very precarious situation, and we had no idea how the Hundes would react. Totally shocked and more than a little frightened by their audacity, we waited in the landcruiser for some signal, some sign of what their intentions were. One of the soldiers came up to the car window and nodded that we could leave. His only comment was that he knew we were MSF, and he had no problem with MSF.

The trucks were turned back, and we continued on the road towards Mweso. We passed the body, lying face down in a pool of blood, and we headed towards home without a word. We were all relieved to get out of there and figured the worst was behind us. Not so.

We arrived on the outskirts of Nyanzale, only to run into a group of Hutu rebels. They were very agitated and obviously very anxious. There were about twenty-five men, all of whom immediately surrounded the car. They accused us of helping the enemy and wanted information about what was happening. One man thrust a grenade in Rink's face and began playing with the pin! Rink was very worried, convinced the guy would slip up and that would be the end of us all. But he was able to speak to the fellow and convince him we'd be more helpful *without* a grenade in our car. The man finally backed out of the window and we breathed a sigh of tremendous relief.

We eventually had to inform the Hutus of where we had been, and we admitted we had seen some Hundes along the way. We were careful not to mention the Hutu who had so recently been murdered in Katwe, as there was no telling how they'd respond. We assured them that we were still supplying their clinic with medicines and material, and that we would continue to support them. After some talking and some reassurances, they allowed us to leave, and we got the hell out of there.

We'd travelled a very short distance when Kambale stopped the car. We yelled at him to hurry up before the group changed their minds and came back for us, but he said he'd spotted his wife, and needed to know what was going on. Sure enough, there was one of his wives — he had three — in Nyanzale visiting family! She couldn't have picked a worse possible time to go visiting, as now she was trapped in the fighting. We told Kambale to stop arguing and pick her up immediately and we'd take her with us to Mweso. At that point, all we wanted was to get out of there as quickly as possible. I told Kambale he should stick with one wife, as I thought three were far too much trouble. He had to agree.

I had warned Rink that travelling so far would be too dangerous. I received no satisfaction in being proven correct.

Chapter 5

The next day, we were called to Goma. The deteriorating security situation was becoming a real concern. We spent four or five days there talking about the situation, discussing the issues and deciding whether or not we could continue, and how.

We weren't the only ones having trouble. Roy, our colleague who also worked in Masisi, had been out near Sake after some fighting and was taken by the locals to see what had been left behind — a decapitated head and two bloody hands sitting on the fence! A rather grisly memento. That evening, while we were sitting down to eat, a colleague complained about having lost his handset. Without blinking an eye, Roy said, "Better to lose your handset than your hands." The whole table became hysterical with laughter. We were developing a rather black sense of humour, but it was the only defence we had.

I needed those days for a little reflection of my own. My resignation from Burundi had actually been quite a blow to my self-confidence. I began to have some doubts about the work and about my position in the team. And in Mweso, Rink and I were encountering some serious difficulties.

Rink had fallen in love with the project the moment we arrived in Zaire. For him, it was quintessential MSF: cutting-edge, dangerous, lonely, urgent. He was prepared to take far more risks than I was for the work. He worked with a passion I found excessive and could not comprehend. He couldn't stand not to be involved in every single aspect of the project, which meant he regularly overstepped his responsibilities and took over *mine*. I felt it showed a lack of trust in me, and his approach did nothing for my self-confidence. I began to feel that my role was insignificant next to his, and I was really struggling for my identity in the work. Discussions with him went nowhere. He saw things a different way, and he wouldn't keep his nose out of my business. Because it was just the two of us, there was nobody else with whom I could speak. We ended up in repeated arguments over this issue, but it went largely unresolved. He listened to my arguments, but somehow we never ended up agreeing. I was feeling left out of my own project, and I couldn't seem to find my way in.

Besides that, the work was just plain tiring. The long hours, the horrendous roads, the isolation and the constant security problems were acutely stressful. Several times, we took dangerous risks that I felt we shouldn't have. Rink insisted that since MSF was the only agency there, we were obliged to do all we could, and that meant checking out every incident that we heard rumours about. I felt that we were ending up in security situations that we could have avoided. It was becoming dangerous, and he didn't seem to realize it. I was growing nervous, and the tension was getting to me. I had been horrified when that man was shot in front of me, and the incident left me shaken. I was not confident that it couldn't happen to us the next time. We had been able to talk our way out of several serious situations, but I was beginning to think our luck might be running out.

By then, the markets in and around ZTM had vanished because it was too unsafe for the people to travel. Our diet was reduced to rice, beans, eggs and canned vegetables. I was so sick of eggs when I left, it took me three months to even look at them again! We were both drinking too much in the evenings, partly because there was nothing else to do and partly because we rarely had an evening alone. There was a constant stream of visitors to our little house — workers from the plantation, nurses from the surrounding clinics coming for supplies, sometimes Marc or one of the other managers. Some of the roads in and out of Mweso had been cut off by the fighters, and we were limited to a few select routes. It was not a positive sign.

Still, it was satisfying to be doing what was very essential work. For Rink it was 'true' MSF work — being alone in the bush, in the middle of the jungle, helping a population in danger. Indeed it was, but I wondered if we'd ever see the end of it. We enjoyed our few days in Goma, but when we headed back to ZTM, the underlying tension remained constant, the fighting continued, and our problems were unresolved.

Chapter 6

Lisette had created 'displaced kits', boxes of medical supplies sufficient for a few thousand refugees to receive health care for a month or longer. We never travelled anywhere without at least one or two of these kits in our landcruiser. It was crucial to be able to give something to the health centres in villages that had just received thousands of newly displaced people. The kits also helped us out of several tricky situations. We never knew when or if we'd be able to return, so the kits were our only way to support the population at times.

One day we were due to visit a very rural clinic for an assessment. The only way there was by a little footpath over the hills. We left Kambale, our driver, with the landcruiser and headed off early in the morning with a guide. It was a long, three-hour hike, and we were pretty tired when we arrived. We checked out the clinic, collected our information, drank banana beer with the chief and aimed to return home before the rain started.

The locals offered us a kitten for a dollar (which became his name), and we headed for the car, Dollar in hand. Unfortunately, he ran away after only a week, joining the ranks of the displaced.

As we drew nearer the village, we saw that the landcruiser was surrounded by about forty Hutu combatants, all heavily armed. I feared that would be the end of the car. Instead, when we arrived, they told us that they had been guarding the car for us and wondered why we were so late. They'd been planning an attack that day and had had to put it off until we arrived. What could we do but apologize for our tardiness and get the hell out of there as soon as we could! I think Kambale was very relieved to see us return. We left them to their attack and headed home in the rain.

Later, passing through the same village on our way to the Hunde stronghold of Kalembe, it appeared that the fighting had escalated. The village looked deserted. As we neared Kalembe we saw the burned truck in the middle of the road, the one that had been stolen in March and had led to the deaths of dozens of people. So much for a sign that the fight was over. We did our assessment in the health centre, dropped off some supplies, and headed back to ZTM.

In no-man's land, between a Hunde village and a Hutu village, Rink stopped and picked me some gorgeous red flowers that were growing on the side of the road. I was thrilled by the gift, but I suspect we shouldn't have wasted that time, because when we returned to the village that we thought was abandoned, we found a group of drunk and agitated Hutus waiting for us. They had put up a makeshift road block, and were adamant that we couldn't pass. If we'd been a few minutes earlier, it might have been different.

They made demands for money, food, cigarettes, et cetera. After a round of discussions, one man grew tired of listening to us. He stood in front of the car, fired off a round from his automatic weapon, and became significantly more threatening than before. Our negotiations took on a new urgency. Finally, Rink left them with a cigarette, and we got out of there as quickly as we could. That evening we spoke to their commander, Erasto, something we'd already had to do more than once. We urged him to control his boys and to give us some guarantee of security. We were having an increasingly difficult time at the various checkpoints these days. Erasto said he couldn't make any promises. That was the last time Rink went picking flowers in no-man's land.

Just after this incident, we had an unexpected visitor in Mweso. Guy was a human rights monitor for the UN and had plenty of experience in Zaire. He spent several days travelling with us and interviewing the commanders, the local chiefs, et cetera. We shared some pleasant evenings with him, listening to good music and drinking his fine whiskey. We enjoyed his company, and his reports on the situation in Masisi were some of the few that we found to be very accurate and professional.

And so our daily routine went on. Several more villages were burned, several others were deserted due to the fighting, and refugees continued to leave Masisi in droves. They had good reason to be scared, and there was little we could do but support those who dared to stay behind. Half of the health centres on our list were now destoyed or abandoned. The few that remained open did so at great risk.

April 24 Update:

Operation Kimya has set up base in the parish here in Mweso. We don't see too many guns these days, but that doesn't mean much to us. We visited Bushumba and tried to go on to Kirumbu. There was a huge tree on the road, and we got completely stuck, so no luck this time. Met Marc on his way to Goma. He might return to ZTM next week, but he intends to go away on leave soon. ZTM is the last business still standing in Mweso. For how long, who knows?

April 25 Update:

Visited both Birambizo and Katsiru. The sisters who had intended to leave are still in Birambizo, and so is Doctor Muke, but the tam-tam says that they've already left, and there are hardly any patients in the hospital.

We had a meeting with Dr. Janniek (the nun responsible for the parish hospitals throughout Masisi). She is pissed at us! She accused us of creating sub-systems and is angry that we're giving drugs to the hospital and financial support to Valentine to get him to stay there. She wants us to stop our work in the hospital unless one of her guys is around. We tried to explain that we are still working, and it's *her* people who have left. If they want to run the show, they can come back any time, and we'll keep our hands off. In the meantime, keeping the hospital open offers the best chance for preventing it from being totally looted.

Dr. Janniek found some military in the hospital, which we'll check out tomorrow. I'll talk to the commander today. But I do not want to deal with this crap from her again. She is no longer involved in Mweso, and we have to do what we can to keep things operational. When and if the nuns return and the hospital re-opens, then she can have her say. We're going to Goma tomorrow.

Chapter 7

We arrived in Goma, stressed, angry, fed up and tired. Or at least I was. Rachel guessed that we had pretty much had enough. She basically ordered us to go to Nairobi for a break, and I was more than glad to take her up on her offer. If nothing else, maybe I could finally get some rest.

Even in Goma, Hotel India was no place for a good night's sleep. Didi kept a virtual menagerie at the place. Between the dog, the chickens, the very noisy rooster, the guinea fowl and the guards trying to keep them all from their early morning rambles just outside our window, we didn't get a lot of sleep. We took to keeping a small collection of rocks on our window ledge to throw at whatever creature happened to be making the most noise at five o'clock in the morning.

Still, I liked Ed and Deirdre, and they always gave us free access to their library. Those books were a lifesaver for me. There was decent food to eat, we could go swimming whenever we wanted, and it was far more relaxing than living right by the office all the time.

We left for Nairobi and spent the night with Tom, the logistical coordinator there. He suggested the beach in Malindi, but aside from gorging ourselves on the excellent lobster, there wasn't much to do there, as it was off-season and pretty quiet.

We found a travel bureau and negotiated for a cheap safari, and off we went to Tsavo and Amboseli National Park. Rink had not been on safari before, and we spent hours in our private landcruiser, gazing at the wildlife and enjoying the scenery. In the centre of the park was a gorgeous Hilton Hotel, beautifully designed as a series of attached rooms raised on stilts, giving it the appearance of several round

African huts. Because of the elevation, it was easy to look down over the watering hole and watch the animals as they came to drink. There was a great view of the surrounding countryside, and we spent a most enjoyable evening there. I wore a slinky dress Rink had bought for me in Malindi to dinner that night, and we managed to seat ourselves at a table with a British couple who turned out to be arms dealers. Talk about a conflict of interest! It turned out to be an interesting (though highly ironic) evening. We had a quiet and peaceful holiday, a world away from the fighting that was now turning into a genuine civil war.

Rink and I got on so well that I never even brought up the issue of our working relationship, which I still felt was not good. Away from the project, things were fine, but when we returned to Mweso, we slipped back into old habits. Rink took over many of my responsibilities, even to the point of giving medical advice to my nursing staff! No matter what I said, he didn't seem to recognize how much I resented his interference. His need to control every aspect of the project was driving me nuts.

Chapter 8

Things in Mweso had really started going to hell. In our absence, Lisette had had a very scary incident in Mushebabwe, where the landcruiser was commandeered by a group of soldiers who forced her at gunpoint to drive them to their destination. I found out much later that they had also threatened to rape her, but the driver had talked them out of it.

By then, I had a new nurse working with me, Kizito, who was very experienced. I really needed her as a counterpart to assist with the training. There was a measles outbreak, and many of the nurses were misdiagnosing the children and treating them improperly. Because of the large number of deaths, we considered a vaccination campaign, but in the end, the insecurity was too big a factor. If we couldn't reach at least eighty percent of the under-five population, the campaign wouldn't work. And at that point we had no way of knowing if the town we planned to go to would still be there the next day. It was frustrating as hell, but there was nothing we could do, except try to teach the nurses and aides how to manage measles properly.

We had a second landcruiser as well, named Echo, and Rink and I usually drove together in one car, with Kambale and Kizito in the second. With the two vehicles, there was a little added security. Still, the situation was changing daily, and we never knew what to expect any more.

The bridges between Kalembe, the Hunde stronghold to the north, and Mweso had been destroyed, and the 'Operation Kimya' commander was withdrawing his forces in failure. Homes around Mweso were set on fire, and tensions were high. Jean-Luc of ICRC was called to see the bodies of a woman and baby who had been hacked to death with a machete — with both the Hundes and the Hutus claiming the other side was responsible. People started disappearing while working on their farms, and the whole region was in an uproar. And then came Mokoto.

On May 13, we heard rumours of trouble at the monastery in Mokoto. Soon after, the monks started arriving in Goma, having fled from fighting in that area. Apparently the Mai-Mai, the Hundes from Kichanga, went to steal some cattle, and the Hutus charged them. The Hundes fled, returning to Kichanga, but the Hutus stayed behind and began attacking the unarmed Tutsis in the refugee camp at the base of the monastery. The monks brought as many people as possible into the church for protection, which proved to be a futile attempt to save them.

The news coming from Mokoto was ominous. Many people were wounded, but many more were killed. We made arrangements with Jean-Luc to travel together the next day to Mokoto to see what, exactly, was going on.

On May 15, we met Jean-Luc in Kichanga. The town was overflowing with Tutsis who had escaped the massacre in Mokoto. The stories they told were dreadful. We were told that the church had been under attack for the last three days, and that more than 100 people had presumably been killed.

We drove in a small convoy, two MSF and two ICRC landcruisers, towards Mokoto, already fearful of what would lie ahead. We saw a few people on the road, survivors heading for Kichanga. About a kilometre or so before the monastery we saw two bodies, totally dismembered, disemboweled and burned beyond recognition. The stench of death was sickening. We didn't see any more bodies on the road, but it was clear from the smell that many people had been killed in the surrounding bush.

As we arrived at the monastery, we saw that the level of destruction was absolute. Nothing had been spared. The yards and lawns were littered with the debris of a thousand people running for their lives: scattered baskets of food, clothing, letters, papers, plastic containers, plastic sheeting and straw mats. The monastery had been utterly destroyed. The vehicles had been smashed beyond repair; the living and working quarters, along with the church, were completely devastated. Debris was everywhere; books, computers, hand carved statues, everything completely ruined. I had a creepy sensation that we were being closely watched, but no one was in sight. Things were quiet in every direction, but I was certain we were being observed.

Bodies were strewn throughout the church grounds — on the altar, behind doors, even in the garden outside. One man had been murdered as he tried to escape up a stairwell, and one of his hands was still outstretched, forever motionless.

We were all silent as we walked through the monastery and outside through the grounds. There wasn't anything to say. We came to the library, which had been one of the largest and most beautiful in central Africa. It was now an avalanche of white, the books and papers torn to shreds and strewn over every surface. The view of the lake from the library had been magnificent, through an entire wall of glass. I could imagine it had been a most peaceful place for meditation, for prayer, for study. Now it was reduced to a shambles that no one would ever return to.

Standing at the top of the stairs, we could hear the buzzing of what we expected to be flies down below, swarming even more bodies. We fully expected to find more bodies. It seemed we stood for a long moment before I took the first step down. It wasn't courage that made me do it, but a desperate desire for this day to be over, and knowing that we were the only witnesses Mokoto might have. We could not leave without seeing everything, though I would have given anything to have avoided those stairs.

At the bottom of the stairs, we discovered dozens of honeycombs thrown on the ground, surrounded by angry bees mourning their ruined beehives. But there were no more bodies. I let out my breath at last.

We were standing in the now demolished living and working quarters. The cheese and food from the kitchens had been stolen or destroyed. The water wheel, which they used for years to supply the monastery, was also ruined. Everything, simply everything, was gone.

The monastery had been filled with some exquisite carved wooden crucifixes, Madonnas and other religious artifacts. All of them had had arms and legs and parts broken off, or had been thrown down and stomped on. As we went back up the stairs I saw Jean-Luc pick up a small carved statue of the Madonna and baby Jesus. The baby's nose had been broken off, but all else was intact. He carefully placed it back on the ledge of the stairwell, as if to say that God would be back, and the evil that had occurred in this place would not overcome all else. One small act of defiance. With all the horrors we saw that day, that gesture alone was the one memory I hoped to retain. All the others I would have loved to have forgotten.

Chapter 9

As we walked out of the monastery, we saw some of the combatants casually going about the business of looting whatever remained. They had indeed been watching us. They paid no attention to us and went on stealing what they could, casual and arrogant, without a trace of regret or a moment's remorse. For a moment, I lost every feeling of humanity, compassion or neutrality I'd ever had. It's pretty hard to remain 'neutral' after witnessing the aftermath of a massacre. They had just killed more than a hundred unarmed men, women and children, and now they stood there and laughed silently. I had never known fury like that, or the helplessness that goes with the knowledge that the murderers would never pay for their crime. The nameless, bloodied, lifeless bodies would disappear in mass graves, or be thrown in to the lake, and there would be no justice done.

When we arrived back at the vehicles, Kambale directed us to a couple of men who had been hiding out in a shed for the last three days. When they saw who we were, they finally dared to come forward. When I asked them what had happened at the monastery, one man explained that the Hutu combatants had taken people from the church out into the bush, stripped them of their clothing, tied their hands behind their backs and killed them with machetes or guns. He himself had been taken out but managed to escape. The second man was very gingerly sitting with his head wrapped in his panga, the type of brightly coloured African cloth seen everywhere. When I asked him what had happened to him, he slowly stood up, turned around, and took the panga off his head.

There was a simultaneous gasp from all of us when we saw what had happened. Someone had, literally, tried to remove this man's head from his neck. He had a huge, gaping wound in the back of his head, almost from ear to ear. It was about four or five inches long, and very deep; by far the worst wound I had ever seen on someone still living. It oozed pus and stank horribly. Kizito and I looked at each other, neither of us having a clue what to do for a partially decapitated man who should definitely not have been breathing. All Kizito said was, "Très mystique, très mystique." It was a mystery to me, too, and nothing short of a miracle that he survived as long as he had.

We cleaned his injury as best we could with material from the first aid kit in the car, then wrapped layers and layers of dressing around his head. There was no water for washing, and when I took my gloves off, the smell of that infected wound clung to me for days. I would smell it again in those very bad dreams I knew I'd be having.

Jean-Luc headed off, picking up the straggling survivors along the road and bringing them all to safety in Kichanga. We packed our man in a sleeping bag and laid him down in the back of the landcruiser that Rink and Kizito would be driving in. Kambale and I would travel in the first car, in the hopes that if we were stopped by the Hutus along the way, they might be less likely to attack a woman, and I might have more luck in talking our way through. It was a highly dangerous thing to be taking a Tutsi survivor out through Hutu territory. Had we been stopped, not only our patient but all of us could have been killed. Luckily, we didn't run into anybody on the trip back to Kichanga, but I warned Rink that our patient would probably die from his injuries along the rough road we had to travel for the next hour. Rink was holding his breath with every bump and pothole, certain that he wouldn't make it. Amazingly, our man survived the ride.

We dropped him off at the clinic and ascertained that there were at least a dozen other seriously wounded and surgical intervention would be necessary. There was little we could do, aside from gathering the necessary information and leaving medical supplies for the clinic. We spoke with the Mwami and arranged for an operating theatre to be set up, which we knew would be essential. There was an old schoolhouse that could be used, and a place for tents in front of the clinic as a post-op ward. We then returned to our little house on the tea plantation to prepare our report for Goma.

Chapter 10

We sent our information about the massacre in Mokoto to Goma immediately. Unfortunately, neither Lisette nor Rachel were there. Both were in Amsterdam for coordination meetings, leaving Roy in charge. This was his first mission with MSF, and he was as unsure as we were about how to handle this nightmare. We probably should have returned to Goma the next day as he suggested, but having lost our objectivity, we made an error in judgment. We elected to stay and continue with the program. Roy made plans to set up a surgical facility in Kichanga to deal with the wounded, using Zairean doctors and an MSF surgeon who would arrive from Rwanda, just across the border. And we would stay in Mweso.

That evening was the worst I ever had. Rink and I barely spoke. There was little we could say after what we had seen that day. What did words mean after all that? I sent a capsat message to Mac, a friend in Toronto, hoping somehow to convey something of what had just happened. Rink wrote a letter to Karel, a friend in Holland. We drank whiskey, we listened to our favourite tape of music that Maaike, our friend from Holland, had made for us. We both shed a few tears, but very few. Tears just didn't seem to bring any comfort or release. I couldn't get clean, and I couldn't get rid of the smell of those bodies that had rotted in the sun for three days. I couldn't rid myself of the image of that dead man in the church, hand outstretched on the stairs, frozen in his attempt to escape. The sight of the man with his head half-severed. The destruction of the monastert; the looted health centre; the emptiness of the camp abandoned in fear by innocent and unarmed men and women, who later died only because they happened to be Tutsis. If I slept, I don't remember it. I only remember that we got up the next day, got dressed, made our radio contact with Goma and started our day as if nothing had changed, when everything had.

There was, I think, a sort of numbness with which I protected myself. Rink and I didn't talk about it again until much later, and even then, we never really spoke of it in any serious way. We went about the business of doing our job and pretended that everything was fine. I didn't write another word in my journal after the massacre.

We talked briefly about returning to Goma that day, but I knew there were dysentery patients in Birambizo, and I wanted to bring them the supplies they needed for the outbreak as quickly as possible. We stayed in close radio contact with Goma and with the MSF team that had arrived in Kichanga to set up the surgical unit. The whole region was extremely tense after what had happened, and people were very nervous and afraid. Had we paid a little more attention to that, we likely would not have gone ahead with the planned visit to Birambizo. The Kichanga team warned us about fighting and that shots had been heard in the area we were heading to, but we decided to try anyway.

The road to Birambizo was busy, crowded with people heading towards the last of the markets. Not much happened along the way until we arrived at a new checkpoint just outside the town. There we saw some of the market women being beaten by soldiers at a new barricade. We heard later that some of the soldiers were infiltrators from the Interhamwe, Rwandan Hutu rebels. They were not happy to see us.

The landcruisers were immediately stopped. The soldiers were very aggressive from the start, demanding to search both vehicles and climbing up on the roof to search for weapons. Rink and I were in the first vehicle and were stopped several metres ahead of Kambale and Kizito. It was for them that I was most afraid, as often the national staff can come under far more intense scrutiny than white expats. But there was no way to communicate with them, or with anyone else. We were on our own.

If the combatants spoke French, they gave no indication. They didn't even seem to speak Swahili, and we were without an interpreter.

In fact, they didn't seem pleased to have us speaking to them at all, and our attempts to communicate with them ended with a gun pointed at our faces.

Things took a turn for the worse when the local people started crowding around the car, trying to see what was going on, or perhaps trying to help us out. One of the soldiers in front of the car suddenly fired off a few rounds from his AK-47, just metres above our heads. Most of the locals fled at the noise. Things were becoming more and more tense, and I was really and truly frightened. I felt, for the first time, that we really had no control over this situation any longer. If we could not speak to these men, if we could not negotiate with them, we would never be able to talk our way out of this mess.

The absolute worst point came when one of the men tried to open the hood of our landcruiser. There was a special catch that he couldn't manage. He motioned for Rink, who was driving, to open it from inside the car. Rink did so, but the soldier still couldn't get the hood open. He pointed his weapon at Rink, became very agitated, and motioned with the gun for him to open the hood. Rink tried to point out that he had done so, and decided to get out of the vehicle to show him how to work it. At that point, the gun was levelled at his head, and he was clearly refused permission. Again, the combatant tried unsuccessfully to open the hood. Angered, he pointed his gun and Rink and for a moment I truly thought he was going to fire it. Finally, he allowed Rink to step out of the car and assist. The gun never left Rink's head as he made his way to the front of the car. He opened the hood, and with that I lost sight of him.

I was trapped in the passenger's seat, a grenade in front of my face and a grim and unsmiling combatant at the side of the car. One of the local people managed to stay beside the car and continued to interpret what I said to the soldier. Whether or not the soldier actually understood, I don't know, but that single voice speaking to me in French, urging me to stay calm, assuring me that we would be all right, was the only thing keeping me sane. To this day, I don't know who that man was or what he said to the soldier, but I am convinced he helped to save our lives. I realized that day how little our lives were worth to these people, and that there was a very good chance we wouldn't get out of Zaire alive. I waited in dread for the sound of the gunshot that would take Rink's life. It was the first time in my experience that I realized *there was nothing we could do*.

Ironically, after I realized the situation was out of our hands, I became very calm. I continued to speak to this lone man outside my car window, telling him that we were MSF, that we were only taking supplies to the hospital, that we never carried weapons. I remained very still, spoke quietly, looked the combatant in the eye and prayed as I never have before or since.

As our vehicle was being searched, so were Kambale's and Kizito's. We didn't dare to look behind us, but I could glimpse in the rear-view mirror that they were having a difficult time as well. Kambale had received a few blows to the head for talking to one of the soldiers. All this time, one of the combatants kept vigil in front of our car, his weapon pointed at my head. He raised the gun once or twice to fire off another round but then returned it to its original position. After what seemed like an eternity — really only about twenty minutes — Rink finally got back into the driver's seat and we were allowed to leave.

I wanted nothing so much as to drive as far away as possible. The hardest thing we ever did was to stop that car after only a few metres. But we would never leave our team behind. One of the soldiers came up to us, annoyed that we weren't leaving, and we explained that we had to go as a team and wouldn't leave without the second vehicle. He ordered us to leave. We refused. He went back to the second landcruiser, and after a short wait, Kambale was allowed to drive forward and join us.

We drove on to Birambizo hospital. I felt almost physically sick. My stomach was churning, my hands were shaking, and I felt as though I had just run a marathon. It was a good thing breathing was automatic, because I'm not sure I could have managed otherwise. Nothing like a gigantic adrenaline rush to really screw up a perfectly normal working day.

We were so close to the hospital that we barely had time to say a word before we arrived. I believe my only sentence was, "I think that's enough and I'm leaving."

Although I have no idea how, I managed to leave the vehicle at the hospital with a smile on my face. I acted calm and pleasant, indeed as if nothing had happened, and went immediately to see Kambale and Kizito. They were both shaken and badly frightened, but they were all right. All Kambale said was that it had been very, very dangerous. Kambale, who rarely said anything, spoke volumes with that statement.

We explained to the local leader what had happened at the checkpoint, and he agreed to return with us to ensure our safety. That time, the boys at the checkpoint merely smiled and waved us through.

We'd had trouble with the radio in our landcruiser due to a faulty antenna tuner, and we tried several times, unsuccessfully, to reach Goma. Finally, we got through and explained briefly that we'd had a "bit of a security incident" and would be returning to Goma the next day, as it was too late in the day to leave immediately. For a change, Rink and I agreed it was time to stop taking risks. That incident was *way* too close for comfort. Personally, I had had enough. I was packing my bags and going to Goma. I did not intend to die in Zaire.

Chapter 11

I honestly don't remember that evening. I barely recall packing my things. There were things we had to arrange: payment for Didas, leaving our warehouse key with someone from the tea plantation, explaining our departure to the rebel commander, locking up the house, promising the hospital staff that we would return. Rink and I had little to say. I think we were both pretty shaken by the incident, and all I really wanted to do was to go home, and as quickly as possible. Unfortunately, that was not to be.

The next morning, we stopped by the hospital in Mweso to speak with Valentine, the nurse. We ran into a group of Hutu combatants in front of the hospital. They were furious with MSF because Radio France had made a broadcast about the massacre at Mokoto, claiming the Hutus were responsible. The information had been released by the MSF-Belgium section working in Kinshasa. We had, of course, informed the other sections about what had happened in Mokoto, but our own section would not issue any information until we were safely out of the field.

The group in front of us didn't deny their responsibility for the massacre, they just didn't like hearing it on the radio. Rink went out to speak with them. I was so irate I likely would have gotten us both killed if I had said a word. As it was, Rink, who rarely gets angry, really lost his temper with them. He started yelling at them, basically accused them of murder, and refused to leave them medical supplies, correctly assuming that they had enough from what they had stolen in Mokoto. We left in a fury for Goma, and I sincerely hoped I'd never be returning to Mweso.

Rachel and Lisette were back in Goma by then, and the team was wonderfully supportive. Rachel, wisely, let us talk and kept the focus on possible solutions rather than the actual incidents. We joined in several staff meetings to discuss the issues, and the whole team was included in the decision-making process. There were no recriminations or reprimands about our unwise decision to travel that day to Birambizo. Nobody could have foreseen what would happen, but we all knew that it had been a very close shave.

The whole team went out for dinner that night, mostly to be with us and to offer support. Eventually, we even danced a while at No-No's, but my heart wasn't in it. Rink kept hearing machetes falling and guns firing with every beat of the music, not exactly what you could call a relaxing evening out.

As much as I wanted to leave, Rachel was wise enough to make us stay. She put us back to work almost immediately, treating us as experienced and professional expats with a job to do. It was empathy, not sympathy, that we were given. So work we did.

Our chief concern was the extremely precarious situation for the rest of the 5,000 or so Tutsis still in Masisi. It was clear from the massacre at Mokoto that they were no longer safe in Zaire. A big public relations push was undertaken, including radio, television and news reporters either calling or arriving for information about the massacre. A press release was issued by MSF encouraging the other UN bodies to assist the Tutsis in relocating to a more secure area. Eventually, MSF helped fund independent local people who agreed to drive the Tutsis, under military escort, to Rwanda. The other aid agencies were not happy with the press statements, fearing retaliation against their own programs, but the whole team supported Rachel in this decision.

The Rwandan authorities, however, initially refused to accept the

Tutsis into the country. And when they were finally permitted to cross the border, they were forced to remain within fifty metres of it, which goes against all international rules for refugees. The humanitarian agencies in Rwanda were outraged at this decision, and none of them wanted to accept responsibility for the Tutsi refugees unless they would be treated fairly. The Rwandan authorities would not back down, and finally a British agency that I'd never heard of, MERLIN (Medical Emergency Relief International) agreed to set up a camp and assume care of the new refugees. UNHCR also agreed to register the incoming Tutsis officially, so that they could receive the benefits of refugee status.

The Tutsis didn't care *where* they ended up, as long as they were alive at the end of their journey. Within weeks, most of the 5,000 Tutsis who desperately wanted to leave Zaire arrived in the Petite Barriere camp, just across the border in Gisenyi, Rwanda.

Our next step was to check up on the post-operative recovery of the survivors in Kichanga. We took two or three trips to Kichanga, separately and together, first to follow up on the surgical cases and then to carry out a vaccination campaign. The journeys to Kichanga did nothing to ease the tension I'd been under since the massacre. I was anxious the entire time, constantly waiting for the next security incident. Some seventeen surgeries had been performed by the time we arrived. The first person to be operated on was our man with half a head. He was also on the first truck out of the country, and later showed up in *Time* magazine, in a well-written article about the situation in Masisi. He became quite famous, our survivor.

After we'd checked on all the surgical cases, Rink and I were asked to stay for a few days and set up a measles vaccination campaign, since there was such an increased number of new arrivals. We planned the event in the course of a day and set up a team of national MSF staff to assist us. Within four days, 4,000 children under the age of five had been vaccinated. It was nice, for once, to carry out a logistical project that went exactly according to the books. We had no trouble, and our estimates were spot-on.

And so the work went on. In the meantime, we never really discussed Mokoto or the following incident in Birambizo. Everything seemed fine on the surface. I hadn't lost my appetite, I still managed to get my work done without much trouble. My only problem was that

I couldn't sleep. For the next couple of weeks, until I left Zaire, I slept no more than three or four hours per night. Either I couldn't fall asleep until dawn, or I woke with bad dreams at all hours of the night.

All my dreams had elements of violence and destruction. Some I recall clearly. In one, an army in tanks and Jeeps, fully armed, was driving across the parking lot of a shopping mall towards my parent's house. In another, I was trapped in a hospital that was under fire, and I knew the only way to safety was across an open field but that I would never make it across alive. The war had invaded my nights, and there seemed to be no escape.

Rachel asked us to try to return to ZTM to collect the things we had left behind, including some of our personal things and some communication equipment. She left the decision to us, but it was not an easy one to make. I was desperate not to drive down that road again, and at one point, we even considered landing a helicopter at the plantation. However, on the last day of the vaccination campaign in Kichanga, we drove back to Mweso. One more thing that had to be done.

Rink seemed pretty relaxed. I guess he thought that the worst was over, and that nothing bad would happen to us again. I dreaded the entire trip, terrified that something might happen again, which I really did not know if I could handle. I felt as if I was walking on the edge, and I didn't think I could endure even one more incident. I just wanted to go home. I was tired of pretending everything was fine. Frankly, I was sick and tired of the whole thing — the violence, the death, the destruction, the aggression, all of it. I wanted that trip to be the last, and then I wanted to leave. Our mission was nearly over anyway, and all I wanted was a ticket out of there. I just didn't *feel* like managing any more.

Luckily we made it to Mweso without incident, except for the fact that two bridges had been destroyed, which we had to repair by hand. The people seemed quite pleased to see us; I don't think they'd expected us back. We delivered money that Marc had sent with us for the office of the plantation, closed down the house and told everybody that we were finished and a new team would be arriving soon. We spoke with the nurses at the hospital; with Erasto, the combatant leader; and with the ZTM clinic staff, who agreed to handle the warehouse keys until the new team arrived. We made it clear that unless the security situation improved, MSF could not continue to work in the area. We packed the last of our things and returned to Goma that day. Again, I swore it would be my last time on that road. Fate would prove me wrong, but that's another story.

A new team of two French people had arrived to replace us. We gave them a verbal handover, and I flatly refused to travel with them back to Mweso, not even for a day. I felt more and more that I had reached my limit. I hadn't been sleeping properly for weeks, and even the valium Roy prescribed didn't seem to help. I was beyond tired, past exhausted, and heading for a nervous breakdown. By the first week in June, we had our tickets in hand and, thank God, we were going home. Then, as usual, just one more thing went wrong.

There had been some skirmishes around Rutshuru, in which several soldiers had been killed. On the day of their funerals in Goma, the rest of the battalion arrived, angry and looking for revenge. As so often happens in these cases, things blew up rather quickly. Within a couple of days, the soldiers had looted shops, burned stores, stolen the vehicles of aid workers and set about generally terrorizing the town. Of course the airport was taken over and closed down, so the agencies were basically trapped in their homes. Nobody was able to travel, all projects were put on hold, and we were stuck. Just when I thought it couldn't get any worse!

For a few days, we were all glued to the radios, listening to the UN and NGO reports informing us about the most recent incidents. Vehicles were stolen, national staff were harrassed, and travelling anywhere was extremely risky. The situation strongly resembled my first evacuation in Liberia. Sure enough, the decision was made that all non-essential staff would evacuate at the first chance. Rink and I, our assignment over, would take the opportunity to leave for good. So we waited, none too patiently, for a lull in the fighting.

When the chance came, we grabbed it. As the airport was out of the question, two landcruisers full of MSF expats drove to the border crossing between Zaire and Rwanda. Come hell or high water, I was getting out of Zaire.

At first, we were refused permission to cross the border. I, however, was a woman on the edge, and I was *leaving*. It didn't really matter too much whether they gave me permission or not; I was getting out that day. I think Rink must have seen how close I was to losing my patience, and he didn't waste too much time in negotiations. A quick bribe of ten dollars, a thorough search by the border patrol, and we were on our way to Gisenyi. Once across the border, we continued on to Ruhengeri, where another MSF-Holland team was working. Fouad, a friend from Burundi, was working there, and we spent the night with him and his crew.

The next day, the rest of the team stayed behind, waiting for the signal to return to Goma, which would come the following day. Rink and I were driven to Kigali, the capital, where the rest of the MSF-Holland team was working. They had arranged a flight out for us from Kigali to Nairobi. We had lunch with the team, and then finally, *finally*, they drove us to the airport.

When I had begun that mission, I could not have imagined evacuating Zaire via Rwanda. It seemed so ironic that even with the genocide there, which was partly the cause of all the trouble in Zaire, it would end up being the safest country through which we could leave.

With enormous relief, we eventually arrived in Nairobi. Tom was there to meet us. At last, I thought, the nightmare was over, and Rink and I could finally go home. But once again, there was yet *another* little problem.

When Rink had arrived in Burundi (had it really been nine months ago?) he had flown with Sabena Airlines. When I went there in December, I came in on KLM. Tom could change our flight plans, but not the airlines. I would have to fly to the Netherlands alone, and Rink wouldn't be able to catch the Sabena flight until the next day.

I was completely devastated. By now it was pretty clear that we were both suffering a little post-traumatic stress syndrome. I couldn't bear the thought of being alone. I didn't even want to go to Rink's house by myself, not even for a single night. He phoned Maaike, who agreed immediately to collect me at the train station and put me up for a night. I didn't intend to face the office in Amsterdam just yet.

The arrangements completed, Rink and Tom prepared to leave the airport. I reassured Rink that I'd be fine and I'd see him the next day. So off they went. And then I decided to have my nervous breakdown, right there in the Nairobi airport. What the hell, I deserved it. I cried non-stop for about four hours. My fellow travellers were quite understanding.

A kind old gentleman brought me coffee and assured me that all would be well. Then I boarded the plane and flew to Amsterdam.

It was an overnight flight, but of course I never slept. I was immensely relieved when we were flying over Europe, and I knew I was finally out of Africa. When I arrived in Amsterdam, I took the first train to Middelburg. Maaike met me at the station. The minute she asked me how the trip was, I started crying again. She basically just fed me and put me to bed. For the first time in what seemed like months, I slept straight through for more than twelve hours. I never dreamed at all.

Chapter 12 - A Long Summer

I told Maaike we'd nearly been killed, but I didn't bother with a lot of other shit. I knew by then that there was no point. Rink arrived, we went to his house, and we might have been on different planets for the distance between us. He insisted on defending our actions in Zaire and refused to recognize how very close we'd come to being killed. For him, we were alive, and the experience was over. His lack of emotional response led me to believe that he didn't really understand what I was going through. I was pretty much alone in dealing with my pain, and I wasn't even home with family or friends or anyone who could help me. It was a miserable summer.

MSF, however, was terrific. We went to Amsterdam several times for debriefings. Wouter, our desk manager for both Burundi and Zaire, was very understanding and took us out for dinner, and for a change I felt we were being taken care of.

We ended up seeing a counsellor a few times that summer, and I'd like to say she was a great help, but in fact, we ended up sorting most of our problems out ourselves. She did help Rink and me face issues of our relationship that we needed to work on. Rink realized that his interference with my work was destructive, not helpful, and that there were more positive ways to give and accept criticism. He learned to have more trust in me. I recognized that Rink's lack of emotional response was his way of dealing with things, that it wasn't personal, or directed at me. We both learned to deal with the fact that no matter what not-so-normal feelings we had, they were over some pretty not-so-normal circumstances. We were 'allowed' to feel that way. Which was good to know, because after an experience like that, there were a few times when you start thinking either you're cursed with bad luck or are times you've just had some *really* bad days.

We did a lot of public relations work for MSF that summer. Rink was on the radio and television and in the national paper, *de Volkskrant*. We wrote an article for *Ins and Outs*, the internal magazine for MSF expats, all about advocacy issues surrounding our response to the massacre in Mokoto. The power of the press took on a whole new meaning, and I learned much more about how to deal with the media — what to say, how to say it and what *not* to say. There is always a sort of love-hate relationship between aid agencies and the press. We need them for the PR that brings in support — meaning donations and funding. We also need a venue for expounding on issues like advocacy and human rights. However, the press can also use relief workers for nothing more than a good story, and the purpose of our work can be ignored or lost in the outcome.

Some of the reporters I had contact with were great, very knowledgeable and experienced. Others came racing in without a clue about the crisis situations they were ostensibly reporting on. Without taking time to find out how things worked, they went about getting 'the story', sometimes putting the months of work we'd put into establishing a good program at risk. I had more than one experience with reporters in Bosnia and Zaire who, albeit inadvertently, put agencies at risk by not following the guidelines set out for them by their host agency and/or the government bodies. Aid workers and the media maintain a necessary but cautious relationship.

When the initial weeks were over, we settled down to a long, hard summer. Rink and I saw friends, visited family. We had a social life. We renovated the house. We got on with our lives. But there remained for a long time a distance between us. I felt hurt somehow. I didn't exactly lose my faith, but it took a serious battering that summer.

As a Christian, I had always believed in the intrinsic goodness of man. Now I believed that men were only as good as circumstances allowed them to be. Change those circumstances, take away all the trappings of civilization that we take for granted, and people become unpredictable. It was not that I didn't still hope for the best, I just no longer expected to find it. I had no illusions about the line between good and evil, right and wrong. There were no lines. The world was neither fair nor equal, and sometimes you were no more rewarded for the good you did than punished for the bad. Justice was something for the rich, a fleeting notion that passed as soon as the headlines changed.

Something cold and hard and far more realistic than a simple faith in the basic goodness of man grew in me that summer. As one friend put it, we had become members of the club: an exclusive club, restricted to those who had gone through something too horrible for most people to fathom. I knew a couple of colleagues, a few missionaries, some UN guys in Bosnia, a journalist or two and a few thousand refugees who were members of the club. They came from all nations, with a thousand different stories and the same look in their eyes. Sometimes we recognized each other. We all had our stories, we all cried out to be heard, and we went largely unnoticed by a world that didn't seem to want to listen. Mostly we learned that it was best not to tell all that we knew. We learned to keep silent, to change the subject quickly, to stick to socially acceptable stories, the ones that made people laugh and smile. Dinner-table stories. But the real truths we kept in our hearts, and kept to ourselves.

Rink and I had changed, and people noticed it. It bothered me that certain people looked upon us as some kind of heroes; some of Rink's family even seemed intimidated by me. I eventually stopped expecting most people to understand, and I began to keep to myself. I stopped laughing at many of the things I'd once found amusing. And I stopped crying almost altogether.

Some people thought that we should quit the business, and I could appreciate their point. It wasn't until the end of the summer that I dared even think about returning to the field. I simply didn't want to risk my life in some country where the people didn't want me there in the first place, and where no matter what we did, we knew it wouldn't last.

Rebecca, my dear friend from Bosnia, took me with her to the Provence region of France. I needed that holiday desperately. The Mediterranean coast was beautiful, so peaceful and gentle. I could finally relax and just enjoy the simple things: good food, good wine, a sunset, a hotel with a pool, an old Roman town, fresh strawberries.

One day in Provence we went to a Benedictine monastery. I was uneasy, not having been in a monastery since Mokoto. Rebecca knew what I was feeling, having had her own nightmare with MSF. She was in Rwanda the day the massacres started in '94. She'd been trapped in the MSF house while the neighbours around them were slaughtered. She and her colleagues had managed to climb the fence and save a small, badly wounded child, but they still felt helpless amid the killing. Somehow, they had survived.

Without a lot of words, Rebecca gave me precious understanding and support. We decided to stay for the evening service.

The robed monks walked up the aisle, stately and singing, and it was more beautiful than I could believe. I kept thinking, "This is how it was in Mokoto, this is how it must have been before." I left the monastery in tears. I could imagine that Mokoto had been beautiful, and that it had served the community for a long time with grace, love and pleasure. I was reassured by knowing that the monks were still alive, and they would go on. Only the monastery itself had been destroyed.

I left Mokoto behind that night. I'd have my own memories to deal with every year in April, but at least I started sleeping better at nights, although insomnia became a pretty regular companion of mine from that summer on.

Mac, a dear friend I had met in the Toronto office, who had been a regular correspondent of mine since Bosnia, wrote a beautiful poem about Mokoto. I felt then that at least some people had been listening, some people had heard and understood. I was glad to know I still had friends who dared to listen, with whom I could share more than the dinner-table stories.

And slowly, over the summer, Rink and I found our way back to each other. We talked, we learned to trust each other again, and we managed to stay in love. In fact, by the end of the summer, we knew we didn't want to risk our lives with anybody else. Nothing like a death-defying experience to bond two people together. We were going to Canada in August, and we decided to get married there.

CANADA

We told nobody about our plans to marry, mostly because it was a very last-minute decision. With everything that had happened in Zaire, we had put our plans on hold. Now I decided that I didn't want to get married in Holland, because it would have taken too long to get my paperwork organized. All Rink needed in Canada was his passport and twenty-four hours' notice.

So we called my sister-in-law, Judy, and she made arrangements for a family barbecue on the evening of August 9. As per our usual luck, we were almost late for our own wedding.

We flew to Toronto first to visit friends and make an appearance in the MSF-Canada office. I ended up doing a newspaper article for the *Globe and Mail*, and we spent a couple days with Sherri, our friend from the Bosnia project. She was trying to sell her old car, fondly nicknamed 'the red slut'. Sherri hadn't found a buyer and agreed to let us use her car to travel around for a couple months. She couldn't vouch for its condition, but we weren't that fussy. We also spent some time with Mac and had a wonderful reunion.

We left Toronto, and after about four hours, the car broke down. Fortunately, a fellow traveller saw us and helped us get to his father's garage, which was just a few miles back. But the part we needed was in the next big town — a mere 100 kilometres away. We waited for several hours until the necessary part was purchased and in place, and with gratitude, we headed for Winnipeg. Being me, I figured we could manage a couple thousand kilometres in two days, so we hadn't left much leeway for errors. We ended up sleeping in a truck stop for a few hours and breaking the speed limit to get to Winnipeg in time.

We arrived (just before closing time) at the wedding shop, where we filled in the necessary forms and paid the fees. We then had twenty-four hours to wait before the wedding. Timing is everything.

The next day we drove around town while I finished running a bunch of errands. We arrived at my brother's house just before the Justice of Peace showed up. My sister-in-law, who never could keep a secret, pulled this one off beautifully. My parents and siblings were taken completely by surprise, to say the least, but the ceremony was lovely, and the evening was wonderful. The spontaneity of it all made the evening that much more special and memorable. No white gowns and grand ceremonies for us. A formal wedding wouldn't have suited us, and we wouldn't have done it any differently. I had Rink, and my family, and that was all I wanted.

We had ordered our wedding rings in Vlissingen, but they hadn't been ready when we were about to leave for Canada, so Rink made us two braided copper rings the night before we left. Total time: about ten minutes. Total cost: about ten cents! After all, a couple should have rings to exchange on their wedding day. At first, I think everyone believed that they were our real wedding rings, but they were too polite to say anything. Maybe they thought it was some strange Dutch custom, or that we'd become unbelievably frugal while in the field.

And with the wedding and all the excitement of being home again, nobody asked very much about Zaire. There was a big Olson family reunion within a few days of our arrival, and once again, the news of our recent wedding superseded any questions about our recent mission. It was just one more mission with MSF, and it was finished.

For our honeymoon, Rink and I took the red slut to the west coast to visit the Rocky Mountains. We had a wonderful trip together, and our time was up too soon. I packed five boxes of my most important worldly possessions, sold most of my things, returned the car to Toronto and prepared to move to Europe.

First, however, we had several discussions about our future with MSF. For Rink, this was the first job he'd had that he felt he was perfect for. He wanted it to be his career. I'd been a nurse for ten years before I'd joined MSF, and I was still ambivalent about returning to the field. Nursing was my career, MSF was just a job. The situation in Zaire had been just about as far as I wanted to go, and I was unwilling to push my luck again. I refused, point blank, to go back into war zones. So I said, and so I honestly believed at the time. But just when you think you've made your plans, God laughs.

MERLIN

Back in Europe, I signed up for a course that MSF offered in Bordeaux, France, called Populations in Precarious Situations (PSP). Rink went home alone, and I left Toronto for Lacanau, a seaside town on the coast of Bordeaux, for a two-week course designed to teach epidemiology and set-up for emergencies. The course was very intense but excellent. A lot of role-playing and decision-making skills were taught, as well as a great deal about the collection of data in emergencies and how crucial this data is as a monitoring tool.

After the course, I returned to Vlissingen, and to my husband, and we sat down to make some decisions. I did miss the field work, but not as much as Rink did. I missed the drama, the excitement, the challenge, the adventure, the passion, the involvement, the risks. I missed it all. But I was concerned about going back. I was nervous about how I would react now in security situations, how I would behave and if I still had 'it'.

'It' is the belief you have, you must have, to do this work. It is the feeling that nothing *really* bad will ever happen to you, and that you will be able to deal with whatever happens, that you will be able to talk your way out of it, and that in the end, it will all be okay. You must have 'it', or you would never go in to the countries that people are running out of, and you would never take such risks to stay and help those who remain. 'It' is the sincere belief that what you are doing is necessary and valuable and therefore worth fighting for, worth arguing over, worth taking risks for. If you don't have that passion, that certainty in your heart and soul, you cannot do this work.

I didn't know if I still had it, but I didn't want to believe that I didn't. If I was to quit the aid business, I wanted it to be on my terms and not because some soldiers in Zaire had given me a hard time. In the end, we decided to return on the condition that we would only accept a mission where we could be together, and preferably in a less dangerous scenario.

Alas, MSF had nothing to offer us at the moment. I believe one of the problems was that Rink had received an evaluation after Zaire that reflected too strongly the problems he'd had in Burundi and not enough on the excellent work he'd done in Zaire. His refusal to sign his evaluation in Burundi was not exactly a point in his favour. Also, I think that since we'd been quite traumatized in Zaire, some people were naturally concerned about whether or not we were ready for the field yet.

So instead, we ended up applying with the British agency MERLIN, which we had first encountered in Rwanda. They were the ones who accepted the 5,000 Tutsis who fled Zaire after the Mokoto massacre. We went to London for a couple of interviews and were accepted as part of their emergency assessment team. Shortly thereafter, we were offered positions with MSF, but we decided to stay with MERLIN for a year and try something new.

MERLIN was organized very much along the lines of MSF, as an emergency medical response agency. It was started by ex-MSF members and was only about three years old, still new and struggling. There were both advantages and disadvantages to working with a young agency. Many of the people had little field experience, and because they didn't have much money of their own, they were very dependent on the donors, meaning they couldn't really start up new projects until they had money in the bank from their sponsors. This made them less independent than an established agency like MSF.

Rink and I were practically the first non-UK members of their emergency assessment team, and they hadn't prepared for foreigners to be in their program. We had trouble finding accommodations, getting visas, making flight arrangements, arranging a per diem for the time we'd have to stay in London, et cetera. Money was a big issue for them, and they were far more strict about payments and financial matters than MSF had been. With MSF, we hadn't worried too much about the pennies, but with MERLIN, we had to consider carefully how we were spending their money.

Still, their enthusiasm was nice to see. MSF was going through some serious changes, and a great many issues were being discussed at the time we joined MERLIN. The president of MSF, Jacques de Milliano, resigned, as did many of the experienced staff. The face of humanitarian aid was changing, and those changes caused upheavals and anxiety for a lot of people at MSF. Whole departments were eliminated and other new ones were implemented. The projects became demand-driven, giving more decision-making power to the people in the field but eliminating many jobs along the way. People were distressed and anxious about their positions, and the tension got higher as the motivation decreased.

For that reason as well as many others, I was glad to be a part of MERLIN. They weren't so well-established yet that they couldn't be flexible, and they were appreciative of the experience and knowledge we brought with us.

Our task would be to fly to any country where there was a population in need due to either natural or man-made disasters, such as earthquakes, war or floods. We would then determine whether or not there was a need for MERLIN to intervene. We'd take a few weeks to do a complete assessment — medical needs, political background, economic situation, security issues, costs, staff, housing and financial needs — then decide what sort of intervention was required. Then we would design a program for MERLIN and make a proposal that included the goals and objectives of the program, the time schedule, the funding required and about a thousand other details. This proposal would be sent to all the relevant donors in the hopes that one would eventually fund MERLIN to begin their project.

It was a challenging job, one that required me to use my accumulated knowledge from both my field experience and my numerous courses. Rink and I were both enthusiastic about taking on a more meaningful and demanding role in the aid business, and somehow with MERLIN we really clicked. All our past arguments and discussions in Bosnia and Africa came together to make us a well-organized and professional team. There was no hint of competition, and we worked extremely well together. We were fast, efficient, and we knew exactly how the other would react and behave. Rink did his logistical assessment and I did my medical one, and though we separated some tasks, we did most of it together. We seemed to have found our niche at last.

Initially, we were expecting to go to Liberia, which at that point was in its post-war, pre-peace stage, so there was a need for more intervention in the health field. Unlike MSF, MERLIN stuck primarily to health needs and stayed away from big logistical programs or feeding centres. If the need was there, they would address it, of course, but they preferred to stick to basic primary health care programs.

However, Liberia was not to be, because that autumn all hell broke loose in Zaire.

THE GREAT LAKES, AGAIN...
Chapter 1

As everyone had predicted, civil war broke out in Zaire that autumn. Laurent Kabila started the conflict in Masisi, determined to overthrow President Mobutu on his march west to Kinshasa. All of the aid agencies had evacuated, many having been trapped in their homes as fighting erupted in Goma. In the end, the last of them drove in a convoy of about forty vehicles to Gisenyi. Goma was then taken by Kabila's men, and most of the homes and offices of the aid agencies were looted and destroyed. The talking parrot, who used to belong to Ed and Didi, however, showed up later in an MSF-France house in Gisenyi.

Trapped between Kabila's rebels and the Zairean army, the Rwandan refugees in the camps had little choice. They could be killed by either side of the warring factions, they could be pushed further in-country by the advancing army, or they could return to Rwanda. Terrified by the prospect of returning, many fled ahead of the advancing army, hiding out in the bush in Zaire. Some were used as hostages or shields, and thousands were killed along the way. The rest returned to Rwanda.

After two years, the largest refugee camps in the world emptied almost overnight. With no agencies to witness the atrocities, hundreds of the people were killed. The rest took to the roads and walked home. Over 500,000 people returned to their country, unwanted and unwelcome. Many had fled to the bush first and had to walk great distances around the advancing army. Some were badly injured along the way, and many walked for weeks to find safety.

MERLIN had a team working in the hospital in Gisenyi, and at Petite Barriere, the camp that had housed the Mokoto Tutsis. Their little health centre was overrun by thousands of refugees returning home. The most seriously injured cases were transferred to the hospital, where a MERLIN surgeon was operating.

Rink and I watched the news every night and we couldn't stand it anymore. As much as I dreaded returning to the area, I couldn't stand to see what was happening there. We finally called up MERLIN and offered our services for Rwanda or Zaire. We knew the area, the people, we spoke French, and we just couldn't refuse to go back if they needed us. They did. Around the second week of November, we flew to Kigali, Rwanda.

The flight was interesting. We made a stop in Asmera, Eritrea, and the passengers were instructed to disembark due to a 'slight problem with the hydraulic system'. As we left the plane, we noticed a huge puddle of fluid beneath the wings. Sure enough, a group of men in coveralls appeared with tool boxes, and we watched the repairs from inside the terminal. Nothing seemed to be effective until one large man took out his hammer and started pounding away underneath the plane. Whatever he did, it finally worked. I'd never seen a plane repaired with a hammer before, and since they didn't replace the fluid that had leaked, I was more than a little reluctant to get back on the plane. However, we survived the next leg of the trip and landed safely in Kigali.

I swore, *I swore* that I would never return to the Great Lakes region, but there I was, getting off the plane and wondering what the hell I was doing back.

We drove from Kigali to Gisenyi, and though the largest mass of returnees had passed by then, there were still thousands and thousands of people on the road heading for the capital. It was an astonishing sight. They walked in a strange silence, hardly speaking; the only sound was that of feet slapping the pavement.

But it was a sad moment. These refugees were returning to a country that was deeply scarred by genocide. They were not wanted, and there would be no forgiveness or understanding for them. They were looked upon as murderers, and they would be subject to retaliation. It was unlikely that the amorphous 'international community' could or would protect them. None of the agencies were even allowed to set up stations along the route. The Rwandan authorities, meaning the Tutsis, refused to allow the returnees to stop along the way. They were to be returned to their communities as quickly as possible. One look at their tired faces, and it was clear that they were anything but glad to be going home.

Chapter 2

We arrived in Gisenyi to an exhausted team, who had been working non-stop for the last few weeks. Their supplies were depleted, and new ones hadn't yet arrived. For a team of fifteen, only one computer was working. The surgeon had completed dozens of operations on some pretty badly wounded people, and those recovering overflowed the hospital wards and were set up in four or five big tents outside the main buildings.

Next door in Zaire, a handful of agencies were slowly being allowed back into the country. One of the seven agencies given permission to return was MERLIN. MSF was also back in Goma, coordinating the medical care. Rink went to Goma with another logistician and a nurse, Nick and Manjit. I stayed in Gisenyi to help out.

Alison, the medical coordinator, asked me to help out in the hospital with the post-op patients. My first impression was rather negative. The Tutsi nurses had not been giving care to the Hutu patients. In fact, military personnel were taking regular tours through the hospital looking for war criminals in the mass of patients. It was not a pretty sight.

Dozens of post-op patients had not had their dressings changed for days. The nurses simply refused to care for them. I was shocked by this blatantly unprofessional behaviour. Usually, no matter where the country is or what the circumstances are, medical professionals honour their oath to care for patients regardless of race, religion, et cetera. However, in this case, that seemed too much to ask. I found a couple of MERLIN national staff, commandeered some supplies, and we spent about four hours doing dressing changes together on some of the worst war wounds I had ever seen: women, old men, unaccompanied children, young boys, all with terrible machete or gunshot wounds. One little six-year-old girl had a machete wound from her groin to her abdomen. Someone had literally tried to slice her in half. It was awful, worse than anything I had seen in Mokoto.

I found a young man to assist and hired him on the spot to start helping with feeding and washing patients. I continued for several days, despite complaints by the head nurse and the director of the hospital. I maintained that those patients had been operated on by a MERLIN surgeon and could therefore be cared for by MERLIN staff. I told the head nurse I could see how very busy her nurses were, and I insisted that we help out. She was furious to see a white woman actually doing nursing care on the patients she refused to assist, but in the end, I think I shamed her into accepting some responsibility for her patients. I continued until a MERLIN expat arrived to take over the hospital supervision.

Unfortunately, many of the MERLIN expat staff didn't speak French, which was a real handicap. Nevertheless, Dale came in with common sense and a good sense of humour, and I left the hospital certain that the patients would finally be looked after.

There were huge problems between the director of the hospital and MERLIN, for a lot of reasons, but I stayed out of it. The poor director had lost fifteen family members in the genocide, and I certainly hadn't the slightest clue what that could do to a person. He was an angry and bitter man, and his attitude made working in the hospital very difficult. He really gave the expats a hard time, to the point where some expat staff quit in frustration.

Next for me was tackling the pharmacy, completing an inventory and rearranging the warehouse to receive the new shipment. Again my experience in Bosnia served me well. In a couple of weeks, some order was made out of the chaos, but the team remained pretty stressed and unhappy. Management from the head office had arrived to implement some changes. Similar to the situation that had occurred in Burundi, positions were rearranged without the knowledge or agreement of the expat staff, which did nothing to bolster an already low morale. Eventually, things settled down, and the team went on with the work at hand, but the general feeling while I was there was not very positive.

One day, Rink returned from across the border with supplies. He was using the 'town' car, a nice European car with one useless feature: a computer program that enabled you to start the car with the push of a button on the keychain, even from inside a building. We were in the house for lunch when Rink started playing with the key chain. Without realizing it, he started the car. It was already in gear and about to drive itself over the ravine when I heard the guard yelling from outside. When I realized what Rink had done, I called for him to get outside and turn it off. He finally got the picture and, thank God, the guard had the presence of mind to put some big stones underneath the wheels to keep the stupid car from driving itself off a cliff. Still, it was a close call. We took Rink's key chain away from him.

Shortly after that incident, I was asked to join the team in Goma for a few days. MERLIN would not be starting a program there, choosing instead to go further in-country, but they assisted as an ambulance service, going up and down the road between Sake and Goma and collecting the survivors that were in the worst physical condition. MSF had set up a feeding centre and clinic in Goma, and it was to them that we delivered our patients.

I crossed the border into the new "Democratic Republic of Congo", and found the team established in temporary quarters in another agency's house. My first view of the empty Mugunga and Lac Vert camps along the road to Sake was unforgettable. I was astonished to see that road empty for the first time in years. Hundreds had been killed in the now-deserted camps, and the debris left behind by half a million fleeing people was horrendous. Another of MERLIN's functions in the area was supporting a local NGO by providing them with shovels, lime and body bags to start the messy but necessary process of collecting the bodies and burying the dead. It was a tragic sight.

One day, we heard rumours of refugees coming from, of all places, Mweso. The fighting had passed there, and we were told there were some survivors along the way. To my dismay, we drove off to investigate along the road to Kichanga, the road I vowed I would never travel again. You can never say never in this job.

We travelled with a couple of reporters from the *Times* and from Reuters. We never made it as far as Kichanga, but met enough people to be reassured that the survivors had already made it to Goma. The reporters went on without us and discovered a multitude of corpses where a temporary camp had been set up just outside Kichanga. Meanwhile, we headed back to Goma. On the way there, we ran into trouble again.

Rink and Nick were travelling in the landrover ahead of me. They saw something happening on the tarmac road, and heard people calling to them, so they drove ahead, with Manjit and me behind in a rented car.

Apparently, a couple of Italian journalists had gone ahead and taken pictures of the Mai-Mai after having been instructed not to do that. Their gear was confiscated, as was their car, and they were stuck at the side of the road negotiating with angry soldiers and praying for someone to arrive and help them out.

Nick went to their aid but was immediately confronted by a soldier who stole his money and threatened both him and Rink. By this time, I had instructed my driver to turn around, and we went further down the road to await the outcome. I was not at all happy leaving the landrover, but that's the policy. No point in two vehicles getting stolen or two teams becoming hostages. I waited, unable to receive a response on the handset. And waited and waited

Finally, Rink answered, and I saw their landrover turn back and head along the road towards me. After the theft, they were allowed to leave, journalists in tow. Same old story. We found one UN vehicle also on the road, and its driver urged us to hurry up, as there had been shooting at the Sake crossroads. Happy to oblige, we headed back to Goma. We almost ran over two grenades left on the road, but somehow all three vehicles managed to avoid being blown to bits on the way back.

The next day and the day after that, we travelled up and down the road collecting survivors. Once, we ended up with fifteen people in the car, including a very malnourished baby, and a very ill woman. All were delivered to the MSF clinic. We also left some supplies at the orphanage and in a couple of clinics around town.

I was pleased to run into some old MSF staff and glad to meet up with Kizito again. We also got to see Piet, from Burundi, in the MSF office in Goma, along with Lisette. But Goma had been thoroughly trashed and was just slowly coming back to life. The camps were finished, and an extraordinary part of the Great Lakes' troubled history was ending. A new chapter was beginning, but none of us felt that it would make much difference to the lives of the people in Zaire. Sadly, a year after Kabila took power, the only change was that his picture had replaced Mobutu's all over the land. The poverty, disease, despair and corruption hadn't changed a bit, and fresh fighting had erupted between government troops and rebel forces who now wanted Kabila out.

Nick stayed behind after we left and regaled us with another horror story after he returned to London. Apparently, he'd been doubting the figures produced by the 'death squad' that MERLIN was supporting, so he went with them one day to check things out. They came to a village in the forest, and he found out, sadly, that they hadn't been exaggerating the numbers of dead. Bodies were lying everywhere. They lifted up a latrine, and to his astonishment, amongst the shit and rotting bodies, there was a live *duck* down there. No joke, a real duck, still alive and quacking. Don't even ask me how they got him out, I don't want to know.

Later, Nick was walking out of the village, and the team started laughing at him, and pointing at his shoe. He looked down to see a *human finger* stuck to his sole. He asked for a shovel, dug a little grave, scraped the finger into it, sprinkled a little lime on it, covered it up, and made the sign of the cross over it. The team just smiled, Nick went home, and Zaire hung around in our nightmares for a long time to come.

ANGOLA
Chapter 1

After our few weeks in Gisenyi and Goma, we were able to return to Vlissingen. I was glad I'd had the chance to return. I knew I could still do this work, and I knew that I had faced my demons in Zaire. If I'd had my way, that would truly have been my final trip to the Great Lakes. I know a lot of people who never went back after one mission. The people of Rwanda are so badly wounded, so damaged, so traumatized, it will take generations for them to recover. One American described working there as 'living under a dark cloud'. She said that Rwanda was the devil's playground, and it sucked the positive energy and enthusiasm and hope right out of you. She might have been right. It was surely the most depressing place I've ever worked in. I was glad to go home.

Our next step was a real assessment mission with Isabel, a lovely red-headed Scottish woman with enormous energy and loads of experience. She, too, was a member of the club, having been beaten and nearly killed in a robbery of the MERLIN house in Chechnya. She was to be our guide in Angola.

She'd worked there earlier with CONCERN, another NGO, and went ahead of us to set things up. Rink and I soon discovered some of the drawbacks of working for a new agency. After we spent ages trying to get our own visas, arranging for photos and sorting out the details that we thought should have been left to the office staff, they screwed up our flight details twice. Not only did we barely have time to collect our visas, but we had to rush like mad to catch an evening flight that they had forgotten to tell us they had arranged! Even worse, after a lengthy flight, we discovered we had arrived without the money! Isabel had taken half the assessment money with her and, as per policy, we were to take the other half. The office insisted Isabel had it all. Not true. So there we were in Luanda, the most expensive city in Africa, with a couple thousand dollars — not nearly enough to cover our expenses.

Isabel was furious and eventually ended up resigning over what she deemed to be outrageous incompetence. We were none too pleased ourselves but started off with what we had.

MERLIN had been asked to do this assessment by the European Committee for Humanitarian Organizations (ECHO), one of the leading donors for humanitarian agencies. Bruno, their representative in Luanda, was to assist us in travel arrangements and background information. We would be looking at three places in one province, Cuanza Sul. Two of the towns were accessible by land and one other, Andulo, by air. For that we could try to get on the World Food Program flights that made regular drop-offs throughout the area. Andulo was accessible by land, but the road had just recently been de-mined, and the security situation in the area was not good. Most people working there travelled by air.

Isabel had found a place for us to stay, an apartment owned by Halo Trust, a British de-mining NGO. There were several de-mining agencies working on the terrible landmine problem in Angola, and Halo Trust was one of the biggest. They were out in the field or away for holidays and would allow us to stay for free for a couple weeks. It was a rather grubby two-bedroom flat on a very noisy street, but at least it was the right price.

I couldn't believe the price of things in Luanda! It was so expensive that all of the agencies ordered their food supplies from their homelands by the container and had them shipped out. Renting a car to drive around the city cost $60 U.S. per day. Travelling out of the country to the towns we wanted to assess cost us $300 per day. The entire city was in the hands of the mafia, and there was no negotiating these outrageous prices. It was clear our funds wouldn't last long. We urged MERLIN to send the rest in the diplomatic pouch of the Netherlands ambassador, who agreed to bring it in, but they sent a money transfer to a bank instead. Except that there was no cash available in the banks, which we tried to tell them. They sent it anyway, and it took us until after Christmas to get our hands on the money, by which time we had procured a loan from Halo Trust and were practically done with our assessment.

December 14, 1996:

Have run around meeting all the NGOs and authorities. I really don't like Luanda. It's sort of a giant urban slum. I guess twenty years of civil war will do that to a country. No nice terraces, no decent restaurants that don't cost a fortune. The one we go to every day gives us greasy chips and a piece of steak for $15 U.S. We hope to rent a 4x4 today so that we can leave tomorrow for the province of Cuanza Sul, to assess Gabela and Quibala. Gabela is in government hands, but Quibala is in UNITA (National Union for the Total Independence of Angola) territory. We will then fly to Andulo, the UNITA stronghold, with either the WFP plane or one arranged by Bruno.

Those are the three areas ECHO will fund a program in, but I get the feeling already that their funding will not be sufficient. I have never been in so expensive a city in Africa! I don't know how the people survive here. Thank God we have the Halo Trust apartment for free (even though sleeping is out of the question, because of the noise); otherwise we'd be finished.

The restaurant we go to is a joke. It's called 'The American Bar', and they keep giving us the menu to read, as if they actually have more than one or two things available. Why not just put the plates down when the food is ready? It's not like we ever get any variety.

When we completed the assessment of the city and had met all the relevant health officials, we headed for Cuanza Sul. We managed to rent a 4x4 to take us to Gabela, the first of the towns on our mission, about an eight-hour drive from Luanda. The roads had just recently been de-mined, so going off the road for any reason was out of the question; it was not the first time I envied the men because the world is their urinal. We ran into a couple of checkpoints, but they didn't give us too much trouble. As we got deeper into the country, the scenery became much more beautiful, green and lush, with rocky hills. The town itself was in pretty poor state, with little running water or electricity, and as in Luanda, the cost of everything in Gabela was enormous. We did an assessment in the hospital there and stayed the night with a local NGO. Luckily, the director spoke German, so Rink was able to communicate with him. Between the driver and the three of us, there were about five or six languages going around, but none of us spoke enough Portuguese to get by.

We also managed to see three or four health centres to complete our assessment. There was a huge need for some teaching for the health staff. Few of them had had any decent training, due to the years of civil war. There was clearly a lot that needed to be done and a definite need for a medical NGO that could offer proper supplies and rehabilitation of the centres. There had been thefts and robberies in the town, and we were told that we would be obliged to pay the local police for protection. How does one put that down in a diplomatic way when asking for funding? Under the heading 'bribes'?

After Gabela, we drove across the frontline to Quibala. This was UNITA territory, and it was in even worse shape than Gabela. UNITA was the faction under the control of Jonas Savimbi, who started the bloody fight against the government after Angola declared independence from the Portuguese in 1975. Support from South Africa, Cuba, Russia and the USA kept both sides going for decades. Finally in Lusaka, Zambia, in November of 1994, a peace accord was signed.

However, when we arrived, disarmament was going slowly, and the United Nations Angola Verification Mission (UNAVEM) forces were encountering numerous problems. The UNITA forces, including Savimbi, refused the government positions offered to them. Indeed, the two sides were anything but united. Disarmed UNITA soldiers flatly refused to become members of a unified government army. Many of the disarmed soldiers were quartered in temporary tent cities, receiving a little food, money and re-education, but all were unwilling to join a united army, and none of them truly prepared to stop fighting.

A quarter of the 12 million people of Angola were displaced or war-affected. Despite large reserves of oil and diamonds, Angola remained one of the ten poorest nations of the world. Peace on paper had a long way to go to become peace in reality.

On we went to Quibala. The bridge dividing the two areas had been blown up by an anti-tank mine. From the sight of the tank and most of the bridge in the river, the mine had obviously worked. We crossed at a temporary bridge further down.

One of the biggest problems with travelling and working in Angola is the incredible number of landmines, an estimated 12 to 20 million. In some areas, one quarter of the population was disabled and crippled by landmine accidents. There were very few safe roads or fields, and road travel of any kind was hazardous.

In Quibala, we drove directly to the airport. We were supposed to meet with Bruno from ECHO and fly together with him to Andulo. Alas, the airport, a ratty little strip totally surrounded by landmines and littered with thousands of shells from previous gunfights, was empty.

Isabel and I decided to wait at the landing strip while Rink went off with the driver to the UN base to see what he could find out. There we both sat on our silver medical kit, at the edge of a gravel runway, eating biscuits and waiting. There was neither a car nor a plane in sight. A ditch-digging UN machine drove past us to do some work at the end of the runway, and the look on the driver's face was absolutely hysterical. Two white women, no mode of transportation in sight, alone on an empty airstrip. He must have thought he was dreaming the whole thing. Issy and I had a good long laugh over that one.

Finally, Rink returned, and with no plane in sight, we headed off to do our own assessment. In UNITA territory, nothing gets done without permission of 'the party' — a very dictatorial approach. We had no freedom of movement and had to be introduced to the relevant members of the party before we were allowed a guided tour of the hospital. The UN people, though, were generous with their time and helped with all the introductions.

Structurally, the hospital was not in bad condition, but again, the staff was poorly trained and unpaid, and what little input there had been was insufficient. There was no running water to the hospital, but part of a water system was in place. Rink dared to walk to the water source on a narrow path through a heavily mined area. Isabel and I stayed behind and hoped he wouldn't do anything stupid, like trip or something.

We hadn't really completed the assessment as fully as we wished when Bruno arrived with the plane, but we flew off to Andulo and hoped to do more there.

Chapter 2

December 26, 1996:

Christmas in Angola. I'm finally over my four days of diarrhea. I still think it's the dysentery I caught in Rwanda that never cleared up properly. At any rate, I feel much better.

Last week's visit was stressful but good. The UNITA areas were bizarre. The 'party' rules, and nobody says a word against them. We arrived by plane in Andulo, and Bruno helped make the introductions to the party members. We had arrived late, so we spent the first night with Africare in their tent camp. Africare is doing the disarmament and re-education program for the ex-soldiers, but they aren't disarming all that fast, I guess. We each had our own little tent to sleep in, but conditions are pretty rough. Still, we spent an evening drinking whiskey with the Africare people and laughed the whole evening. Rink even managed (don't ask me how) to get me a UN Brazilian peacekeeper's cap for a birthday present.

The second day there, they took us to Chillesu, one of the saddest hospitals I've ever seen. It was in dismal shape: mud walls, dirt floor, no windows, an operating table with three-and-a-half legs — the half supported by stones. Yet it's the referral centre for the whole area, and the nursing care was surprisingly good, I think. Man, could these people use some help!

Rink got into a heavy discussion with one of the party members, fighting for a more independent program than the sort they would approve of. Still, it's going to be tough to do, as a 'big-brother-is-watching-you' feeling prevails.

We were able to catch the WFP flight back to Luanda before Christmas, but just barely. Rink and Tony, the Africare doctor, didn't get on the WFP manifest, and we thought they wouldn't be allowed on the plane. They had decided to take the road, which is pretty dangerous, but in the end, we all got on the plane; Rink and Tony were listed as cargo. Serves them right! The weather was pretty bad, and the plane was really skidding in the mud when it arrived. We thought it might not be able to leave at all, so I'm glad we all succeeded in getting out.

There is much to be done in Andulo, but it's hard to even know where to begin! There is no infrastructure, and the level of health education is dreadful. These people have a long, long way to go, and in UNITA territory it's twice as difficult, because we aren't permitted to choose or hire our own staff. We are obliged to use the people the 'party' gives us, which means lots of spies but probably not many good nurses in the bunch.

Luanda is such an unattractive city. It's loud, crowded, dirty, sprawling with ugly, rundown buildings, bad roads, beggars, only occasional water and electricity, and absolutely no systems that work. Next to the squalor you see all these mafia types with their Rolexes and Mercedes cars, their mobile phones in hand. Weird.

Anyway, we enjoyed Christmas afternoon on the beach, where Rink spent his time watching the smallest bikinis known to mankind parading about. At least one of us had a good time! We had a nice dinner together then, but tonight's was better. We had a real feast with CONCERN — turkey, dressing, mashed potatoes, Christmas pudding, the works! What a nice treat that was.

We also met up with Tony again. We had a drink together and met his sister, whom he lives with when he's in town. He's quite enamoured with Isabel and even managed to present her with a diamond. Not bad for a first date! Of course in Angola, there are a lot of diamonds floating around. Too bad few of the civilian population profit from them.

At long last, the money transfer has come through! Rink's looking for a 4x4 so we can go back to Quibala next week and finish the assessment. Isabel's already working on the proposal, but I suspect it will be an expensive undertaking. I doubt London will be able to find donors, and besides, Luanda is not exactly the sort of place I'd like to be working. We'll see. For now, it's too insecure to travel the roads. Holidays are always bad times, so we're stuck in town. In the meantime, we'll try to kill Erasto, the rat. He's living somewhere in this house and actually getting into the refrigerator and eating our food. We saw him shimmy up the TV antennae like a pro. Ugly creature!

January 6, 1997:

I've been working on the proposal all week. It's quite new for Rink and me, and there's so much information that has to be included. We haven't killed Erasto but have cleaned and closed off the refrigerator so he can't get into the food any more. We had a nice New Year's Eve. Back to the beach for the afternoon, bought lobster to cook for dinner, which was fantastic. Tony and his sister, Celia, brought us to this very expensive night club for dancing, and the next day we had dinner at Tony's house. He's a lovely man, and he really is quite smitten with

Isabel. However, she's about to break his heart, because we ought to be leaving soon.

We also heard the horrible news about the six International Red Cross staff members killed in Chechnya. Isabel knew some of them, and we are all devastated by the news. One was a Canadian nurse, and I believe another was Dutch, so this is a bit close to home. It's frightening to see how aid workers are becoming targets more and more often. Our flags and stickers used to protect us, but now they seem to attract some of these lunatics! This just after three others that were killed in Rwanda in November, right after Rink and I left. Christ, this is scary. Would somebody tell me again why I'm doing this?

At any rate, we got our vehicle and returned to Gabela and Quibala to complete the assessment. Spent one miserable night in a lousy hotel in Gabela being eaten alive by mosquitoes, all of us crabby and irritated.

In Quibala, the UNITA people are hopeless, worse than in Andulo. Total idiots assigned by the party as committee members for health, education and other programs, with absolutely no knowledge about their roles. Public health is a joke! We might be given a bit of freedom to move around but not much. We'll be assigned a house and given workers, so we can't even hire our own people. This could definitely be one of the most difficult, challenging places to work in, and MERLIN had better have some pretty strong-minded people in charge. I can foresee a lot of arguments between us and UNITA regarding an independent program, as UNITA is not very keen on the word independent.

We stayed at another quartering area for disarmament in Quibala, but this was completely different from Andulo. The whole group working there is quite mad! Not at all like they were in Andulo. They had no tents planned for us, refused to share their food and were generally not very welcoming. One of the commanders took a liking to Isabel but ended up being quite irritating and a bit threatening. She was so uncomfortable with his advances that Rink kept the handset on all night just in case we had to reach her. A very strange situation, and not very pleasant.

Anyhow, we finished what we had to do, and I think we're all pleased to be returning to Luanda. On the return trip, we had a close encounter with a group of military personnel. They tried to block the road, probably in hopes of stealing the vehicle, but they eventually waved us on without any problems.

We made it back to Luanda and finally met Paul from Halo Trust, whose home we had been squatting in for the previous few weeks. He was great fun and enjoyed telling us about the expected visit from Lady Di in the next week. He joked that he'd have to go blow up some mines with her, which we laughed about at the time. Later, after her tragic death, we saw him several times on television, when Diana's visit to Angola was shown worldwide. Who could have known it would be one of her last visits?

Rink and I now had some experience working with MERLIN and seeing how they operated. The incident with the money was only one example of things we saw that indicated their lack of professionalism and inexperience. I felt it was a shame that they should lose Isabel, who was such an experienced expat, over the incident of the money. But nobody in the office ever assumed responsibility for it, and none of them apologized.

Still, Rink and I were enjoying the experience of doing emergency assessments and planning and designing new programs. The challenge of the work was enough to make up for any shortcomings we may have noticed. Besides, Angola was a place to remember — our second mission as part of an emergency team.

Chapter 3

Upon our return, we presented our proposal and spent the next couple of weeks refusing to give in and accept what the agency considered a more reasonable cost structure. MERLIN, lacking any funding of their own, simply couldn't find a donor at the price we knew would be necessary. The cost of the program would amount to at least two million dollars and, when measured against the expected outcome, was more than MERLIN could manage. So there was no project in Angola, but plans were made for our next assessment. Rink and I would be heading for Liberia, and I was really looking forward to going back.

In the meantime, we returned to Vlissingen for a while. We had several visitors over the weeks; Rebecca and Paul from Bosnia and Piet and James from Burundi. It was only when we were with our friends from the field that we really felt we could be ourselves. We shared memories that we otherwise kept to ourselves, and the talk would go late into the night, full of laughter, stories, discussions, plans, ideas, disagreements, politics, economics, the present, the future, the past. When we were together, we felt alive, we felt a part of things that others did not share. We were with friends, and we loved them, and they were the only ones who understood. That was to become the pattern of our lives. We led one life that our regular friends and family saw and one that we saved for our friends from the field. We couldn't seem to get the two lives to merge.

In February, we returned to London in preparation for Liberia. We were also able to attend Isabel's farewell party. She had joined MSF and was on her way to Sarajevo to work on the project there. We spoke to new recruits at the London office on their 'induction night', where new people are welcomed. We gave a talk about our assessments, how they work, the reason and rationale for them, the methodology. The talk was well received and gave us a chance to become better acquainted with the MERLIN office staff and other expats. Then we started getting ready for Liberia.

BACK TO LIBERIA
Chapter 1

On February 10, 1997 — almost three years to the day from my arrival in Liberia for my first MSF mission — Rink and I flew out of London, heading for Sierra Leone, which would be our starting point for the Liberia assessment. MERLIN had a team working in Kenema, Sierra Leone, establishing feeding centres, health centres and a Lassa fever program. They would help us make flight arrangements to Monrovia and would be our contact people in case of trouble. Actually, it turned out to be the other way around, but that was yet to come.

I was happy to be returning to Liberia after all these years and hoped to see some old friends. I was also very curious to see how the peace process was actually coming along. Needless to say, I had my doubts, as did everyone, but I was delighted to be going back.

After I had evacuated Liberia in 1994, the situation had deteriorated dreadfully. It was more than a year later before aid agencies could begin returning to the Gbarnga area. That, too, didn't last. In 1995, a new peace accord was drawn up, bringing all factions into the transitional government. Still, hostilities escalated, with the ECOMOG troops unwilling or unable to intervene. An attack on Monrovia, the capital, on April 6, 1996, led to the deaths of some 1,500 people and the evacuation of 2,000 aid workers and foreign nationals.

Paul, our friend from Bosnia, had been one of the evacuees. He'd been more than happy to share his war stories with us, knowing we were on our way there. I couldn't help but remember his tale as we left London.

Following the enormous loss of vehicles and property by every agency, many were reluctant to return. Those aid organizations who did choose to return made a combined effort to provide aid in a rather new and innovative way.

Liberia was the first country I'd been in where humanitarian aid was carefully coordinated under a joint policy of operations (JPO). Every agency, new and old, had to agree to provide only limited and essential intervention, as stated in the contract. The idea was to coordinate all aid work and limit the risk of further property losses. This meant that nobody had brought in new vehicles, nobody was hiring new staff, and aid was limited to emergency care only. No long-term or developmental work was encouraged by the JPO.

The drawback to this plan was that Liberia was truly in a transitional phase. Elections were slated for the end of May, and many of the agencies were refusing to move to a more developmental phase of work until after they were held. Once bitten, twice shy, as the saying goes. Everyone was naturally afraid that the outcome of the election might be a return to civil war. MERLIN was arriving at a key period. The problem would be to devise a plan that fit in with the 'limited intervention' policy but would be adaptable to a more developmental approach if things went well with elections. Any program we established would have to begin with limited staff and new vehicles, and it would have to incorporate the plans and goals of a new government. I love a challenge.

At any rate, we had an easy start with our arrival in Freetown. I found the landing quite amusing. Our plane landed at Lungi airport, and we then had to catch a connecting flight by helicopter to the mainland. The helicopter was an old Russian machine that definitely had seen better days. It had no windows! But we arrived safely in Freetown and met some of the expat staff for the Sierra Leone project. They had a large house/office, and we quickly settled in.

We had a few days before we could catch our flight to Monrovia, so spent the next three days enjoying Freetown. The team took us to the most amazing beach, which I was told was called the 'Bounty' beach. After relaxing there, I had the chance to chat with a few of the agencies in Sierra Leone and some old friends, including Steve, a friend from the MSF-Toronto office who was the head of mission in Freetown. We got the names and numbers of some of the agencies in Liberia who could give us a hand getting started, and before we knew it, we were on our way.

Chapter 2

I'd only been in Monrovia once before, when I'd evacuated with Gerda, who was ill at the time. I didn't really know the town at all, so there were a few surprises this time.

For starters, it was a slight shock when we arrived at the airport to have our passports immediately confiscated. It turned out to be an easy procedure to get them back — we simply made the rounds of all the officials, got our stamps, and we were out — but not without about a dozen introductions.

We spent the first couple of nights at the Mamba Point Hotel, the only decent hotel in the city. We were quickly able to hire an old taxi and driver and started making our rounds. Before we knew it, the ACF team offered us the use of their apartment for the duration of our stay. It had housed two expats, both of whom were away, and the apartment hadn't been rented out yet. They even offered to let us retain the services of the cook and cleaner, a married couple who took very good care of us. ACF were very generous and wonderfully helpful, and we became good friends with all of their staff.

Within days, we had made the acquaintance of all the NGOs in town — ACF, MSF, SCF, Medecins du Monde (MDM), Tear Fund, Oxfam, International Rescue Committee (IRC), plus all of the UN agencies. The UN had a big role in Liberia, and there was a UN-HACO (United Nations Humanitarian Aid Coordination Office) that met regularly with all the aid agencies to coordinate who was doing what, where, when and why. We also met the US embassy staff and put our names on their NGO list, which got us into cheap movies at the embassy every Wednesday night, with popcorn. Besides, in case of another evacuation, it helped to have your name known.

After we'd done the NGO rounds, we met all the national health representatives, the Minister of Health (who used to work for MSF), the UNICEF representatives and numerous other significant people. There were a lot of names, a lot of meetings, and a lot of social events in the first couple of weeks. We got to know several restaurants, Kendeja beach, and the olympic-sized swimming pool at the Coconut

Plantation (a residence where several different NGOs lived). Of course, we also became regulars at Papa Johnson's 7-11, the 'Number One Watering Hole' in Monrovia.

I had a fantastic reunion at the MSF office with a lot of old friends from Gbarnga. To my surprise, none of them had forgotten me, and we spent some time reminiscing, while receiving plenty of requests for work. MSF had really scaled down its projects after the April 6 disaster, and many of their old staff members were losing their jobs. Finding suitable and well-trained workers would certainly not be a problem in Liberia.

Most of our travels around town were made with our less-than-trusty taxi, but for our planned field trips we'd need something better, a 4-wheel drive. Because of the JPO rules, very few of the agencies were using new vehicles. Most of them were well worn and prone to breaking down regularly. The only chance we had of finding a decent used 4x4 was in the car lots which, by European standards, were nothing more than scrap yards. Nevertheless, we made our rounds and tried to see what we could pick out, either to rent or buy. In the end, we borrowed a 4- wheel drive vehicle and a driver from the International Rescue Committee.

Having determined by this time what areas could use the input of a new medical program, we made our first field trip to the hospital in Buchanan.

Chapter 3

It was only a couple hours' drive to Buchanan, but it felt a little strange to me to be driving that far without any signs of a checkpoint. During the war, there had been dozens of them along the way. We crossed what had been the frontline, and there we could see the scars of the war, but we never encountered any trouble on our journey.

The hospital was partially rehabilitated and in pretty good condition, but we had been warned about the corruption within. Sure enough, many of the supplies that arrived ended up in one of the seventeen private pharmacies owned by hospital personnel. The only way we could realistically intervene would be to replace all the staff with people we could hire ourselves and trust, which was against both the JPO regulations and the wishes of the Ministry of Health (MOH). The next day, we returned to Monrovia, thinking of a second plan.

There were at least two other counties that required medical intervention, as none of the other agencies had ventured that far out of Monrovia yet. We planned two more field trips, to Nimba county in the northeast, and to Lofa county, far in the northwest.

In both of these areas, the UN had set up disarmament and rehabilitation programs for ex-fighters. Roads, bridges, schools and clinics were being rehabilitated by ex-fighters, who were paid a meagre salary for their services, and the goal was to keep them away from the still-strong influence of the combatant leaders.

There were a few scattered clinics being re-started by the MOH with the assistance of UNICEF, and MERLIN was encouraged to consider the rehabilitation and re-training of MOH staff in several clinics along the way. We were invited to stay with the UN people, and were heartily welcomed to set up a base near them, since there were no other agencies prepared to start upcountry yet.

We took a couple of weeks to complete our plans and see all the clinics and hospitals that needed our input. The roads were, as I recalled, not that great but manageable. The main problem was that the vehicle we were using was old and not in top condition, so we ended up having three flat tires between Lofa county and Monrovia. Fortunately, the last one occurred just as we arrived in the town of Gbarnga, so we were able to get it repaired at one of the tire shops.

Along the way, we were helped by the various NGOs. People assisted with radio contacts, places to stay, advice, suggestions, rooms, meals, vehicles and drivers. The assistance we received was invaluable and freely given. I was truly impressed with how the NGO community worked in Monrovia, and we couldn't have asked for better colleagues.

In the end, we devised a plan that fit in nicely with the JPO but could expand to incorporate the goals and objectives of the new government. It would be directed towards the primary health care sector, something MERLIN found ideal.

We planned to set up a central base in Monrovia and two secondary bases, one in each county where we would be working. Our first base would be in Voinjama, the provincial capital of Lofa, and the second in Gbarnga. We'd start rehabilitating and retraining MOH staff in each centre and would pay the staff already in the field a salary close to what the ministry was paying, so as not to undermine their programs. We'd use MOH people to assist in teaching and workshops and would use the EC-funded cost-recovery drug distribution system already in place in Monrovia. As in Zaire, there was a long-term cost-recovery drug distribution system in the early stages of development, which meant the clinics we supported could buy their own drugs from the National Drugs Service (NDS). Patients in our clinics were encouraged to pay for their drugs at a reasonable cost. The money was then used to purchase more drugs from NDS, with enough of a profit for each clinic to keep it operational. We would require new vehicles, because of the long distances and the road conditions, but would hire minimal staff and follow all the national health guidelines for training, which were also the WHO-recommended guidelines. We'd start with about six clinics in each county, laying the groundwork to increase our numbers to a total of eighteen or nineteen health centres.

It took about a month for us to complete our full assessment, and though it was a long, hard month, it was also one of our best assessments and a lot of fun for us both. There was a great social life in Monrovia, all the agencies seemed to get along fairly well, and there was little competition. There was rarely an evening that we were free, since there were constant invitations to the Holiday Inn for dancing, the 7-11 for drinks, and the various houses for dinners and parties. It was also a refreshing change that the Liberian nationals were a full part of that social life, and there wasn't the distance between the expats and the nationals that occurs in some areas.

We even arranged for funding for our program prior to leaving the country. It was a real bonus to be able to return to London with both a plan on paper and a willing donor. We spent about two weeks revising and refining our program, planning the budget and selling the idea to MERLIN. Eventually, it was settled, the draft was sent to various other donors, and the wait for approval began. In the meantime, we could finally return to Vlissingen and get some rest.

On March 19, we returned to Vlissingen. On March 24, we left again, this time for Albania. The problem with being part of an emergency assessment team is that you never get to choose your emergencies.

ALBANIA
Chapter 1

Albania is an unusual place. It used to be one of the most closed countries in the world. At one point, it had strong ties with China, and then later with Moscow, but from the end of the Second World War until the late 1980s, those ties were broken, and ties with the west were virtually non-existent. Slowly, Albania opened up to the rest of the world. In 1991, the first multi-party elections were held, and a massive influx of humanitarian aid followed. A market economy was introduced, and the lifestyle of the Albanian people changed dramatically. Then, as some real money began circulating in the economy, the opportunity for get-rich-quick pyramid schemes appeared and raised the hopes of Albanians that they could quickly achieve a lifestyle similar to their western European neighbours.

Alas, these pyramid schemes collapsed at the beginning of 1997, after many Albanians had lost their life savings over the course of a few months. Since the government had allowed the schemes to proliferate for years, the population held them largely responsible. Demonstrations began, followed by clashes with the police and the violence quickly escalated. Some of the most serious violence occurred in Vlorë, in the south of the country, where the largest investment schemes had been based. Gangs of people looted military depots, burned down police stations and government buildings, and assisted in the release of some 1,300 prisoners. To make matters worse, some government officials opened military caches themselves and distributed arms to the people!

Though President Sali Berisha refused to resign, the government quickly lost control over the situation. Due to Berisha's already poor reputation (a rather dubious record concerning unfair election proceedings in 1996 and the imprisonment of his chief political opponent for fraud), he was seen to be most at fault for the economic crisis.

When we arrived, some 200 people were officially reported as killed in the violence and some 12,000 had fled to Italy. Nearly a hundred more were killed when their boat sank after being rammed by the Italian navy, who were attempting to deny the refugees access to their country.

Many of the government-run services were still trying to work, in spite of the fact that none of the 1997 budgets had been approved, leaving them without funds at a precarious time. The civilian population had most of the weapons, many of the police and military had deserted and joined armed gangs around the region, and what was left of the government sent out an urgent request for UN intervention.

Some gangs had organized themselves in certain cities, running their own checkpoints. We eventually learned that much of the unrest and violence had ceased to be against the government and was now between rival gangs and mafia using the opportunity to strengthen their positions.

So we arrived to a large group of armed civilians milling about with their AK-47s and tanks and absolutely no idea how to use them. People were nervous and tense, but nobody seemed to be leading any actual rebellion. And not a single person we spoke to blamed anybody but the government for their financial troubles, though I doubt they were forced at gunpoint to invest in stupid schemes. I thought that what the country really needed was a couple of good accountants, but hey, you want an assessment, you'll get one.

Chapter 2

Before we left London, we got the name of a local NGO, Hamlet Trust, whose people would be kind enough to collect us at the airport and show us to our home for the next three weeks, Hotel Europa in Tirana, Albania.

We quickly met up with some of the other NGOs in the area and heard pretty much the same thing from all of them — Albania didn't need medical assistance, it needed financial support. Most of the hospitals were still functioning, and the infrastructure was really in pretty good condition. There were hundreds of local NGOs and several international ones throughout Albania, and there had been a lot of input over the last several years to improve and re-direct the health system.

We met the Minister of Health and several of his colleagues, and it became clear that the health system was struggling under the economic crisis, but that the basic structure was very much intact. Though some hospitals had been looted and some supplies taken, none were destroyed. Staff were still working, and most of the essential drugs that were needed in the immediate aftermath had been replaced.

Many of their drugs were produced in Tirana itself, though some of the supply routes to certain areas were still insecure. They had a very decentralized system, with each hospital receiving its own budget, buying its own supplies and paying its own staff.

They even had the National Social Institution, which reimbursed patients for medication that they had to buy in the pharmacies and paid monthly support to the unemployed and pensioned people. The people in other countries where we've worked should be so lucky! Compared to some places, this was a dream.

After a week or so, it was clear from the Minister of Health, from WHO, and from all the other agencies that the last thing Albania needed was more drugs. We contacted MERLIN and notified them that no shipment of emergency drugs was required. They had been standing by, ready to ship emergency medical supplies in, and they weren't that happy to hear that the situation didn't require any. We were instructed to keep looking for some way to assist the population in this less-than-dire 'emergency'. I still supported the accountant idea, but it didn't go over well.

By this time, we'd gotten to know our way around Tirana pretty well, not that there was much to see. Big ugly square buildings around a big, ugly central square, and about a thousand coffee shops in a couple of blocks. It was clear that these people had no clue about thriving in a free market economy. Anyone who had invested their money and managed to gain a little something from it had immediately reinvested everything in a coffee shop. There were little phone-booth-sized shops selling sweets and coffee and snacks everywhere in the city, as if they were waiting for thousands of tourists to start pouring in any minute. There were also a few new extravagant hotels, which were pretty much empty the entire time we were there, even with the influx of the media.

Having spoken with all the key people and agencies in Tirana, we decided it was time to head north and see for ourselves if all we'd heard was true. For that, our colleagues at Hamlet Trust couldn't help us.

We soon found ourselves a taxi driver, Jimmi, who spoke not a word of English but was happy to drive us to Shkodër for a reasonable fee, and a translator, Emin, who agreed to come along. We were fortunate to find two people willing to leave Tirana, because most of the people there were very paranoid and anxious about the current situation, so many refused to leave the city. Besides, CNN had ruined the market for drivers by agreeing to pay outrageous sums of money for a ride to Vlorë — something like a thousand dollars. This meant that unless you had your own car and driver, you could forget about doing an assessment there, as it was too much money for any aid agency to pay.

The north was a barren, rocky, not very scenic region. We spent the night in Shkodër, interviewing hospital directors and public health directors and viewing several hospitals and clinics along the way. We found that the 'emergency' was basically over. The police had restored some order, and the number of wounded had greatly decreased. The supplies had been sufficient for the emergency, and though they were out of some materials, they were expecting more from the central pharmacy, taking a line of credit to purchase what was needed with the approval of the MOH.

The wounded we saw were mostly accidental shootings, both adults and kids who had shot their hands, feet and faces because they were playing with guns or grenades that they didn't know how to use. There was an outrageous number of powder burns from the accidental discharge of weapons. Maybe they learned raiding the military stores hadn't been such a great idea after all.

At any rate, the need for emergency intervention, from a medical point of view, was slight. We did find some unusual problems in some places. For example, in one town they wanted to get credit from the bank, but the bank had been looted and the safe was lying out on the sidewalk with a hole in its side, which made any such transactions pretty much impossible. Some areas hadn't received their supplies from Tirana and had had to set up private arrangements from across the border in Macedonia or Former Yugoslavia. In Lehzë, we learned that the director of the primary health clinics had fled to Italy, leaving the entire region without medical supervision. But still, although we received a lot of legitimate requests, the end result was that no emergency medical intervention was necessary.

The one serious medical problem we did discover was that there was a threat of contagious disease due to the lack of chlorinated water. In 1994, there had been cholera cases involving seventeen out of thirty-seven districts: not a very good record. The pipe systems were old and worn out, and there was no international funding for a long-term program. In Tirana, they were using double the standard amount of chlorine to make up for the poor pipeline system and numerous leaks. The system suffered from several crossed lines of water and sewage, which didn't help the situation. Every region was running out of chlorine.

Chapter 3

When we returned to Tirana, we gathered at our favourite pizza restaurant and discussed the possibility of a country-wide chlorine distribution program sufficient to tide the country over for a few months, until the situation was calmer and new supplies could arrive.

Rink and Emin spent the next four or five days researching the idea, collecting very specific data from every region, which was no easy task. Many of the places could only be reached by phone, and Emin spent hours at the post office using one of the few public phone lines to try to gather information. Rink visited the sanitation engineers in Tirana, and I collected all the public health information on infectious diseases I could find.

In the end, we had a beautiful program with very detailed information — population data, litres of water used per month, amount of chloride used per litre, amount of calcium hypochloride required per district per month, et cetera. We even found an implementing partner, Catholic Relief Services (CRS), who would distribute the chlorine for us and collect follow-up data. A proposal with a budget was sent to London, and we waited to hear the result.

The answer was no. Nobody was interested in funding a water and sanitation program at that time. Don't ask me why — maybe it wasn't dramatic enough for the donors, or maybe it was too much money for a single intervention, or maybe nobody really wanted to get involved in Albania, because social unrest is not as moving as a civil war.

At any rate, we donated our well-researched proposal to the other NGOs in Albania before we left and hoped that somebody could use the information we had collected at some point in time. No sense in wasting good research.

Before we left, we spent a lovely day with Jimmi and his wife and kids at the beach in Durrës. We played among the dozens of concrete bunkers that dotted the entire country. Some had been converted to homes, chicken coops or storage facilities One farmer used his for growing mushrooms. It was amusing to see big new homes cropping up in regions where there were lousy roads, no running water and a failing infrastructure, or a brand new Mercedes driving down dirt side streets next to a horse and buggy.

On April 15, we left Albania for the London office. We were both a bit disappointed that our proposal hadn't been accepted, considering the work we had put into it and considering that it met the criteria for emergency intervention. It was also one of the few proposals that the MOH agreed with. Still, there was not much we could do about the whims of donors, and it was not the first time we regretted that MERLIN relied entirely on outside funding.

On a more positive note, we found out that approval for our Liberia project was in the works, but nothing was finalized, so we returned home to the Netherlands to wait for our next mission. A few weeks later, the funding came through and we were asked to return to Liberia to set up the program we had designed. We were delighted to be going back and looking forward to getting things started, but we had already informed MERLIN that we'd be leaving Liberia after two months, as we had plans in the Netherlands that we couldn't avoid. They were a bit annoyed with our announcement, certain that there was no way we could set up an entire new program in two months. We decided to prove them wrong.

We intended to quit the aid business for a year after this project. I wanted to get settled in the Netherlands, which meant taking a year off and going to Dutch classes to learn a new language. I had been living in Vlissingen for nearly a year, and I hadn't had time to unpack my boxes from Canada yet! Besides, it was time to stop for a bit, catch our breath, and try our hand at a 'normal' life for a change. There had been times in the last six months when I had wakened not knowing what country I was in, or what language I'd be speaking that day! As much as Rink and I both enjoyed the independence and freedom that goes with doing assessments and project set-ups, it was stressful work, and a lot of responsibility. I'd been at aid work for nearly four years and was beginning to feel too far removed from 'the real world'. I didn't know if we could truly ever return to that world, but I felt it was time to try.

LIBERIA, FULL CIRCLE
Chapter 1

On May 5, Rink and I flew to Liberia. In a sense, I felt that I had come full circle by having my career as a humanitarian aid worker end where it had begun. I couldn't help but look back at my first trip for MSF and see how far I'd come, how much I'd learned along the way. We were going back to set up a program we had planned and designed; I would be returning as the head of mission, something I had barely imagined I'd ever be able to do when I first began. I remember arriving in Liberia the first time with twenty-six kilograms of luggage. Now I travelled with no more than twelve kilos, including a sleeping bag, and that was everything I needed to survive for months. If nothing else, I'd become an expert at packing light.

Our first stop was in Freetown. The team in Kenema had just evacuated the area because of serious fighting in the region. Nobody knew then how serious things were to become, but it was not a good sign. We stayed for a couple of days, then flew on to Monrovia to get things started. Our good friends from ACF had their driver pick us up at the airport, and they put us up in their house — actually the old French embassy — for the first couple of weeks. It was quite a mansion, with a swimming pool, a separate library that still housed thousands of books, and two bedrooms that we could use. We were quickly assimilated back into Monrovian NGO life.

The first few weeks were an incredibly hectic blur of renewing acquaintances and catching up with the present military, political and humanitarian situations. We spent a great deal of time running about, attending meetings, planning our project with the MOH and generally making ourselves known to the other NGOs. We also started looking for a house and office from which we could work. Again, our colleagues came through for us. SCF owned another empty apartment in the same building we'd been in previously, and they offered it to us for a few weeks, until we could find our own place.

Monrovia seemed to be the generator capital of the world. The entire city-wide electrical system was destroyed, so no agency could function without a generator. The machines ran day and night, and their constant noise took some getting used to. The telephone system was intermittent, so most people relied on satellite phones for communication. Water had to be ordered and trucked in by an EC agency that had set up huge tanks throughout the region. Rebuilding Monrovia after this war was not going to be an easy task.

It was also a place where there were more meetings than you could shake a stick at. Every Monday there was a security meeting in which the UN and ECOMOG would meet with all the other agencies to discuss security issues from the last week. Then there were bi-monthly regional meetings for each county, and MERLIN was working in two of them. There was also a bi-monthly NGO meeting; the donor coordination meeting every two weeks, where donors met with recipients to determine how effective the programs were; food and nutrition meetings; agricultural coordination meetings; education committees; an epidemic control task force; a local NGO coordination meeting; a seeds and tools committee; a health services coordination committee, and dozens more. As the head of mission, I was obliged to attend most of these meetings, and they consumed much of my time. We were living in a part of town that was at least half an hour's drive from the UN compound where most of the meetings were held. Sometimes I found myself travelling the same road two or three times a day.

It wasn't long before we found a house that was big enough for the planned team, where the ground floor could be used as an office. Rink had to sort out the endless logistical problems with the house — the rent, power, water, security, et cetera — and we also had a zillion things to arrange for the project. We had to open new bank accounts, transfer money, arrange for permits, even find legal representation to coordinate all the official documents necessary to get established as a new NGO.

Then there was the matter of hiring new staff for the house and the project. Every day, dozens of hopeful applicants arrived at the SCF apartment, desperate for work. Many of my old MSF staff ended up at our doorstep. We hired John Dennis, my old MSF colleague from Gbarnga, as our local logistician, Rink's counterpart. We also ended up with a couple of our old drivers, including Saah, who had been my driver back in Gbarnga, in good old 'Charlie 5'.

There was also a huge amount of work to be done in preparation for the actual clinics. Every morning, there were at least a thousand things that needed to be done before breakfast. Sadie, who was to be our expat nurse for Nimba county, arrived within a few weeks to get started.

The political situation in Liberia was changing. The first democratic elections had been postponed until July 19, and the planning and preparation for the elections was dismal. The Elections Committee was terribly underfunded, and voter education was scandalous. The rainy season had made many upcountry areas inaccessible, and a lot of people doubted that their vote would be a secret, or that the elections would be carefully monitored. Threats had been made in some places against people who dared to vote for the 'wrong' party, and few refugees risked returning to the country until after elections, making them ineligible to vote.

Political campaigning by all the parties took place in Monrovia and the outlying regions, leading to stone-throwing and clashes with the police and ECOMOG troops. Tensions were high. To make matters worse, some of the parties named certain NGOs as suppliers of food, shelter, et cetera, in their election campaigns. None of the agencies knew they'd been named until it was too late. Votes were bought with a sack of food and promises that could never be fulfilled.

Some of the ex-fighters had formed 'building societies' through which they demanded NGO supplies and goods be sent. The transitional government also put pressure on the agencies to hand over money, a percentage of goods, and bogus fees for registration before the actual new government could assume its responsibilities. It was certainly a tricky time to be setting up a new project.

Chapter 2

By the third week, we'd gotten some crucial things accomplished and were well on our way to getting our base established. However, on May 26, all that changed.

We received an emergency call on our satellite phone from the head of mission in Freetown. A *coup d'état* had taken place in Freetown in Sierra Leone, and the Freetown team, along with hundreds of other expats, was forced to take refuge in a hotel. President Kabbah fled the country, and the city was in the hands of the rebels. The house and office were abandoned and contact with the Kenema team lost. Within days, the Freetown team evacuated the city, leaving their teams upcountry without a support base. We were asked to assume responsibility for the stranded Kenema team and ensure their evacuation.

Along with several other NGOs in Monrovia, we were now responsible for getting our colleagues out of Sierra Leone. Two committees were formed in Monrovia over the next few days. One was the Security Committee, which was responsible for devising a security plan for Monrovia that included acquiring updated high frequency and very high frequency radios and details on agency 'safe houses', with lists of supplies available for people. It was clear that Monrovia could easily be affected by the neighbouring turmoil. Refugees were already crossing the border, putting a strain on supplies and material meant for the local population. With elections looming, the chance of unrest and tension grew ever larger, and we all knew the added trouble in Sierra Leone could spark a disaster. Nobody wanted to be unprepared this time.

The second committee was the Emergency Committee, which would look into the logistical capacity of the Liberian agencies to respond to any emergency brought about by the *coup d'état* — disease outbreaks, an influx of refugees in Lofa county, a return to fighting in Monrovia.

The MERLIN team became very busy over the next few days, attending all the security meetings and trying to find a means of getting our people out of Kenema. Our first attempt involved Minister Pronk, the Minister of International Development from the Netherlands, who was in town to assess the projects that were funded by the Dutch government. Rink, being a good Dutch citizen, approached the minister's people for the use of the Pronk's private plane. After an evening of drinking (for which I duly suffered the next day), we obtained permission to use the plane, only to be informed the next day that permission to fly into Sierra Leone had been revoked due to the insecurity.

Next, we got our hands on a pilot who agreed to fly into Kenema for a not-too-unreasonable fee. But at the last minute he refused to go, fearing it would be too dangerous an undertaking. We became increasingly anxious to get the Kenema team across the border.

At least the situation in Kenema itself remained relatively stable. We had daily contact, either by radio or with the satellite phone, but it was the first mission for almost all of that team, and I feared they really didn't grasp the severity of the situation. They were quite prepared to remain, thinking everything would 'blow over' quickly. Having evacuated from nearly every project I'd been on, I was familiar with that notion but far more aware that things would probably not calm down enough for the aid agencies to go back in until a month later.

We continued to hear the stories out of Freetown and they weren't good. Looting had started in the city, and most of the agencies were targeted. Nigerian ECOMOG soldiers stationed upcountry had been killed. Both civilians and military personnel were killed in Freetown. The UN base and the U.S. embassy were attacked. The ECOMOG troops, who were supposed to stay in Liberia until well after the elections, were deployed to Sierra Leone, leaving the Liberian population vulnerable at a crucial time.

In Guinea, refugees were arriving to a hostile welcome. Many had been refused when they tried to enter Guinea, or forced to pay outrageous amounts of money to cross the border. Agencies trying to reach the Sierra Leonean refugees were denied access. A 10 P.M. curfew was in place in the border towns north of Lofa county. Things were tense all over, with incidents occurring upcountry in Kenema and Bo, where the expats were waiting evacuation. I got the feeling that this wasn't going to blow over any time soon.

We also faced the problem of poor communication from the outgoing head of the mission in Freetown. Before she left and made us responsible for the Kenema team, she informed us that in addition to the six MERLIN staff, there was a man named Casper, the boyfriend of a MERLIN expat, who wanted to be evacuated along with the others. The trouble was, she only told us she was working for a 'local' NGO, and the message was sufficiently vague for us to assume that we were being asked to evacuate a Sierra Leonean national.

Rink and I spent a couple of sleepless nights worrying about how to get this person out. It's impossible to evacuate national staff during these situations, so we didn't even bother informing the London office about our concerns. They would have refused to consider evacuating him, and we had enough experience to know dismissing these problems was never that easy.

We spent several days trying to get the UN personnel in Monrovia to fly into Sierra Leone to evacuate our expat staff there. They had evacuated their own UN staff but made it very clear that they had no legal obligation to assist the NGO community. It took many days of negotiations and pressure from ACF, SCF and Merlin before the UN staff would budge, but they eventually agreed to evacuate our expats.

We listed Casper as a Kenyan national and hoped for the best. We'd already warned the team that it could be very dangerous to bring him out, and that the UN had the right to refuse to allow him on the helicopter. Guy, one of the logisticians in Kenema, who had become our main contact person, insisted that the team refused to leave without Casper. I made it clear that this was not a request, it was an order. Having spent days arranging this evacuation, I had no intention of allowing them to *not* get on that helicopter.

The UN had set out numerous conditions that would have to be met before the plane could leave Liberian airspace. Arrangements were made between the soldiers guarding the airfield in Kenema and the UN pilot. We gave instructions as to what to do with the local staff, how to pay them and what precautions to take in case MERLIN couldn't return any time soon. An assessment team from MERLIN had already arrived in Conakry to determine when and how the project could be restarted, and other NGOs had their emergency teams standing by. MSF and ACF were planning to have their teams flown out from Bo that same day.

Finally, all was ready. On the morning that the helicopter was to leave, we had our last radio contact with the Kenema team. It was only then that we were informed that Casper was the proud owner of a *British* passport! With great relief, we told them they had nothing to worry about, though by that point I'm sure they thought we were slightly nuts for making such an issue out of a misunderstanding. I still haven't figured out what went wrong or why the outgoing head of mission was so unclear with the information, but we were very pleased to get everyone out safely.

When the team arrived in Monrovia, they were collected at the UN base and driven to our little apartment. Though we only had three bedrooms, we'd made arrangements for sleeping and food well ahead of time. It was with much relief that we greeted our guests that day.

However, the fact remained that Monrovia was not the best city to evacuate to. With the upcoming elections and the insecurity that went with the whole process, it wasn't exactly a safe haven. We had numerous discussions with the London office about the team, and once again, MERLIN's inexperience with these matters became painfully clear.

Nobody from the office even bothered to phone us in Monrovia to talk with the Kenema team, to ask how they were doing, or to offer reassurances. That job fell to us. MERLIN simply sent a fax requesting that all of them prepare to return to London as soon as possible. The team, naturally, was angered by MERLIN's apparent lack of interest in them, and they dug in their heels, prepared to stay. There wasn't a lot we could do except look after them, explain repeatedly how an evacuation works and reassure them that none of it was personal. The project in Kenema was over. No one would be allowed to return to Freetown, and nobody could give any guarantees about when or if MERLIN would be returning.

The London office left Rink and me pretty much alone to deal with the team, which was fortunately not a problem. There wasn't enough work to keep everyone busy, but we paid them their per diems, showed them the way to the bars, restaurants and swimming pool, and got them to assist when we finally moved into our new house.

In the meantime, we tried desperately to keep our own project in mind. There were no positions for the Sierra Leone team, except for Guy, in Liberia. As much as they wanted to help out and be a part of the project, it was only to stay close to Sierra Leone, and their hearts were not with Liberia. Everyone was very emotional about having to leave Africa, and we had some difficult talks with upset team members and did a lot of explaining on behalf of the London office. In the end, everyone reconciled themselves to leaving, except for Guy, who agreed to stay for another month and leave with Rink and myself in early July. We were happy to have another good logistician for awhile.

There was one last snag with headquarters when Casper and his girlfriend tried to get new plane tickets issued. The original ones had been left in the safe in Freetown and were totally inaccessible. MERLIN refused to pay for new tickets, and trying to get new ones issued in Monrovia was a nightmare. MERLIN was rather inflexible on this point, for reasons I could understand, but it was one more thing that infuriated an already frustrated and disappointed group. Casper and his girlfriend persevered and finally managed to persuade the airline to re-issue their tickets, but MERLIN's lack of support took a toll on everyone.

After two weeks, the last of the Kenema team bid a sad goodbye. MERLIN would be returning to Kenema, but not for months to come. And we now had less than a month to complete the set-up of our project.

Chapter 3

A day after the last of the Sierra Leone team left, the expats for our project arrived: Simon, who would replace me as head of mission; Jenny, the financial controller; Anna, the nurse for Lofa county; and Rupert, the logistician for Lofa county, Guy was soon joined by Derrick, and the two would work with Sadie in Nimba county for the time being.

Simon was one of the few MERLIN expats that had enough experience to pick up the ins and outs of NGO life in Monrovia quickly. He soon made himself at home and started attending all the meetings with me, and getting to know the other agencies.

Jenny spent the first week in a state of high anxiety. Rink and I were never that brilliant when it came to finances, and she had her work cut out for her. But she hung in there and pretty quickly made order out of our chaos. She even managed to get Rink and John Dennis to produce their receipts for a change — with the correct codes and everything! I was impressed.

Sadie helped Anna get familiar with the drug distribution system, the data collection forms and the drug consumption records. Though it was Anna's first mission, she learned quickly and was soon attending meetings for Lofa county and getting a handle on the situation there.

Rink and John Dennis had their hands full trying to get the house in order and our vehicles out of the port so that we could get our first clinics in Nimba county up and running. The actual running of the house and office offered numerous problems. Though we found sufficient house staff, they didn't always get along that well. The electricity was a nightmare, with the generator frequently breaking down, leaving us without a schedule to work with. Not only could we not count on the computers to function when we needed them, we had no idea when or if we'd have water, which annoyed the house staff to no end. Even when the generator worked, we had to plan a schedule of activities to correspond with both the times it would run and everyone's separate priorities.

Until the cars were available, travel and transport became a matter of luck and a few radio calls to friends with whom we could catch a ride. We had four new vehicles sitting in the port, but we'd been warned that getting them released could take months. Rink and John Dennis may have set a world record in speeding the process up — five days, $700 worth of bribes, and thirty-nine different signatures.

In between my countless meetings, I now had to give an orientation to each new arrival, while Rink and Simon worked to devise a new security plan, with special attention paid to what should be done during elections. Many of the agencies were planning to send their people out of the country, and we decided to do the same. Emergency stocks had to be collected and drug supplies kept in the house in case something happened during elections. Those expats remaining behind had to be prepared for any contingency.

New handsets for everyone and new codes for each person were arranged. We'd been given the call sign 'Wizard' by the Oxfam people, and even our license plates had the title of Wiz 1, Wiz 2, et cetera. With the incoming staff, we'd already gone from Wiz 3 to Wiz 7! Each new person had to be introduced at the American embassy and given an embassy card which entitled them to more than just movies each week; it meant they were listed with the embassy in case another evacuation would be necessary in July.

Finally, the plans were completed with the MOH and the Nimba county health team. On June 6, Sadie, Derrick and Guy drove to Tapeta with a crew of MOH staff and instructors. Our first workshop was held over the course of three days. In the end, the distribution of materials, medicines, data collection forms and instructions was completed. Our three clinics in Nimba county were operational. Derrick and Guy started the renovations in Sanniquellie Hospital, and our plan was in action.

On June 16, Rupert, Anna and Simon made a similar trip to Voinjama, in Lofa county. Again, three clinics were given supplies, materials and instructions, and Anna officially assumed her role as medical officer for Lofa county.

As we had hoped, the project we had planned and devised and created was up and running within two months. Only one thing remained to be done. We had to throw a party.

Nobody is really 'in' the NGO community until they have their first party. With a little creative financial planning (party falls under the heading PR), we hosted sixty or seventy friends from various NGOs. It was a great success, everyone enjoyed themselves, and MERLIN was officially a part of the NGO community. Our project eventually became one of MERLIN's biggest, and MERLIN became one of the leading medical agencies in Liberia. At the time, I just thought we'd gotten it off to a pretty good start.

Chapter 4

Once the party was over, it was time for us to leave. For Rink and me, the parting was bittersweet. We were proud of what we had accomplished in Liberia and pleased that our program met the needs of an isolated population and was approved by the MOH. What we had started could eventually be continued by the Liberian people without the input of expat staff. It might not happen quickly, but Liberia was going to be okay. Peace really had broken out. But the Liberia project had been our baby, from its conception to its implementation. We would have loved to stay, and saying goodbye was not easy, as we had so many friends there now, especially ACF's Dalton base (named after their mangy dog, who used to chase our cars). They'd taken us in from the first, fed us, educated us, helped us with so many things. Introduced us to dancing at the Holiday Inn, the beautiful Kendeja beach, picnics in their hidden little cove and, of course, Papa Johnson's 7-11.

We had made some good friends, and had some wonderful times together. I had especially enjoyed the reunion with the local staff from MSF. Seeing them all again had been very special for me. We had achieved our goal: MERLIN's program was established in Liberia. It was time to leave.

All flights out of Monrovia now went through Abidjan, in the Ivory Coast. Having said our last goodbyes, drunk our last beers, had our last party and hugged our last hugs, Rink, Guy and I headed for the airport. Our plane was sitting on the runway, and the weather was finally clear. There were just two little problems. One was a rather large dip in the runway, which was now filled with water, cutting the takeoff distance for the plane almost in half. The second problem, Rink pointed out to me, was that the plane had two different engines! I asked him if that wasn't a bit dangerous. He just kept saying things like 'My God!' I assumed it wasn't a good thing.

We boarded the plane, and had no serious qualms until the engines started. A huge burst of flames shot out of the engine on Guy's side. He looked over at us, his eyes wide. We just nodded reassuringly, trying not to panic yet. Eventually, the fire went out. A smoky mist came through the overhead ventilation into the plane, but that, too, slowly vanished. And then we were up. However, every plane in Africa is far heavier than it is supposed to be, and carry-on luggage takes on a whole new meaning there. I doubted we'd get up before we hit the flooded section of the runway, and I knew there were no other planes that day, but somehow, miraculously, we did it.

We arrived in Abidjan to find that our flight to London had not been confirmed, due to a computer glitch in Monrovia. We wouldn't know for certain whether we could get on the flight until shortly before we were due to leave. After a lengthy discussion, we left our passports behind and headed for town. We had a lovely dinner together and spent a few hours in Abidjan before heading back to the airport.

The final Catch-22 came when we found out we weren't going to have our passports returned until we had a boarding pass, but we couldn't get our boarding pass without our passports. Rink chatted with the KLM representative, who realized he'd have to put us up in a nice hotel for three days if we didn't get on this flight and stepped up his efforts to help us. The problem was that Monrovia didn't have computer access to Abidjan, but the airline was able to confirm our flight in London. We got the last three seats at the last minute. Typical.

In London, we spent only a few days in the office. Our reports were finished, the Liberia project was operational, and we were leaving MERLIN, maybe for good. Some of the office staff took us out for a drink on our last day, but many didn't even realize we'd be returning to the Netherlands for a year. It all seemed to be over before we knew it. It had been a terrific nine months, and it had flown by. Now we were on our last flight. We were going home.

NOT QUITE THE END

For the first time in years, we were actually home on time, as planned. I doubt Karel and Ingrid knew how miraculous it was that Rink was actually *present* to stand up at their wedding. But Karel was one of Rink's closest friends, and Rink wasn't about to miss that wedding. It was the first time in years that anything had worked out according to plans. We had a great time together, meeting new people, getting reacquainted with Rink's old friends and finally relaxing after the hectic last months.

No sooner was the wedding over than we headed off to Sarajevo for holidays. We drove there to visit Isabel and Piet, and it was a rather odd experience. The scenery hadn't changed much, except for the fact that there were no checkpoints any longer, no obvious frontlines and no blue helmets. UNPROFOR had been replaced by stabilization forces (SFOR), all wearing military green, well and visibly armed.

Issy was having a tough time there, and we were glad for the chance to spend some time together. Sarajevo not under siege was a lot more interesting than before. We actually climbed the hill with the radio tower, the one that had been under constant fire during the war. Not a single sniper to be seen. Amazing! We returned to the same restaurant we'd been in after we drove across the frontline in Elvis. Sarajevo was coming to life again, in spite of the enormous damage it had received. We even ran in to Roel and his new wife, Liljana. They'd been married a few months before and were immigrating to the Netherlands. They were one of several couples that had met in the MSF-Bosnia project, and not the only ones that ended up married and living in the Netherlands!

We continued on to Livno to see Catherine, another friend who'd been in the Liverpool school with me. She was stationed with SFOR, and we made a quick stop there. Then finally, it was on to Banja Luka, via a road that had been impassable before, one we had only dreamed of being able to travel. It was a strange sensation to be returning, past the old towns that had been utterly destroyed and through villages we had fought and pleaded for access to.

I got the distinct impression that not much had changed in Banja Luka. At least not in the attitude of the people. I can honestly say that we were probably the first people to actually go to Banja Luka for *holidays*. We were, of course, greeted with suspicion and distrust at the hotel we checked into. And though there hadn't been a frontline to cross, I could feel the difference the minute we landed in Serb territory.

But our old staff had certainly changed. Sanja had taken the Health Emergency Preparedness/Logistics Training course in Amsterdam, the same one I had taken before heading to Liberia, and just received her first mission with MSF as an expat in Azerbaijan. Shy little Gordana, who didn't know a capsat from a computer before she joined MSF, was the office manager for a Swedish agency. We went to see our old friend, Borislav, and found the years of self-imposed exile hadn't done him any favours; he was having a difficult time adjusting to a normal life. It was nice to see his brothers safe and sound, and to visit his parents again. The old man had had a stroke, but he was recovering, thanks largely to his daily bottle of slivovitz and vodka, or so he still claimed. It was with great pleasure that we could finally take Borislav out to dinner at the castle, in public, without worrying about who might see. Even the waiter at the restaurant remembered us. I wonder if he remembered that little shooting incident from the last time we were there. We ended up writing a character reference for Borislav before we left, and he actually got his first job helping out during the elections.

To my surprise, it was nice to go back. I was delighted when the pictures of Radovan Karadzic that were put up around town during elections were just as quickly ripped off by a population who obviously didn't look upon him as their hero anymore. There were a few familiar faces in the UNHCR office, including Julian and Vladimir, who, along with their staff, were astonished to see us again. Vladimir, who had spent all his time during the war trying to get the minorities out, was now trying to persuade them to return! Maybe peace really had broken out.

The most amazing thing was to see that our three agencies, who had struggled so hard to provide aid during the war, had increased in number to about forty-six. I couldn't help but wonder where they all had been when we were begging for some help just a few years back. Still, Banja Luka seemed to have finally accepted international aid, if not with good grace, then with resignation. The people may not have truly felt at peace, but the evidence was all over. It was time to rebuild.

For us, the real pleasure came in sharing our stories and memories of "Blue Lagoon". The time when it had been just a handful of people working long days, longer nights, weekends and holidays, trying desperately to get supplies out to more than fifty hospitals. How eventually we managed to laugh and enjoy those memories. Whatever else we had or had not achieved in that place, our old staff received us with pleasure and looked back upon their work with pride. We had shared something together that would never be forgotten and could never be replaced. To them, we mattered.

That wasn't quite the end. We left Banja Luka, travelled through Italy and France for holidays and returned to Vlissingen to unpack and make a home for ourselves. Rink found work as part of the management team in a refugee asylum centre, and later as its director. I learned Dutch and later worked as a nurse in the medical department of another refugee centre. We renovated the house, settled down and had a 'normal' life again.

And still, the only time we ever felt alive was with our friends from the field. Only then did our eyes light up, when the whiskey came out and the talk went on until the wee hours of the morning. We talked about everything, the things that mattered to us, about life and death, politics and policies, economics, about changes in the office, shared memories, future plans, our work, the people we'd known, the missions we'd had. Those terrible moments that we'd gone through and the joy and laughter that went with working on the edge. For all we'd changed, and for all we'd lost, in the end — we missed it.

It's a strange life, the world of international aid, a unique and special life indeed. And in the end, it matters. Not what we go through to get there, not what we do to make it all come together in the end, not the endless bureaucracy, the paperwork, the petitions and prayers and plans. Not the danger, the fear, the difficulties, the distance. What matters is that we were there. We did something when something needed to be done. It may not have always been enough. We may not have always made the right choices or the right decisions. But we were there. And we reacted, and we responded, and we cared.

We were neither heroes nor fools. We chose the greatest adventure we could have, because we wanted to make the greatest difference that we could.

Sometimes now, I watch the disasters of the world unfold on television with an interest I never had before. I see those aid agencies on CNN, I check out the T-shirts, and I smile to myself. Nobody who receives the food, the shelter, the medicine, the aid that they offer, has any idea what the agencies have probably gone through to get there. I know.

And I'm glad they got there.

GLOSSARY OF TERMS

AFL	Armed Forces of Liberia (official Liberian army)
A(I)CF	Action (Internationale) Contre la Faime
APC	Armoured personnel carrier
ASRAMES	cost-recovery drug distribution program
BCG	vaccine for tuberculosis
CRS	Catholic Relief Services
CSB	corn-soya-blend (cereal)
CUC	Cuttington University Compound
DPT	vaccine for diphtheria, pertussis, and tetanus
DSM	dry skim milk powder
DSP	Zairean presidential armed forces
DZ	dom zdravja (hospital)
EC	European Community
ECHO	European Committee for Humanitarian Organizations
ECOMOG	Economic Community of West Africa Ceasefire Monitoring Group
EPI	Expanded Program of Immunization
FBU	Burundian currecy
HF/VHF	high frequency/very high frequency
ICRC	International Committee of the Red Cross
IRC	International Rescue Committee
IV	intravenous
JPO	joint policy of operations
LDF	Lofa Defense Force
loggie	logistician
LPC	Liberian Peace council
LWS	Lutheran World Services
MERLIN	Medical Emergency Relief International
MDM	Medecins du Monde
MOH	Ministry of Health
MSF	Medecins Sans Frontieres
MSF-H,-B,-L,-F	MSF-Holland, -Belgium, -Luxembourg, -France

NATO	North Atlantic Treaty Organization
NDS	National Drug Services, cost-recovery drug program
NGO	Non-governmental organization
NPFL	National Patriotic Front of Liberia
OR	operating room
PR	public relations
PSF	Pharmacien Sans Frontieres
R & R	rest and relaxation
RPG	rocket-propelled grenade
SCF	Save the Children Fund
SFC (SFP)	supplementary feeding centre (program)
SFOR	UN Stabilization Force
sitrep	situational report
TB	tuberculosis
TFC (TFP)	therapeutic feeding centre (program)
TT	tetanus toxoid
ULIMO	United Liberation Movement (of Liberia) for Democracy
UN	United Nations
UNAVEM	UN Angola Verification Mission
UNDP	UN Developmental Program
UNHACO	UN Humanitarian Aid Coordination Office
UNHCR	UN High Commissioner for Refugees
UNICEF	UN Childrens' Fund
UNITA	National Union for the Total Independence of Angola
UNMO	UN Military Observers
UNOMIL	UN Observer Mission in Liberia
UNPA	UN Protected Area
UNPROFOR	UN Protection Force
UNPRONA	The Union for National Progress
USAID	U.S.A International Development
WFP	World Food Programme
ZTM	Zairean Tea Management